BEYOND THE BIG 5-0
WHAT YOU NEED TO KNOW . . .

- Menopause may cause sleep problems, but insomnia doesn't have to make you suffer.
- A Mayo Clinic physician gives five top recommendations for keeping healthy . . . and at least one is going to shock you.
- New cosmetic surgery can safely get rid of broken capillaries, age spots, cherry angiomas, and varicose veins . . . permanently.
- One common B vitamin may be your best bet to prevent cervical and colorectal cancer . . . but most American women don't get nearly enough.
- Medical studies can let you in on the latest drug discoveries—or confuse you. Find out the best journal for getting information you can trust.
- You don't have to suffer the discomforts of menopause or the long-term risks with new treatments, including estrogen bypass, the latest alternative to hormone replacement.

WHAT TO EXPECT IN YOUR FIFTIES

What to Expect in Your Fifties

A WOMAN'S GUIDE TO HEALTH, VITALITY, AND LONGEVITY

JUDY MANDELL

A Dell Trade Paperback

A DELL TRADE PAPERBACK

Published by
Dell Publishing
a division of
Bantam Doubleday Dell Publishing Group, Inc.
1540 Broadway
New York, New York 10036

Library of Congress Cataloging in Publication Data
What to expect in your fifties : a woman's guide to health, vitality, and longevity / [compiled by] Judy Mandell.
p.   cm.
Includes index.
ISBN 0-440-50810-X (pbk.)
1. Middle aged women—Health and hygiene.
I. Mandell, Judy
RA778.W325   1998
613'.04244—dc21   98-15264
                         CIP

Book Design by Barbara Berger

Printed in the United States of America

Published simultaneously in Canada

October 1998

10 9 8 7 6 5 4 3 2 1

BVG

For Jerry, Jim, Elizabeth, Joshua, Zachary, Pam, Scott,
Kim, Kira, and Cranberry

And to the wonderful physicians
and scientists who grace this book:

Thank you.

Thank you for your explanations and revelations.
Thank you for your dedication and inspiration.
Thank you for your kindness and generosity.

Thank you for caring.

Despite overwhelming workloads, crowded waiting rooms,
and grant deadlines, you graciously answered my questions.

Your only payment was the satisfaction that you might help
the readers of this book.

For that I am grateful.

Acknowledgments

First and foremost, I wish to thank my daughter-in-law, Elizabeth Hope Berger Mandell, M.D., who scoured my text for errors and kept me on the straight and narrow.

Thank you to friends and relatives who graciously read and commented on sections of this book. They include Helen Abramowicz, M.D.; Mark Abramowicz, M.D.; Jayne Charlamb, M.D.; Sandra Levison, M.D.; James Mandell, M.D., Ph.D.; Gerald Mandell, M.D.; Sylvia Mandell; Deborah Rhodes, M.D.; and Elaine Rubenstein.

I am especially grateful to Susan Lattman, my dear friend and sister-in-law, who was enthusiastic about this book right from the beginning. Her editorial comments were always insightful, valid, and honest.

Thank you to those who offered advice, encouragement, and, most important, leads and referrals to top physicians and scientists. They include Stephen G. Baum, M.D.; Florence Berger, Ph.D.; Toby Berger, Ph.D.; Jeffrey Blumberg, Ph.D., F.A.C.N.; Fran Carpentier; Robert Clark, M.D.; Peter Densen, M.D.; William C. Dement, M.D., Ph.D.; Herbert DuPont, M.D.; Margaret Wright DuPont; Eda Elbirlik, D.D.S.; Rina Freedman, Ph.D.; Julie Gerberding, M.D.; Eugene T. Giannini, D.D.S.; David Gilbert, M.D.; Jerome Gold, M.D.; Sara Horton; Sandra Levison, M.D.; Elizabeth Mandell, M.D.; Gerald L. Mandell, M.D.; James W. Mandell, M.D., Ph.D.; Pam Mandell; Scott Mandell; Aviva Must, Ph.D.; Miriam E. Nelson, Ph.D.; Kim Perzel; Judith Riven; Elaine Rubenstein; Merle Sande, M.D.; Neil Steigbeigel, M.D.; Charles Steinberg, M.D.; Paul Stolley, M.D.; Katherine Tucker, Ph.D.; Claudia Valentino; Peyton Weary, M.D.; and Myron L. Weisfeldt, M.D.

In addition, I wish to thank Longstreet Press, which provided me with books about arthritis, and Woodward White, publishers of the annually updated *The Best Doctors in America*.

And finally, I want to thank Mary Ellen O'Neill, my excellent editor at Dell.

Grateful acknowledgment is made for permissions granted by the following:

Helen Abramowicz, M.D.
Mark Abramowicz, M.D.
Robert Amonic, M.D.
Donald Bliwise, Ph.D.
Jeffrey Blumberg, Ph.D., F.A.C.N.
Reay H. Brown, M.D.
Raymond Coll, M.D.
Alan Dalkin, M.D.
Ellen Shaw de Paredes, M.D.
Robert Dobie, M.D.
Robert L. DuPont, M.D.
Jerome L. Fleg, M.D.
Kathleen M. Foley, M.D.
Roy Geronemus, M.D.
Eugene T. Giannini, D.D.S.
Michael H. Gold, M.D.
James S. Gordon, M.D.
Gerald Imber, M.D.
Richard Jackson, M.D.
Lawrence G. Lazar, D.P.M.
Sandra Levison, M.D.
Patricia L. Maclay, M.D.
Elizabeth Mandell, M.D.
Aviva Must, Ph.D.
Miriam E. Nelson, Ph.D.
Michael O'Shea, Ph.D.
JoAnn V. Pinkerton, M.D.
Mark B. Pochapin, M.D.
Norman Relkin, M.D., Ph.D.
Deborah Rhodes, M.D.
Maj-Britt Rosenbaum, M.D.
Richard Santen, M.D.
Katherine Tucker, Ph.D.
Hansen A. Yuan, M.D.

Contents

Foreword

In recent years, efforts to improve the health of women have gained widespread public attention and assumed an unprecedented eminence in public and private initiatives in the United States. With the new awareness of women's health issues, increased attention is also being given to improving the health of women over the entire course of their lives.

Today, in most industrialized nations, women live longer than men. In the United States, women make up approximately 59 percent of Americans over the age of sixty-five, and 72 percent of those age eighty-five and older. In fact, the greatest rate of increase in the American population has been among those over the age of eighty-five. If present trends continue, in the coming decades three-quarters of elderly Americans will be women. The importance to our nation of maintaining good health in women during the postmenopausal years has never been greater.

The aging of America's population is creating enormous challenges for many individuals and institutions in our society, including families, health care and social service institutions, and those engaged in medical research. The emotional rewards—as well as the emotional, physical, and financial burdens—of caring for elderly women frequently fall upon their daughters or other female family members, who themselves are, in many cases, beginning to experience the health problems that can occur during women's postmenopausal years, typically the sixth decade of life.

In light of these demographic trends and the emotional, physical, and financial costs associated with illness and debility, preserving the health of women in their middle and postmenopausal years must be at the top of our nation's health care and health-research priorities. Unfortunately, at present we know more about the prevalence of health problems that may be experienced by women during their menopausal and postmenopausal years than we know about how to prevent or treat those problems.

In order to understand better the interplay of biological, social, and behavioral factors that contributes to illness among women, and to address gaps in our knowledge of women's health across the entire life span from childhood through the later years of life, the National Institutes of Health (NIH) established the Office of Research on Women's Health (ORWH) in September 1990. The Office fosters and supports a multidimensional approach to women's health and research: an approach that calls for an integration of basic science and clinical investigation, from molecular medicine to the application of scientific breakthroughs in the clinical study of diverse populations of women across the life span. Through its policies and programs, the ORWH also seeks to increase opportunities for women to pursue and advance in biomedical careers.

Differences exist among some populations of women with regard to health status and health outcomes associated with some diseases, disorders, and conditions. In many cases, the complex reasons for these differences have not been well delineated. The ORWH and the institutes and centers of the NIH support a number of studies aimed at elucidating such differences in health status among diverse populations of women in order to understand better the ways in which socioeconomic status, access to health information and care, educational background, individual behavior and attitudes, attitudes concerning health care and health care providers, cultural background, and race and ethnicity influence women's health and the decisions they make that can affect their health.

The NIH is conducting and supporting investigations to determine both normal development and health status of girls and women across the life span, as well as ways of preventing debility and disease through behavioral change and improved health interventions. Through both basic and clinical research, investigators are seeking to establish what constitutes normal growth and development in females, as well as interventions and strategies to preserve good health over the life span, particularly during the menopausal and postmenopausal years. For example, the NIH-sponsored Study of Women's Health Across the Nation (SWAN) is a multi-site investigation of the biological, psychosocial, cultural, and lifestyle factors that influence the health of women of diverse ethnic backgrounds as they make the transition from pre- to peri- to postmenopausal status.

The SWAN study, which is looking at health among five racial/ethnic groups of women (African American, Chinese American, Japanese American, Hispanic, and Caucasian) has three components: focus groups, a cross-sectional survey, and a prospective cohort study. The cardiovascular component of the study is testing the hypotheses that, independent of aging, changes in reproductive hormones, marked by cessation of menses, lead to alterations in levels of lipids, lipoproteins, fasting insulin and glucose, and clotting factors that affect women's cardiovascular health in the postmenopausal years. The psychological, social, and cultural measures of SWAN focus on how stress, factors that have been shown to protect against stress, and culturally induced attitudes and beliefs about menopause influence its basic parameters, symptomatology, and the treatments that women know about and choose. The study of functional limitations in SWAN explores whether the menopausal transition is associated with functional limitations, and examines women's performance of social roles and their perceived quality of life. The lifestyle measurements in SWAN examine the effects of diet, physical activity, smoking, behavior, socioeconomic status, and occupational and reproductive factors on participants' health. Successful strategies for managing and minimizing symptoms, including obesity, are also included.

In addition to hot flashes and other immediate symptoms of menopause, rates of heart disease, stroke, osteoporosis, and cancer increase in women after menopause. The NIH-sponsored Women's Health Initiative (WHI) is designed to determine which of the common, though as yet unproven, interventions and strategies are most effective in preventing these and other diseases that afflict postmenopausal women.

The WHI is a fifteen-year study that involves more than 164,500 postmenopausal women of diverse racial and ethnic backgrounds between fifty and seventy-nine years of age in large and small communities nationwide. Like SWAN, the WHI has three components: a randomized controlled clinical trial of promising but unproven approaches to prevention; an observational study to identify predictors of disease; and a study of community approaches to developing healthful behaviors. The prevention component of the WHI is examining the benefits and risks of long-term hormone-replacement therapy, the role of low-fat diet modification using behavioral change, and calcium and vitamin D supplements in preventing the major causes of death and debility among postmenopausal women: cardiovascular disease, cancer (particularly breast and colorectal cancers), and osteoporotic fractures. The WHI also has the goal of identifying the most effective means of encouraging women of diverse backgrounds to adopt healthier lifestyles so that women can contribute to the improvement and preservation of their own health.

The SWAN study and the WHI are but two of many NIH-supported studies under way to provide scientific data to answer some of the most commonly asked questions that women have concerning their health as they approach midlife. While the medical community still lacks definitive answers about how women can best preserve their health during the postmenopausal years of life, it is clear that much can be accomplished with the knowledge available to date. Seeking reliable health information is important for every woman as she approaches midlife. Just as the NIH and the biomedical community are seeking to resolve many questions about women's health through research, so too should women strive to be well informed concerning what to expect during the perimenopausal and postmenopausal years and the health interventions and prevention strategies now at their disposal. Reading books such as *What to Expect in Your Fifties: A Woman's Guide to Health, Vitality, and Longevity* can be the first step in gaining the knowledge that women need to lead healthier, more productive lives in their fifties and the years beyond.

—Vivian W. Pinn, M.D.
Associate Director for Research on Women's Health
Director, Office of Research on Women's Health
National Institutes of Health

Introduction

When my mother was in her fifties, menopause was in the closet. Cartoonists and comedians characterized women over fifty as irritable, wrinkled, and sexless. The sixth decade was viewed not only as the end of a woman's reproductive life but a time of degeneration and disease—a dreadful picture and quite fearsome. Most women "of a certain age" were passive, fatalistic, and avoided the subject of growing old.

There were no midlife women's centers or books on menopause. Mom would go to her gynecologist (a man, of course, since female physicians were almost nonexistent) for an annual Pap smear, but her complaints of insomnia, night sweats, hot flashes, and migraine headaches were mostly ignored. She probably was considered a malingerer. Menopause was viewed more as a pathologic and neurotic state than a normal evolution of a woman's reproductive life.

Today baby boomers have brought a new attitude to aging. This vocal generation of 77 million people born between 1946 and 1964 has pushed the years of vigorous life ahead. Discussions of hot flashes, vaginal dryness, and cosmetic surgery are now commonplace. There is a new approach to women's medical care. Women's midlife health centers have popped up all over the country, and there are more female physicians to choose from.

Each decade of a woman's life includes unique challenges. The fifties is a time of profound change for a woman.

Menopause is a key issue for women in their fifties, but it is far from the only problem. The fifties can be a period of psychological and physical upheaval. Grown children may have returned to the nest, and ill and aging parents may need help. Divorce is rampant. We may not feel as good in bodies that are beginning to show signs of age—or we might just not feel good.

Health care choices in this decade can be confusing. Many gynecologists advise their menopausal patients to take estrogen to lessen their symptoms and possibly decrease the risks of heart disease and osteoporosis, yet no one is certain of the long-term risks. It seems that every day there is a new announcement either for or against estrogen replacement. With the release of a recent study here, contradicted by another study there, a woman could go a little bit crazy trying to sort it out.

Whether it's about estrogen replacement and breast cancer, salt and hypertension, or cholesterol and heart attacks, the rapid release of new medical reports through the media confuses the public. Often we are advised not to make changes until the results of randomized, placebo-controlled studies are available. So what does all that mean?

I've asked the experts to clarify medical studies and many other issues relevant to women in their fifties. *What to Expect in Your Fifties* emphasizes wellness while it addresses almost every subject that is appropriate to women of this decade.

I asked top scientists and physicians to answer questions that a typical woman of this age would ask about her health and well-being. I posed what I thought were fifty- to sixty-year-old women's most-asked questions about problems they encounter. Should most women take estrogen? Do they need to get a bone scan? When? Why? How should they deal with the physical symptoms of menopause, aging and fear of aging, aches and pains, illness, insomnia, sexual problems, addiction, and more.

I interviewed leaders in their fields, who are on the cutting edge of research and knowledge. I found my experts by asking their colleagues for recommendations and by reading *The Best Doctors in America*, published by Woodward White, as well as "top-physicians" lists selected by magazines such as *American Health for Women*, *New York* magazine, *Atlanta* magazine, and several other major-city magazines.

What to Expect in Your Fifties is a medical guide that will help women make health care decisions. Readers will learn how to interpret studies and data. Although much of the material applies to all women in that age group, those with specific interests can seek out certain chapters.

When a scientific term or answer was confusing to me, I assumed the reader also might be perplexed, so I probed until the explanation was clarified. I asked the experts to define, clarify, and illustrate concepts, to reveal "the truth" about controversial issues as they see it, and to justify the basis of their opinions. I always asked interviewees to fill in what I might have left out.

I asked almost every expert, "What is the best way for a woman in her fifties to stay healthy?" or "What do you advise women in their fifties who want to live long, happy, healthy lives?" Therefore, almost every chapter ends with general advice and/or philosophy, so that readers can find the viewpoints of respected scientists and physicians quickly and compare them.

The information in this book is "straight from the horse's mouth." Although the physicians and scientists that I interviewed were "up to their eyeballs" with clinical work and research, they willingly and graciously answered all my questions, discussed the latest research studies, discussed problems encountered in women of ages fifty to sixty, and offered free advice. They received no payment beyond the knowledge that their invaluable information might help my readers.

What to Expect in Your Fifties is fact-filled, but at the same time it is full of diverse opinions. I often asked the same question of different specialists. Many times they gave me differing opinions, all based on the facts as they see them. Highly trained scientists may disagree on important issues. It happens in life and it happened in this book. What is the lesson here? We must become informed and educated so that we can draw our own conclusions.

—Judy Mandell

SECTION I
Women's Health Today

1
Changes in Health Care
for Women

Sandra Levison, M.D.

Sandra Levison graduated from college in 1961 with a major in zoology. After earning a medical degree from New York University School of Medicine, she completed her internal medicine internship and residency at the State University of New York (SUNY)–Downstate, Brooklyn Kings County Medical Center, and New York University, Bellevue Hospital Center. She subsequently took subspecialty training in nephrology at SUNY-Downstate. She is board certified in internal medicine and nephrology. Dr. Levison is a professor of medicine at the Medical College of Pennsylvania (MCP)–Hahnemann School of Medicine, and chief of the Divisions of Nephrology at Allegheny University of the Health Sciences, MCP, and Hahnemann Hospitals. She is also the director of the Women's Health Education Program in the Institute for Women's Health at MCP-Hahnemann School of Medicine. She is cochair of the National Academy on Women's Health Medical Education. She has published many book chapters and articles on women's health and recently coauthored a monograph titled *Tips for Talking, A Guide to Inclusive Communication for Physicians, Medical Students, and All Health Care Providers.*

Q. Tell me about previous inequities in medical care.

A. Gender inequities in medical care existed prior to the 1980s because women's care needs were not understood and were thought to be similar to those of men. While we will never know exactly why this was, the fact that men dominated medicine and medical research and the absence of women as patient activists probably played a role. For example, the symptoms of menopause became medicalized. Because of a lack of information, they were treated as a disease rather than a normal change in a woman's body. While estrogen replacement has been available for almost fifty years, there is still very little known about its effects on women.

Until recently breast cancer was never treated as a high priority in terms of diagnosis, treatment, or research. A colleague who specializes in infectious disease put it this way: "One out of nine women will develop breast cancer over her lifetime. In my specialty, statistics like that would be called an epidemic and a major war would have been mounted." Yet that kind of energy was never applied to breast cancer, a disease that is a significant cause of premature death in women.

Q. Give me examples of research that failed to include women.

A. The aim of the Baltimore Study on Aging, which began in 1958, was to examine aging. The first phase involved data collected from more than 20,000 men over the course of twenty years. No women were included, even though women constitute more than 60 percent of the aged population. So that phase of the study didn't teach us anything about women and osteoporosis, breast cancer, menopause, or other issues specific to women. The study currently includes about 40 percent women.

The Physicians' Health Study was completed in 1988 to determine the safety and efficacy of aspirin in preventing heart attacks. During the course of the study, most doctors were men, so the study population included 22,000 men and no women. Results showed that men who took daily doses of baby aspirin substantially reduced their risks of heart disease and stroke. The inference was that this was probably true for women, but we didn't know that for a fact. The Nurses' Health Study provided some tentative conclusions in this regard, but the definitive results await studies in progress. The Multiple Risk Factor Intervention Trial was a long-term study initiated in 1982 to examine the influence of lifestyle, diet, and exercise on heart disease. This study included no women. The exclusion of women as research subjects illustrates a mind-set that ignores the potential differences in the care of men and women.

Q. When and how did these unfair practices begin to change?
A. In the 1980s and early 1990s the gender inequities began to be appreciated and dealt with as women became more empowered in medicine, politics, government, and consumer activism. Patricia Schroeder was elected to Congress from Colorado and Bernadine Healy, M.D., was appointed director of the National Institutes of Health. As women in positions of power understood that changes were needed, an appreciation of inequities in women's health began to surface. Schroeder wrote and helped enact legislation. She was later joined by Nita Lowey and the Congressional Women's Caucus. She also supported women's reproductive rights. Healy created the Office for Research in Women's Health and launched the Women's Health Initiative.

Q. Tell me about the changes in health care for women.
A. There were three types of changes—research, treatment, and the training of physicians.

Q. How did research change?
A. In the early 1980s Schroeder called for Congress's General Accounting Office to formally investigate whether women were being included in the medical research being conducted. Not only did the investigators discover that women were being omitted from the studies, but breast cancer and estrogen research were being studied in *men*. From that time on there was strict enforcement of regulations that mandated that women had to be recruited and included in significant numbers in federally funded projects. In addition, women of color also had to be included.

5

Q. Why did researchers previously exclude women from their studies?

A. The mostly male investigators probably didn't include women because they believed that women would complicate the study design, necessitating more subjects. They may have been afraid that women's menstrual cycles would affect the outcome or cause obscure results. Young women could become pregnant, which could also be reflected in the results, or new drugs could adversely affect the development of the fetus. In laboratory experiments, only male rats were used in order to avoid any influence of the estrous cycle.

Q. How did the government help?

A. When Dr. Healy became the director of the National Institutes of Health, she made women's health a priority. She set up an Office of Research in Women's Health, appointed a director, Vivian Pinn, M.D., and funded $625 million toward the Women's Health Initiative, a fifteen-year study. The Women's Health Initiative is looking at the effects of estrogen on osteoporosis; of estrogen and progesterone on the development of heart disease and the subsequent risks of breast cancer; of the effects of simple dietary changes on colon and breast cancer; of the benefits of antioxidants such as vitamin E; and at other interventions that could affect women's medical care.

Q. Why were women unhappy with their medical care?

A. Women felt that their voices were not being heard. Issues that were important to them were not perceived so by the physician. Their first complaint was a lack of communication with the physician. We now appreciate that there is an unconscious difference in the way men and women talk, particularly when the health care provider is a man. Several studies have shown that men tend to dominate the conversation and often interrupt female patients. The dissatisfaction women felt with their physicians and the health care community resulted in a self-help movement and such publications as *Our Bodies, Ourselves*, by the Boston Women's Health Collective.

Women also were treated differently from men. Frequently their symptoms of angina or coronary artery disease were ignored. Only now do we recognize that the symptoms of these diseases are often different in women and men. While some women experience chest pain, others may be pain free but might feel weak or dizzy, or experience gastrointestinal problems. As a result, many women with heart attacks were turned away from hospitals and/or received delayed treatment. It is also believed that women received fewer interventions like coronary bypass surgery, angioplasty, or thrombolytic therapy and that their survival rate from heart attacks was poorer.

Q. What problems in medical education had an effect on women's health care?
A. The classical model in medical education was the 70-kilogram (154-pound) male. With the exception of reproductive issues, men and women were considered to be similar. The field of gender biology did not exist. Issues that related specifically to women were reserved for instruction in obstetrics and gynecology (ob/gyn). Sex and gender differences were ignored. When women were mentioned in textbooks (or the classroom), it was usually with respect to their reproductive function. Illustrations in anatomy and physical diagnosis texts rarely showed women. As women became a larger proportion of medical students, they recognized the gaps in medical education.

Q. What improved medical education?
A. Belief in the concept that women's health is more than just reproductive health and that it involves the whole spectrum of maintaining wellness as well as attending to disease. Women's health is the responsibility of all physicians, not a few specialists.

Q. Tell me about women's health centers in the United States.
A. On the increase are fully integrated women's health care centers that are characterized by a primary care physician and an ob/gyn who provide the full spectrum of care. They offer one-stop health care, where a woman can get her total preventive care: a physical exam including a breast exam, pelvic exam, and mammogram; bone densitometry; psychological support; social service support; nutritional sup-

port, and other needed services. The office should have abundant reading materials and information about women's health.

Q. What should a woman look for in a women's health center?
A. She should know exactly what the facility provides. She should ask questions. The primary care practitioners should provide total well-woman care including expertise in menopause, preconception counseling, contraception, adoption, and abortion. Are bone densitometry and mammography available? Is there an expert in plastic surgery, a psychologist or psychiatrist, a cardiologist who is interested in female heart disease, and a gynecologist available? Can you get advice about exercise, stress management, and nonpharmacological forms of health maintenance?

Q. What's best—a women's health center for one-stop shopping or a regular primary care physician who could direct a patient to a specialist?
A. Not all locations have women's health centers, and some centers are just marketing tools. It is most important to develop a good relationship with a competent, concerned physician. The physician should know and understand the needs of the patient. If the physician is not interested, the woman should look elsewhere for health care. In the managed care setting, nonphysician practitioners should be available for interdisciplinary support.

Q. What do you advise a woman in her fifties who wants to take the best care of her health?
A. Prevention should be the focus. Women should read and become informed since they can still influence their health at this age. Don't wait for something bad to happen. As soon as menstrual periods begin to change, make an appointment with a physician who is knowledgeable in women's health and can help with understanding the options.

Make a checklist of preventive behaviors. Continue to use sunscreen and avoid sunbathing. Watch your diet and include green leafy vegetables. Get the calcium that you need. Try not to put on the weight that seems inevitable. Continue to do breast self-exams and get a yearly mammogram. Be sure your stools are periodically tested for blood—at least yearly. Have a sigmoidoscopy or colonoscopy performed regularly, depending on your family history. If you are at risk for osteoporosis, get a bone density test. Have yearly pelvic exams and Pap smears. (Some say every two years.) Have your cholesterol and lipid levels measured. Take hormones if and when you need them, based on an analysis of your individual medical and family history.

Understand the killers. While many women are worried about breast cancer, they forget that coronary artery disease is the biggest killer of women. Try to stop smoking tobacco. If you are in an abusive relationship, get help to get out. No one deserves to be hurt physically or emotionally. You can change things, even at fifty. There are increased resources for women and children who are targets of violence. There are also laws to prevent stalking.

This is a good time to "stop and smell the roses" to decide what is important and where you are going. Don't go for medical fads. Don't be the first person on the block to try something new. Don't take "mega" doses of anything.

In our highly consumer-oriented culture, we all want to look young and beautiful. People who venture into plastic surgery should be knowledgeable and cautious. If you become depressed, seek help. Counseling and medication are very effective. Analyze, with professional help if necessary, why you feel you need surgery and what the real benefits will be. Above all, become an educated consumer of health care. Read and become informed. If you are knowledgeable, you'll demand what you need and become a partner in your health care.

Q. What are some of the challenges of the future?
A. Health care must be made available for all women and children regardless of ability to pay. Medical care must include a knowledge of racial and cultural issues. Ensuring prenatal care, care for those with disabilities, adequate nutrition, and preventive health services for women and children should be another goal. Since aging may be associated with disabilities, falls, and fractures, rehabilitation must address these issues. We also need to make sure that lesbian patients feel comfortable with health providers so they access health care. We need

to recognize the impact of global health issues on our future. Health care occurs within a cultural and political context. Good medical care must approach these issues as well as the biology of health and disease. Educating patients to be full partners in their health maintenance is a goal.

2

A Prescription for Women's Health

Elizabeth Berger Mandell, M.D.

Elizabeth Mandell graduated from college in 1984 with a degree in biology. After earning her medical degree at Cornell University Medical College in 1988, she completed her residency in obstetrics and gynecology at Lenox Hill Hospital in New York City. In 1992 Dr. Mandell became assistant professor of obstetrics and gynecology at the University of Virginia Health Sciences Center in Charlottesville.

Q. How does the health of a woman in her fifties differ from that of a man?
A. Although men and women share many of the same health concerns as they enter their sixth decade of life, there are some important differences. The most obvious difference is the abrupt shift in the hormonal environment that women experience during these years. Men undergo hormonal changes during their life span, but these tend to be gradual.

For women there is an identifiable signpost—menopause—which is associated with a significant decline in the production of estrogen. Menopause occurs in this country at an average age of fifty-one. Prior to menopause, a woman's ovaries secrete large amounts of estrogen. Following menopause, the amount of estrogen production is minimal. The physical and emotional effects of this estrogen withdrawal can be quite dramatic. The majority of women in their fifties will notice signs of estrogen deprivation. Symptoms can include hot flashes, night sweats, insomnia, memory loss, mood swings, genital discomfort, joint pain, and fatigue. No naturally occurring hormonal event in men approximates this experience.

Another common problem faced by women in their fifties is menstrual irregularity. Hormone imbalances can lead to extremely heavy bleeding in some women. This can be inconvenient as well as frightening. Obviously there is no parallel condition for men.

The most significant health issue facing a woman in her fifties is her increased risk of heart disease. Heart disease is the most common cause of death for both women and men in this country. Most people are surprised to learn that women are more likely to die from heart disease than from breast cancer. In fact, for every woman in the United States who dies from breast cancer, five women will die from heart disease. Prior to menopause, women are protected from heart disease by high levels of estrogen secreted by the ovaries. Estrogen helps to keep the levels of "good cholesterol" high, which reduces the risk of cardiac disease. Starting at age fifty-five, however, women start to catch up with men, and by the time they reach eighty, women and men are at equal risk for death from heart disease.

Osteoporosis is a prime example of a disease process that impacts a fifty-year-old woman more directly than a fifty-year-old man. Although women and men will both undergo a gradual loss of bone density in the later decades of life, women undergo an especially rapid decline of bone density in the decade following menopause. For this reason, osteoporosis prevention is a serious concern for women in their fifties, whereas it is rarely a problem for men of that age. Additionally, women have lighter skeletons than men to begin with, which serves to heighten the differences in risk for this serious condition.

Q. Why is it important for women, especially mature women, to be treated medically as a whole person?
A. Life is a balancing act. So is medicine. Prudent decision making requires a careful assessment of risks and benefits, and nowhere is this more salient than when treating midlife women. You can't prescribe

estrogen to treat a woman's bones without considering its effects on her breasts and her uterus. You have to look at the big picture.

Although this is the time of life when women are prone to develop illnesses such as hypertension, diabetes, and arthritis, it is also the time they can take definite steps toward preventing, or at least diminishing, many health problems associated with aging. Health care in your fifties is exciting because there are multiple areas available for intervention. The changes and uncertainties surrounding menopause are sure to cause an uproar, but this presents the perfect opportunity for positive change. Now is the time to begin an exercise program, or stop smoking, or take a low-fat cooking class.

One of the most challenging but fascinating aspects of treating women in this age group is that they bring their whole family with them even though they are the only patient in the room. Women who are in their fifties tend to lead complicated and varied lives. Some still have young children at home. Others are already grandmothers. Some are married, some are single, some are widowed. Compared to women of previous generations, today's fifty-year-old woman is more likely to be divorced. She is also more likely to work outside the home and more likely to be taking care of an elderly parent. These stresses and demands are essential parts of the health care equation.

Q. Baby boomers are beginning to enter middle age. How will this affect medical care for women?
A. Aging boomers are the best thing that could have happened to women's health care. First of all, they command attention by the sheer strength of their numbers. There are more people entering their fifties than ever before in history, and half of them are women. Second, many women in this generation entered adulthood as revolutionaries, and they're not about to step into middle age any more quietly. They have focused public awareness on issues that are important to them and have put women's health in the spotlight. And the medical profession has responded. Research in areas such as breast cancer and osteoporosis has skyrocketed. Women's clinics, designed to accommodate the unique needs of this population, are becoming increasingly popular. It is no longer taboo to discuss hot flashes. The boomers have taken menopause out of the closet.

Q. Why do women need midlife health centers?

A. Midlife health centers offer convenience in the sense that most of their services can be coordinated with respect to place and time. The idea is that a woman can combine a mammogram, a nutrition consult, a cardiology appointment, and a gynecology exam in one morning.

Q. How can a woman coordinate a medical program that meets her needs if there isn't an integrated women's health care center close to her town?

A. If you don't have a "midlife mecca" of this sort in your neighborhood, don't lose hope. Family medicine doctors, internists, gynecologists, and/or nurse practitioners are all excellent places to start. What matters most for success in midlife health is a commitment on the part of your doctor to help you assess your individual situation and your willingness to act as your own advocate. Even if everything cannot be available under one roof, you can create your tailor-made health care plan. The areas to pay attention to include cardiovascular health (focusing on blood pressure and cholesterol), cancer screening (in particular, Pap smears, mammograms, and sigmoidoscopies), osteoporosis prevention, diet and exercise advice, stress reduction, and smoking cessation (if needed). This is the short list. You may have other medical problems that need special attention and need to be factored into the equation as well. Of course, you may not need to address all of these issues at every doctor's visit, but you and your primary care provider should have an overall sense of where you are and where you are going in terms of your health in the decades to come.

Q. What is the status of integrated health care programs for women? Are women's midlife centers in the beginning stages of development, or are they flourishing throughout the United States?

A. Specialized clinics for midlife health are, to my knowledge, quite a recent phenomenon. A handful of dedicated specialists laid the groundwork, but I believe that the "one-stop shop" concept is new. These clinics have evolved to meet the needs of a unique group of patients. Women in their fifties tend to be in transition. Often they have drifted away from the health care system after finishing their childbearing and don't resurface for a decade or more. Midlife clinics have seized the opportunity to reconnect with this group of women. There is currently a mix of established clinics and fledgling clinics, but very few of them have been around for more than a decade. We're certainly not at the point where there is a clinic on every street corner, but the idea is rapidly gaining in popularity. These clinics tend to be progressive and innovative, and they often rely on the patients themselves to suggest improvements. This is an exciting area now—funding is increasing, research is blossoming, and it seems as if new products and options become available every week. All of this leads to better health care for women in their fifties.

Q. How would you advise women in their fifties to protect their health?
A. Prevention is the best protection. You are standing on a threshold. Now is your chance to make decisions that will impact the rest of your life. Examine your lifestyle with a critical eye. Are there some factors you could change that would significantly reduce your health risks? Do you eat too much? Drink too much? Sit too much? Smoke too much? Work too much? Getting older is frightening—there are many things beyond your control. But you might as well try to positively influence the areas you can affect. In the arena of health care, you don't do yourself any favors by being passive.

Next, go out and find a physician who is genuinely interested in issues of midlife health. But don't expect to get all your answers at once. Keep in mind that medical knowledge is continually evolving. People often are disappointed that their doctors can't answer questions definitively. "All those years of medical school and she can't figure out why I'm so tired all the time?" "Stacks of journals on the shelves and he still can't give me a simple yes or no about the estrogen question?" "Panels of experts and still nobody can tell me how often to get my mammogram?"

Rather than getting frustrated, I think women should use these gray zones as springboards for discussions. Someone who offers quick and easy answers probably isn't taking the time to regard your case individually. A doctor who takes the time to explain what is known and what is not known is more likely to give your question thoughtful consideration. Also, make sure your physician keeps you up to date.

15

When you have your yearly checkup don't forget to ask, "So, is there anything new that I need to know about mammograms?" "Any new breakthroughs in estrogen replacement therapy?" "What vitamins are you recommending these days?" And so on.

Remember, the more information you bring to the visit, the more you'll take away. Do your research. Learn as much as you can about your family history. Telling your doctor that your grandmother died of "some kind of internal cancer" will not separate you from the crowd. However, if you can report that it was colon cancer or ovarian cancer or stomach cancer, then you will set the stage for a personalized discussion. Specific information like this will enable your doctor to discuss risk factors, prevention strategies, and screening techniques for diseases that are particularly relevant to you.

The keys to protecting your health are motivation, luck, and a successful partnership with your physician. You deserve a health care provider who is excited by the challenge of solving your unique equation.

Q. What are your hopes for the future of medical care for women?
A. I am encouraged by the recent burst of research attention directed toward women's health, and I hope to see it continue. In addition to traditional medicine, I believe there is much to be learned about nutrition and alternative therapies. At this point there is a severe lack of solid science. I would like to see some rigorous controlled studies evaluating plant estrogens, for example. Certainly I think women need to be included more often in studies of heart disease, cholesterol, and hypertension. Of course, it would be wonderful to have definitive answers regarding the estrogen–breast cancer connection. There is some exciting but very early evidence suggesting a preventive role for estrogen against Alzheimer's disease, and I am looking forward to watching this science unfold. We have a long way to go but we are on the right track.

Q. What is your prescription for a long, happy, healthy life?
A. It's essential to remember that optimal health involves a synthesis of physical and emotional well-being. These are intertwined inextricably.

A crucial factor that is missing from so many people's lives is exercise. It's my favorite all-purpose prescription. We all know that exercise is good for our hearts and our bones and our figures, but even more important, it's one of the best things you can do for your mind and your mood. There is a scientific basis behind the "runner's high"— physical exercise releases chemicals in the brain called endorphins. These chemicals, which are "100 percent natural," are similar to opiate drugs such as heroin and morphine. No wonder people who get started on an exercise program find it addicting! Many people suffering from fatigue, stress, and blue moods (not to mention insomnia, weight gain, and constipation) can find more relief from a walk around the block than from a hormone pill or an antidepressant. Exercise can do wonders for your self-esteem and body image as well. Active people live longer than their sedentary peers. Go for a walk. It's the cheapest, safest fix you'll ever find.

3

Understanding Menopause

JoAnn V. Pinkerton, M.D.

JoAnn Pinkerton graduated from college with a degree in psychology. After graduation, she attended the Medical College of Virginia in Richmond. She completed her obstetrics and gynecology residency at the University of Virginia School of Medicine in Charlottesville, where she joined the faculty in 1985. Dr. Pinkerton developed a specialty in menopause and hormone replacement therapy. She has been medical director of the University of Virginia's Women's Midlife Center since 1995.

The Midlife Center is a multidepartmental, academic-based center that provides a comprehensive approach to women's midlife health through prevention and early diagnosis of common health problems such as osteoporosis and heart disease.

Q. **As the medical director of a women's midlife health center, you see thousands of women who are approaching or in their forties and fifties. Please paint a picture of a typical patient.**
A. Sally is forty-nine. She is at the peak of her profession and is balancing career, husband, and children. Her father died two years ago and her mother has just been diagnosed with breast cancer. Her older sister had a nonfatal heart attack at fifty-eight. Sally has begun skipping four periods a year. She is very irritable premenstrually and has been on the verge of tears during recent meetings with her boss. She has recently developed hot flashes ten times a day and night

sweats that interfere with her sleep. She has gained five pounds per year over the last four years, going from a trim size 8 to a size 14. Her self-esteem is dropping. She knows she is eating due to stress but can't help it. Her last period caught her unaware and unprepared, and she ruined her favorite suit. She is embarrassed by her inability to cope because she has always been "strong" and in control. She comes to the Midlife Center hoping for a miracle—to feel the way she felt ten years ago.

Q. Let's talk about menopause. What is menopause?
A. The word "menopause" literally means the cessation of menses (menstrual cycles), but it's actually a series of changes that occur as a woman's body gradually loses estrogen. A woman is truly menopausal six to twelve months after her last normal menstrual period.

Q. When do most women become menopausal?
A. The average age of menopause is fifty-one, plus or minus five years.

Q. How have attitudes toward menopause changed?
A. In the "old days," women didn't often survive past menopause. It's only in recent years that women have begun to outlive their menopause.

The male scientists of the seventeenth century described menopause as a character disorder, a chronic disease, or a sign of female weakness. In the nineteenth century, investigators began to study menopause, but they dwelled on negative emotional traits, such as melancholy, mood swings, and irritability. Women were valued primarily for their childbearing capabilities, so menopausal women were thought of as useless, sexless, and undesirable. Back then menopause was considered to be the end of meaning to a woman's life. In 1929 scientists isolated the hormone estrogen, which ushered in our current understanding of the physiologic processes of menopause.

Today women live into their eighties, nineties, and, it is hoped, into their hundreds. Midlife has been redefined as ages forty to sixty-five. The average woman will live about one-third of her life post-menopausal. Although myths still abound in a society where youth is prized, women are quickly changing the negative image of menopause as a disease, a tragedy, and a sign of old age. Instead of hot flashes, women now have "power surges." Menopause is viewed as a natural transition.

Q. What is perimenopause?
A. Perimenopause is the five to ten years preceding menopause when women begin to have irregular periods, hormonal fluctuations, and never quite know what to expect from month to month.

While most twenty- and thirty-year-old women have regular menstrual cycles—they usually can pinpoint when their periods will arrive each month and how many days the flow will last—menses become erratic for women in their forties or early fifties, with frequent cycles—every twenty-one to twenty-three days—followed by one or two missed periods, followed again by a forty-day or sixty-day cycle. One period may be heavy, lasting only three days, the next a lighter ten-day cycle. Women at this stage begin to develop menopausal symptoms. We now know that the perimenopause is the hardest time for women because of the fluctuations in hormones and erratic symptoms. Once women are menopausal, it is much easier.

Q. Why do these changes occur as women get older?
A. In their late thirties and early forties, women begin to have fluctuation of ovarian function, causing estrogen levels to decline. Eventually the ovary completely fails to ovulate. It's a complicated process. The pituitary gland, which is located at the base of the brain, works with the ovary. As the ovary begins to produce less estrogen and fewer eggs, the pituitary tries to stimulate the ovary to work harder. This process continues, causing menstrual fluctuations—a woman might have normal ovarian function for three to six months or even a year, skip several cycles and not make an egg, and then make another egg. There are 2,000 to 4,000 eggs remaining at menopause, but these seem no longer to respond to stimulation by the pituitary gland.

Q. What are the common symptoms of menopause that may cause upheaval in women's lives?
A. The most common symptoms are hot flashes, night sweats, irregu-

lar bleeding, weight gain, premenstrual syndrome and mood swings, depression or depressed mood, heart palpitations and anxiety, insomnia, memory changes and concentration problems, headaches, joint and muscle aches, changes in urination, changes in sexuality, vaginal dryness, and skin changes. Often, at the same time, women may experience significant stress with career changes, marital problems, issues of aging parents, and dealing with teenagers or an empty nest. This is often referred to as the "Big Squeeze."

Hot Flashes

A hot flash is the perception of warmth, usually starting from the head downward, which may be associated with sweating. It can be mild or profuse. Temperature changes in the body can be documented. When the temperature goes up, the body perceives that it's too hot and dilates the blood vessels so that the temperature will drop. We don't know the actual trigger. We used to think that hot flashes were due strictly to decreases in estrogen levels, but we now know that's not true. However, fluctuations in estrogen levels are part of the trigger.

About 70 percent of women get hot flashes. Hot flashes are minor for some people, with occasional warm feelings. Some women never experience them. We don't know why.

Other women can have five, ten, twenty, even forty hot flashes in a day. They can last from thirty seconds to fifteen minutes and may persist for three to five years.

Night Sweats

Night sweats can be as mild as waking up in the middle of the night just feeling warm or as extreme as producing enough sweat to soak the sheets. The majority of women who experience night sweats have them for less than three to five years.

Irregular Bleeding

Heavier, mildly irregular bleeding patterns (every twenty-one to thirty-five days) prior to menopause are bothersome but not usually a cause for worry. Erratic bleeding can respond very quickly to treatment with cyclic progesterone. (This progesterone is a medication prescribed by the physician, not the cyclic progesterone that your own body makes. If your own body was making cyclic progesterone, you wouldn't have bleeding problems and therefore wouldn't need the medication.)

Persistent or heavy bleeding could be a sign of polyps in the uterus, fibroids, or cervical or uterine cancer, all of which require further evaluation. The physician may perform an endometrial biopsy—a scraping of the lining of the uterus—or a vaginal ultrasound, which utilizes sound waves to visualize the female organs; both are office procedures. Saline instilled in the uterus improves ability to visualize pathology in the uterus. A hysteroscopy, in which the doctor looks into the uterus with a lighted tube, may be done in the office or in the hospital. A dilatation and curettage, commonly referred to as a D & C, in which the doctor scrapes off the lining of the uterus to look for abnormal cells, may be needed for persistent bleeding. Hysteroscopy combined with D & C is usually an ambulatory case, not a prolonged "in-hospital" procedure, and usually does not require overnight admission.

Weight Gain

For many women in their fifties, metabolism declines as well as physical activity. Women may be more sedentary than they were in their twenties and thirties. The two together can cause dramatic weight gains—ten pounds a year, forty to fifty pounds over a ten-year period. Weight gain is a problem that can hurt a woman's self-esteem.

To avoid or minimize weight gain, a woman must burn more calories than she consumes by focusing on exercise patterns and watching caloric intake and daily amount of fats. If we begin to see an increase in weight—say, of five to ten pounds—we try to help women look at what's going on in their lives and help them increase their exercise. Weight gain in midlife can be very frustrating. It may take six months of exercise and decreased calories before a woman sees weight loss occur. The first goal often is to stop the gain, then attempt gradual weight loss through exercise, activity, and decreased calories.

Premenstrual Syndrome and Mood Swings

Premenstrual syndrome (PMS) can worsen during perimenopause. PMS normally begins about the week before menses, when women may feel irritable, sensitive, and cry more easily. These women are fine for two to three weeks, but during the fourth week any problem stresses them out. The symptoms can escalate to the point that some women can't function. Other symptoms may include bloating, water retention, headaches, insomnia (often early-morning awakening), excessive fatigue, mood swings, or depression. Regular exercise and avoiding caffeine and salt may help PMS. Vitamins such as B-6 or E are commonly used. New antidepressants that affect serotonin levels are also effective.

Depression

Mild or major depressions often coexist with menopause; either the depression is associated with menopause or it is an exacerbation in women who have had chronic problems in the past. Menopause per se doesn't cause depression. There's probably an interplay with serotonin receptors in the brain during menopause that makes depression more likely. (Serotonin is a brain chemical—actually the chemical that Prozac works on.) Also because women in midlife have multiple responsibilities to children, spouse, aging parents, work, community, or church, there is more chance of situational depression, which may be exacerbated by losses seen at midlife.

Heart Palpitations and Anxiety

If women have experienced heart palpitations, they may become more frequent at this stage. Although we don't feel that anxiety and nervousness are caused by menopause, some women have anxiety prior to their menses, which worsens into panic attacks. At menopause, panic attacks may increase in women who are predisposed to them. Sometimes both antianxiety agents and estrogen are needed.

Insomnia

Insomnia can be a major problem. Menopausal women often have early-morning awakening and difficulty going back to sleep. This seems to be separate from being awakened by night sweats or hot flashes. Some researchers think the pineal gland (located in the brain, associated with light and dark) might be involved. There may be a decrease in REM (rapid-eye-movement) sleep. Although some patients have tried melatonin to cure insomnia, there are no research studies substantiating its benefits. Yet insomnia may explain to some degree why menopausal women are more irritable or feel that they have less capability to cope. There are a number of nonmedical ways to approach this, including herbal teas and relaxation techniques. Hormone therapy may help.

Memory Changes and Concentration Problems

Some women note memory changes, often the worsening of short-term memory recall or difficulty with concentrating. It's unclear if this is linked to estrogen levels or whether insomnia worsens the problem. These problems often improve with hormone therapy.

Headaches

A change in headaches may occur during menopause. Menstrual migraines are felt to be hormonally related. Because menopause is a hormonal event with fluctuating estrogen and progesterone levels, headaches may begin or worsen during this time, particularly migraines. These headaches may improve or worsen with estrogen therapy. Excessive medication for headaches actually can worsen the frequency or intensity of headaches, due to the rebound effect. Menstrual migraines may disappear once women are through menopause.

Joint and Muscle Aches

Joint and muscle aches seem to worsen as estrogen levels drop. The etiology is unclear. No link has yet been found between arthritis and lowered estrogen levels.

Changes in Urination

The bladder contains estrogen receptors. With menopause and decreased estrogen levels, the bladder becomes less able to distend, which can lead to urge incontinence, in which the woman may get the urge to go but leaks urine before she can get to the bathroom.

Women who sneeze or cough also may leak small amounts of urine. During and after menopause, the loss of estrogen and the thinning of the epithelium (lining of the bladder) may cause a worsening of this so-called stress incontinence. Kegel exercises and vaginal estrogen may improve stress incontinence. A number of surgical procedures are also available.

Changes in Sexuality

Loss of sex drive or decreased sexual response is a common complaint. It's very difficult to know if this loss is due to decreased estrogen or testosterone (the male hormone) or related to a hormonal event, a fatigue event, or a midlife event. Many perimenopausal women have multiple life stresses, which may affect desire. Some women's sex drive improves when they are given estrogen or combination estrogen and testosterone. Medications such as antihypertensives and antidepressants also can decrease sex drive and sexual response.

Vaginal Dryness

Most women don't note vaginal dryness unless they're having intercourse. Vaginal dryness is associated with loss of estrogen, which causes thinning of the vaginal tissues. This can cause pain during intercourse—pain just from penetration, a feeling of friction or burning during intercourse, or a feeling of rawness or burning in the vagina following intercourse. Over-the-counter topical lubricants or moisturizers can help. Topical or oral estrogens also may be prescribed.

Q. Which menopausal symptoms will estrogen-replacement therapy (ERT) help?
A. Virtually all of them. Estrogen can dramatically relieve insomnia, hot flashes, night sweats, and mood swings, usually within two weeks or less. Difficulty with concentrating and memory changes may improve with estrogen. It also may prevent the pain that women have during intercourse, and it has been found in some instances to help menstrual migraines, joint pains, muscle aches, and urinary problems. Estrogen can give women a sense of well-being. Estrogen helps maintain skin elasticity and therefore may help cause less dryness and wrinkling, but it is not truly an antiaging hormone.

Q. What are the long-term benefits of estrogen replacement?
A. Prior to menopause, the estrogen produced by the ovaries exerts a protective effect against cardiovascular disease. After menopause, when the ovarian production of estrogen is significantly diminished, the risk of cardiovascular disease increases. Estrogen replacement has been clearly shown to decrease the risk of heart disease by 40 to 50

percent. It also will help maintain bone density and therefore prevent osteoporosis. And there's very exciting but still early work that estrogen may decrease the incidence or severity of Alzheimer's disease and possibly decrease the risk of colon cancer, stroke, and macular degeneration (leading cause of blindness).

Q. If estrogen is so great, why not give it to every woman?
A. Actually, some physicians look at menopause as an estrogen deficiency and think that every woman should be on estrogen. But some women have risk factors (discussed below) that make us hesitate to recommend estrogen. Other women are hesitant to take estrogen either because they prefer "a natural menopause," prefer to avoid the use of medications, or are afraid of taking estrogen.

Q. Why do many doctors prescribe hormones as women are entering menopause?
A. There is an acceleration in bone loss as women go through menopause. Once women are five years postmenopausal, bone loss will have occurred already. If they begin estrogen therapy as they are entering menopause, that precipitous bone loss can be prevented. In addition, women lose the protective effect of estrogen after menopause and their risk for heart disease increases. Ten years after menopause, a woman's risk for heart disease equals that of a man. Women become symptomatic as they enter menopause, and estrogen relieves the menopausal symptoms. One can choose to begin hormones during perimenopause, menopause, or postmenopause.

Q. Who, without question, should take hormones?
A. There is clear-cut benefit from estrogen for women who are at risk for heart disease or osteoporosis.

Q. Who should not take hormones?
A. Women with current breast cancer, women with palpable breast lumps that have not been diagnosed, women with current endometrial cancer, women who have suffered an acute stroke or blood clot, or women whose menstrual migraines are worsened on estrogen. Estrogen may make gallstones more symptomatic and should not be used

with active liver disease. Prior history of breast or endometrial cancer requires extensive discussion regarding risks and benefits.

Q. Does estrogen replacement increase a woman's risk of uterine cancer?
A. If a woman takes estrogen by itself for a prolonged period of time, she will increase the chance of developing precancer or cancer of the uterus. There is a 20 percent risk of developing hyperplasia (a buildup of the lining that can lead to precancer) if estrogen is used by itself (at 0.625 mg, a low dose) for one year. We can safely guard against this problem by prescribing adequate amounts of progesterone for adequate lengths of time each month. We can prevent or reverse most cases of uterine precancer with adequate progesterone.

Q. How long do women take hormone-replacement therapy (HRT)—the combined estrogen/progesterone replacement?
A. The length of time a woman takes HRT depends on the reason she is taking it. If she is using hormones to help with menopausal symptoms, then she may use them for three to five years and then begin to taper off.

If she is using them for prevention, then the risks and benefits should be evaluated periodically. Potentially, some women will stay on HRT for life. In the future, new hormone products will be developed and natural products will have been tested, I hope. This will give women more options in the future. Raloxifene has just been approved by the FDA for prevention of osteoporosis. It improves bone density and lowers cholesterol, although the magnitude of the effect is less than that seen with estrogen. However, it appears to decrease the risk of uterine and breast cancer. Three-year safety data on raloxifene shows a 50 percent reduction in breast cancer for women on raloxifene versus placebo (dummy pill). We now have specific nonestrogen treatments for prevention of heart disease and osteoporosis with cholesterol-lowering agents and agents that improve bone density, such as alendronate and miacalcitonin. Phytoestrogens are plant estrogens that are being studied at this time. Populations with high levels of soy intake have lower rates of coronary heart disease, breast cancer, and osteoporosis. Soybeans are a rich source of phytoestrogens. These have both estrogen and antiestrogen effects. In addition, low-dose (half-dose) HRT may be enough to maintain bone density and lower cholesterol and may be an option for women choosing long-term HRT. Additional research is ongoing for improved ("designer") estrogens that will help the heart, bones, and brain without increasing the risk for uterine or breast cancer.

Q. How can physicians monitor bleeding problems to be certain that a woman on hormones has not developed uterine cancer?
A. Women taking cyclic hormones should have regular cycles. On continuous HRT (daily estrogen and progesterone), her bleeding should stop after six to nine months. If a women develops abnormal bleeding, we can perform a transvaginal ultrasound in the office, in which we look at the lining of the uterus to see if it has thickened. In that case, we can instill saline, which distends the uterine cavity and allows visualization of endometrial tumors, polyps, or cancer. We also can do an endometrial biopsy in the office, where we take a sample of the lining of the uterus to make sure that precancerous cells are not developing. Another option is an office procedure called hysteroscopy, where we use a lighted instrument to look inside the uterus for abnormal areas.

Q. Can estrogen cause breast cancer?
A. We don't know. That's the million-dollar question. The studies on estrogen and its link to breast cancer are confusing and conflicting. Most of the studies are not randomized or controlled. With conflicting results, the analysis of the potential risk for breast cancer is difficult. We do not believe that we will know the answer soon about whether there's an increased risk for breast cancer. Studies do suggest that high dosages of estrogen for long periods of time may increase the breast cancer risk—that is, at double the normal dose for ten years. But even these data are conflicting. Until we know, women need to be aware that there may be an increased risk of breast cancer, particularly after long-term use. The NIH-funded Women's Health Initiative may answer the question.

Q. What if a woman has risk factors for breast cancer—a mother or sister with breast cancer, for example?
A. These women are already at increased risk for breast cancer, particularly if the cancers were premenopausal. We don't yet know whether adding estrogen increases a woman's risk of breast cancer if she already has an increased risk from her family history (that is, if there is an additive effect). A family history of breast cancer needs to be considered in the risks/benefits analysis. The new designer estrogens may be an option.

Q. What if a woman has been recently diagnosed with breast cancer?
A. Most physicians don't give estrogen to someone who has just been diagnosed with breast cancer.

Q. Should women who have had prior histories of breast cancer take estrogen?
A. Some breast cancers have estrogen receptors. If a woman had an estrogen receptor breast cancer, we may be increasing her chance of a recurrence by giving estrogen. Again, studies are conflicting. We know there is not a dramatic short-term increased risk of recurrence. A small number of studies have shown that women on estrogen when diagnosed with breast cancer have longer survival and do better after breast cancer than women who are not on estrogen. And then there are the issues of preventing heart disease and osteoporosis. And also the issue that local vaginal estrogen may improve the quality of life or allow continued sexual functioning. So across the country, experts provide varying answers.

Q. What about a woman who is five or ten years out from a very early breast cancer and has bone loss or the risk of heart disease?
A. Many physicians will give estrogen to such women after extensive discussion of risks and benefits. Some doctors recommend estrogen to all women with breast cancer because they feel that the benefits outweigh the risk of recurring breast cancer. A woman with a localized node-negative breast cancer has a 90 to 95 percent chance of five-year survival. Therefore, long-term health risks and potential prevention of

heart disease or osteoporosis become important. Designer estrogens may be an option in the future.

Q. What are other concerns about taking estrogen?
A. Some women feel it is not natural. They don't want to take something that the body's not making. However, women take thyroid replacement if their thyroid malfunctions. In menopausal women, the ovary is no longer making premenopausal levels of estrogen.

Estrogen may increase the risk for symptomatic gallstones. Estrogen is metabolized through the liver, which is one of the ways that it lowers cholesterol, but it also has an effect on gallstones and gallbladder function. It is not recommended for women with acute liver disease.

There has been a long-term concern about whether estrogen therapy increases the risk for stroke or blood clots. Birth control pills, particularly the high-dose pills used in the past, have increased the risk for blood clots and stroke. That risk has decreased as the amount of estrogen in the pills has decreased. When we're talking about estrogen therapy, we're talking about much lower amounts than that seen in the pill. We think that low-dose hormone therapy slightly increases the risk for blood clots or stroke. We would not recommend starting estrogen therapy in the face of an acute stroke, an acute blood clot, or for people who have an abnormality in the clotting system that makes them a high risk for blood clots. We do feel comfortable putting women who have had prior strokes and prior blood clots on hormone therapy. Early evidence suggests that estrogen may decrease the risk for stroke by 30 percent. Transdermal estrogen (by patch) is theoretically safer.

Q. How does estrogen lower the risk of heart disease or osteoporosis?
A. With regard to the heart, estrogen decreases the total cholesterol and improves the good cholesterol. It also decreases the amount of cholesterol-related plaque that forms on the heart vessels (thus the vessels are cleaner) and improves blood flow to the heart and the flexibility of the blood vessels.

When women enter menopause, there is an exaggerated loss of

bone density for the first five years. Estrogen started at menopause decreases this loss and helps preserve bone density. It is most effective if started at the time of menopause. If started later, it will still decrease the risk for fracture although it may not improve bone density.

Q. Are there alternatives to estrogen that can treat women's menopausal symptoms and help lower their risk of heart disease and osteoporosis?
A. Women can decrease their risk of heart disease by not smoking or stopping smoking, by eating a low-cholesterol diet, and by exercising. They can try to prevent osteoporosis by taking calcium and by doing weight-bearing exercises. Vitamins and herbs may help women with the menopausal symptoms. Plant estrogens are currently being tested. Antioxidants are being tested. Women on estrogen need 1,000 milligrams of calcium; those not on estrogen need 1,500 mg of calcium. The preferred form is calcium citrate or calcium carbonate.

Now new medications called bisphosphanates are on the market that are *not* hormones but are FDA approved to treat or prevent bone loss and significantly decrease the risk for fractures. Calcium, vitamin D, and weight-bearing exercise are key ingredients in *all* plans to prevent osteoporosis. By themselves, however, they are not enough for most women.

A nasal form of calcitonin, another nonestrogen, is FDA approved for treatment of postmenopausal osteoporosis. Extended-release sodium fluoride is being tested. Estrogen, low-dose alendronate, and raloxifene are approved medications for prevention of osteoporosis.

Q. Do you believe that products such as soy and ginseng are helpful, or do they merely provide a placebo effect?
A. Many compounds, such as found in soy products, ginseng, and dong-quai, have estrogenic activities. We don't know yet whether they prevent osteoporosis or heart disease, but they may relieve menopausal symptoms. Early studies are in progress. There is a clear placebo effect for many women. If a person takes soy, ginseng, or vitamin E and her menopausal symptoms get better, it doesn't matter whether it's a placebo effect or a direct effect, as long as symptomatically she is

better. We don't know if there is a risk of uterine cancer or breast cancer with these compounds.

Q. Why would a woman choose estrogen therapy or the alternatives?

A. The severity of her menopausal symptoms usually determines whether a woman chooses estrogen therapy or nonestrogen alternatives of menopause. Any decision she makes can be changed at a later date. If estrogen doesn't work to relieve her symptoms or she doesn't want to stay on it, she may elect to try other alternatives. Or if she prefers to avoid medications, she may try alternatives first. If her symptoms are not relieved, she may then decide to try estrogen. If she has no symptoms, then she must look at her risks of medical diseases such as osteoporosis or heart disease to decide if she should take hormones.

Q. Tell me about cyclic versus continuous hormone replacement therapy. Will women on HRT ever stop bleeding?

A. Women in their fifties don't usually want to continue to have periods. With cyclic estrogen/progesterone replacement, where women take estrogen alone either twenty-five or thirty days per month with twelve to fourteen days of estrogen combined with progesterone, most women will continue having bleeding, although it may get lighter and lighter and eventually stop. But with continuous hormone-replacement therapy, where you take both estrogen and progesterone 365 days per year, 75 percent of women eventually will stop bleeding, usually after six to nine months.

Q. Why does continuous estrogen/progesterone cause the bleeding to stop?

A. The constant progesterone causes the lining of the uterus to become very thin, and there's not enough growth of the cells to cause bleeding. It also protects against the development of hyperplasia. Even if a woman stops bleeding on the continuous regimen, she is still protected from developing hyperplasia as long as she continues to take both estrogen and progesterone.

Q. How do physicians determine the proper dosages of hormones?
A. Some physicians start everyone on a low dose and then go up. Others start at a higher dose and then go down. I normally start with a low estrogen dose equivalent to 0.625 mg conjugated estrogen. That dosage will control many women's menopausal symptoms at the same time as it protects against osteoporosis and heart disease. Some women may need higher dosages to eliminate symptoms of menopause.

There are three types of estrogen found in women—E1, E2, E3. E1 is estrone, E2 is estradiol, and E3 is estriol. It's difficult to measure and to know accurately whether a specific type or level of estrogen is protective of the bones and the heart.

Once women are through menopause, we prefer to have them on low levels of estrogen, the level that does not seem to be associated with any increased risk for breast cancer. We are now studying even lower doses—half-dose and three-quarter-dose—that we hope will still prevent bone loss and heart disease but have even less potential to cause breast cancer.

Q. Why don't physicians test women for the amount of their natural estrogen?
A. One reason is that estrogen varies during the cycle. Also, serum levels do not necessarily correlate with how a woman is feeling. Many women with low estrogen levels have no symptoms. Other women with high levels do have symptoms. There is some evidence that an estradiol level of 50 μg (micrograms) is protective against bone loss in otherwise healthy women.

Q. What would you advise a woman who is entering menopause? She's fifty and experiencing irregular bleeding, hot flashes, and night sweats. What should she do?
A. I strongly encourage her to find a gynecologist who is interested in and knowledgeable about menopausal hormone replacement. Together they can discuss her symptoms, needs, health risks, family history, and the benefits and risks of hormone therapy. After a medical examination, doctor and patient can try to evaluate her risks of osteoporosis, heart disease, Alzheimer's, colon cancer, and breast cancer. The physi-

cian can then decide whether to recommend hormones. The woman is a partner in the decision.

I almost always recommend a trial dose of hormones when a woman becomes symptomatic during menopause. If she's strongly against hormones, I provide information about alternatives. We will have new and different types of estrogen and progesterone products in the future. If a woman elects not to take HRT, I recommend a bone density test and lipid (cholesterol) profile. We can then follow these over time.

Q. When is hysterectomy an option to cure menopausal symptoms?
A. Many problems will improve or resolve after menopause. A woman should not have her uterus removed simply so she won't have to deal with bleeding unless it is excessive or she is anemic. There are risks and even deaths from hysterectomies. Heavy, irregular bleeding or an enlarging fibroid uterus are valid reasons for a hysterectomy. Hysterectomy may be needed to treat uterine or cervical cancer.

Q. Is concern about pregnancy and birth control an issue for women who are fifty?
A. Fertility begins to decline for women in their midforties. Some cycles may make eggs and some may not. But risk for pregnancy does not necessarily go to zero when you're fifty. Women have delivered babies at fifty and fifty-one. I think the oldest recorded spontaneous pregnancy was a fifty-seven-year-old Irishwoman. Recently a woman who received a donor egg delivered in her sixties, but she did not conceive spontaneously or even use her own eggs. So women need to be concerned about birth control until they are through menopause. Dr. Leon Speroff, an expert in gynecological endocrinology, has recommended that if a woman's FSH (follicle-stimulating hormone) remains above 30 IU/ml (International Unit per milliliter), her chances of getting pregnant are slim. At that point women can discontinue birth control. (FSH is a blood test to measure how well the ovaries are functioning.) We usually recommend birth control until women are through menopause for a year—that is, they have had no periods for a year before they discontinue birth control or their FSH remains greater than 30.

Q. How can a woman feel comfortable without birth control if she takes estrogen and bleeds each month?
A. Just because a woman is bleeding doesn't mean she's fertile or produces eggs. Hormones cause the cyclic bleeding. This would be a pharmacologically induced event, not an indication of fertility.

In order to feel safe from pregnancy, we need to prove that the FSH is above 30. This can be tested periodically as a woman becomes perimenopausal. A woman on birth control needs to be off the pill for five days in order to get an accurate test. The test is usually done during the last week of the pill pack (since these are placebo pills). Once the FSH is above 30, I recommend condoms and a recheck of FSH three months prior to the discontinuation of contraception. If a woman is having menopausal symptoms, I often have her switch from birth control pills to HRT when the FSH remains above 30, or at age 50.

Q. Tell me about the different types of estrogens and progesterones on the market.
A. Conjugated estrogen, which was the first of the estrogens, came from pregnant horse (mare) urine. It is still used extensively in this country and is probably the best studied. We also have synthetic estrogens, including estradiol (E2), estrone (E1), or a combination of those. Estrogen is available orally, by patch, by vaginal cream, or by vaginal ring. If a woman has had her uterus out and doesn't need progesterone, she may very well take estrogen by patch. We'll probably have a progesterone in patch form soon. There's also a combination of estrogen and testosterone for women who have had their ovaries surgically removed or for women who need more of the male hormone testosterone, frequently evidenced by fatigue or loss of sexual drive. Estrogen is also available by pellets that are inserted subcutaneously—under the skin. Natural forms of estrogen available are compounds and may include various amounts of E1, E2, and E3 (estriol). Although there are reports that estriol is protective against breast cancer, this has not been proven. It is a weak estrogen and requires a higher dose to be effective.

Progesterone is used in conjunction with estrogen in patients who have not had their uterus removed, because it helps to offset stimulating (and possibly cancer-causing) effects of estrogen on the uterus. It is also a second-line treatment option for hot flashes in patients who cannot or will not take estrogen.

Progesterone is available in oral form, in creams, and in suppositories. Two synthetic forms are medroxyprogesterone and norethindrone. It is also available as a natural micronized progesterone that is compounded but not FDA approved. Progesterone precursor is found in wild yams.

Q. Tell me about the estrogen patch.
A. Medication in transdermal patches is absorbed more efficiently into the body than oral medications because the estrogen is not immediately metabolized by the liver. The patches are ideal for women who have had a hysterectomy and need a steady amount of estrogen or in cases where there is a prior history of venous thrombosis (blood clot). Some women tolerate patches much better than estrogen in oral form. It also may better control their menopausal symptoms, particularly menstrual migraines.

Q. What is a vaginal ring of estrogen?
A. The vaginal ring is a local estrogen therapy designed to relieve vaginal and urinary symptoms associated with postmenopausal estrogen deficiency for a full ninety days. It exerts its effects locally in the vagina and bladder and has not been shown to have significant effects elsewhere in the body. It provides relief of local symptoms only. The ring releases estradiol, a form of estrogen, into the vagina in a consistent, stable manner for ninety days. It is a soft, flexible ring that is placed by the patient in the upper third of the vagina and worn continuously for ninety days. The most common problem with the vaginal ring is discharge seen in 12 percent of women.

Q. What are the best things women can do who are entering menopause to stay healthy?
A. Women entering menopause should find a gynecologist who is interested in menopause and knowledgeable about hormones, who can help them make intelligent decisions.

They should take calcium supplementation (1,000 to 1,500 mg per day) with 400 IU of vitamin D.

They need to have a regular exercise pattern, decrease their caloric intake, and watch the cholesterol and fat content of foods, because their risk of heart disease will go up as they go through menopause. Preferably the exercise should be aerobic and weight-bearing. They want to maintain their weight or minimize excess weight gain.

Stress reduction is very important. Many women at menopause are caught between taking care of elderly parents and teenage or younger children. How women handle stress may be very important to their health.

Women need to learn about their own health risks from their own physical examinations and by looking at family health patterns. With the help of their physician, they should determine their own risk for osteoporosis, heart disease, Alzheimer's, and different types of cancers.

Routine health care is essential: Pap smears once a year; monthly breast self-exams, mammograms every one to two years; tetanus vaccinations updated (should be done every ten years); periodic blood work, including cholesterol, thyroid function, and stool testing—we start looking for bleeding in the stool at fifty. Bone density testing can identify early bone loss. A sigmoidoscopy, looking through a flexible endoscope into the rectum, every three to five years after fifty is used to detect colon cancer.

Mental health is a major key to good physical health. Exhaustion and burnout can turn into a major depression. Are these women becoming overwhelmed and exhausted? Are they trying to do too many things? Do they know how to say no?

Midlife is the ideal time to evaluate one's own health risks and lifestyle and develop a program of preventive health to maximize life expectancy and delay or prevent the development of serious medical illnesses such as heart disease and osteoporosis. Hormones and other medications or products are available to assist women. The goal is to remain active, alert, and healthy and continue to learn and grow.

4

Estrogen Bypass: Alternatives to Hormone Replacement at Menopause

Richard Santen, M.D.

Richard Santen graduated from college in 1961 with a major in philosophy. After earning his medical degree from the University of Michigan Medical School in 1965, he worked for two years as a resident physician in internal medicine at The Cornell–New York Hospital in New York. He returned to the University of Michigan as a senior resident from 1967 to 1969, went to the University of Washington in Seattle as an endocrinology fellow, and joined the faculty of the Penn State University Medical School in Pennsylvania in 1971, where he climbed the ranks from assistant professor to professor to Evan Pugh professor. In 1993 he became chairman of medicine at Wayne State University. Dr. Santen joined the faculty of the University of Virginia in 1995, where he is now professor of medicine and associate director for clinical research of the Cancer Center.

Q. Tell me about women in their fifties and their thoughts about estrogen.
A. Most women over fifty who have gone through the menopause are

very confused about hormone-replacement therapy (HRT). They read that estrogens can cause cancer of the uterus but if they take progesterone with estrogen that won't happen. They're also worried about breast cancer and the side effects of estrogens and progesterone.

Q. Under what circumstances would you advise perimenopausal or menopausal women not to take estrogens?
A. Women who have had a diagnosis of breast cancer probably should not take estrogen because it could make their cancer return and grow more rapidly. There is also concern that estrogen could cause a second breast cancer. Most physicians are conservative in recommending estrogens and consider a history of breast cancer a contraindication. I also might discourage estrogen replacement in women with a family history of breast cancer or if they have any other condition that could increase the risk of breast cancer.

Q. How can a woman protect herself from the risk of osteoporosis, heart disease, and Alzheimer's if she doesn't want to or really shouldn't take estrogen? Can other medications bypass the need for estrogen but offer the same benefits?
A. I'll tell you about the medications that can be used to bypass the need for giving estrogens systemically (that is, to the whole body). Let's divide the symptoms of menopause into four categories.

One category is vaginal symptoms—vaginal atrophy, pain on intercourse, itching or burning, or increased frequency of urinary infections. A soft, plastic ring called Estring can be placed in the vagina that delivers a very small amount of estrogen only locally to the vagina constantly over a three-month period. This method bypasses the need for systemic estrogens. It treats local symptoms without allowing estrogen to get into the body. Vaginal estrogen creams also can be used at a low dosage to provide local delivery without systemic estrogen effects.

The second category is the bones—osteoporosis prevention. We think estrogen is the most effective way of preventing osteoporosis. But some nonestrogen medicines may treat osteoporosis and prevent it to the same extent as estrogen. These drugs are called bisphosphonates. Alendronate, commercially known as Fosamax, is now available in the United States. After three years, alendronate can give a 7 percent average increase in bone in the spine and hip. Estrogen alone would increase bone density in spine and hip by about 3 to 5 percent. So, in fact, there may be a greater effect from the nonestrogen than the estrogen. A woman who is at risk for osteoporosis or who has osteoporosis can get around the need for estrogen with alendronate. Another way is to use a hormone called calcitonin, with a preparation known as Miacalcin. This is given by nasal spray that is used daily.

The next category is hot flashes. A blood-pressure-lowering drug called clonidine may reduce or control hot flashes in 50 percent of women. Clonidine works by blocking adrenaline-mediated mechanisms in the brain, a possible cause of hot flashes. Megace, a progesteronelike medication, is another way of controlling hot flashes. In appropriate doses, this drug will substantially reduce hot flashes.

The final category is preventing heart disease. A woman who is at a high risk for heart disease because of high cholesterol levels and a family history can take drugs that will lower her cholesterol and triglycerides and decrease the risk for cardiovascular disease. Drugs known pharmacologically as statins will bypass her need for estrogen. Examples include Mevacor, Zocor, Pravachol, and Lipitor. These drugs lower cholesterol to a greater extent than estrogen and can prevent heart disease.

Besides its effect on cholesterol, one of the ways estrogen prevents heart disease is through its effect on the blood vessels. Interestingly, tamoxifen, the drug used to treat breast cancer, acts like an estrogen on the blood vessels yet acts like an antiestrogen in the breast. Tamoxifen appears to reduce the risk of heart disease in women who can't take estrogen. Thus drugs such as tamoxifen are another way of bypassing estrogen.

Q. Are any drugs being developed that could be used as antiestrogens?
A. Several designer antiestrogens are being developed that act as estrogens on some tissues and as antiestrogens on others. These are called SERMs (selective estrogen receptor modulators). Raloxifene (Evista) was released in January of 1998 for use in postmenopausal

women. This is an antiestrogen that may reduce the risk of breast cancer. It acts like an estrogen to block the loss of bone and results in a 1 to 2 percent increase in bone after two years of administration. Its effects are similar to those of tamoxifen but less than those of estrogen or Fosamax. Raloxifene also lowers cholesterol levels and would be expected to reduce the risk of heart disease. Unlike tamoxifen, it doesn't cause cancer of the endometrium or uterus. The only drawback is that raloxifene does not relieve hot flashes or symptoms of urogenital atrophy. Its main use, then, is likely to be for the prevention of osteoporosis and heart disease. Recently available information from an early study in 7,000 women given raloxifene for an average of thirty months showed a 70 percent reduction in new breast cancers. Raloxifene is an antiestrogen on the uterus but acts as an estrogen to lower cholesterol and to reduce the risk of osteoporosis.

Q. Are there estrogen bypasses to prevent Alzheimer's disease and colon cancer?
A. Although there's a good deal of indirect evidence that estrogen may prevent or reduce the severity of Alzheimer's, there are no strong direct data now. As yet we don't have drugs to bypass this possible benefit of estrogen. The issue of estrogen in preventing colon cancer is up in the air at this point.

Q. What are the side effects of the various drugs one might use to bypass estrogen?
A. The vaginal estrogen causes virtually no side effects.

The side effect of Megace, the drug used in estrogen bypass to prevent hot flashes, is weight gain. Most women don't like that. Clonidine can lower the blood pressure too much, but that's easy to test for.

Cholesterol-lowering drugs have very minimal side effects.

The side effects of tamoxifen, the currently available antiestrogen used to prevent cardiovascular disease and osteoporosis, are uterine cancer and hot flashes—very substantial indeed. However, uterine cancer can be prevented by taking progesterone at the same time. The new antiestrogen, raloxifene, does not cause uterine cancer.

Q. What is your take on estrogen bypass versus estrogen?
A. Most physicians think that estrogens are the better way to go. But we are in the era of patient choice. My approach is to inform women of everything I know about the benefits and risks and let them make the choice. Surprisingly, many women don't want to take estrogen. For women with a history of breast cancer, nearly all women and most physicians would favor not giving estrogens and recommend a form of estrogen bypass.

Q. If a woman doesn't want estrogen, why give her anything?
A. The choices are not just estrogen bypass or estrogen. A substantial number of women don't need anything. We must determine if there's a problem that needs to be treated.

We'll recommend a bone scan. A woman who has osteoporosis or who has low bone density needs alendronate, Miacalcin, or estrogen because she is at risk of developing fractures. A woman whose bone density is high doesn't need any one of those drugs.

A woman who doesn't have hot flashes or symptoms of vaginal atrophy doesn't need treatment.

If she has no risk of cardiovascular disease, based on cholesterol measurement and family risk, she doesn't need medications.

Q. What would you advise women who decide not to take estrogen or estrogen bypass drugs?
A. The most important advice is to take in enough calcium so her bones will not break down.

She should be on a moderate amount of exercise—we recommend twenty minutes or more, three times a week.

Women must be careful not to take drugs such as steroids, thyroid medications, and antacids in doses that are too high, which could cause osteoporosis.

I don't recommend frequent bone scans. For women with border-line risk of osteoporosis, I'd recommend a DEXA (dual energy X-ray absorptiometry) scan down the road.

Q. What is your recommendation to perimenopausal and meno-pausal women in terms of hormone replacement?

A. I usually recommend estrogen unless there are contraindications. But I also provide information about the alternatives—we have other ways of treating menopausal symptoms, and we can design a regimen for the specific needs of each patient. On the other hand, some women will do well without estrogens. These are women without symptoms, without risk factors for heart disease, and without loss of bone density. These women are advised to follow a good lifestyle, take enough calcium, and exercise regularly.

5

Healthy Breasts

Richard Santen, M.D.

Richard Santen graduated from college in 1961 with a major in philosophy. After earning his medical degree from the University of Michigan Medical School in 1965, he worked for two years as a resident physician in internal medicine at The Cornell–New York Hospital in New York. He returned to the University of Michigan as a senior resident from 1967 to 1969, went to the University of Washington in Seattle as an endocrinology fellow, and joined the faculty of the Penn State University Medical School in Pennsylvania in 1971, where he climbed the ranks from assistant professor to professor to Evan Pugh professor. In 1993 he became chairman of medicine at Wayne State University. Dr. Santen joined the faculty of the University of Virginia in 1995, where he is now professor of medicine and associate director for clinical research of the Cancer Center.

Q. What do you recommend to women in their fifties who want healthy breasts?
A. I recommend a healthy lifestyle that includes exercise, moderate fat intake, moderate amounts of alcohol, no smoking, hormone-replacement therapy when needed, and beyond those things, it's early diagnosis. Breast self-examination and screening mammograms are vital.

Q. Let's talk about hormone-replacement therapy (HRT) as it relates to women's breasts. Many women worry about taking estrogen because they fear an increased risk of breast cancer. How do you feel about that?

A. This is a very controversial topic both among physicians and patients. About half of the thirty or so published studies showed that there is a slight increased risk of breast cancer for women on HRT. The other half showed no increased risk. I tend to be very conservative. I believe the best way to deal with this is to think of the worst case and accept the fact that estrogens could possibly cause breast cancer.

Q. What are the chances of a woman developing breast cancer when she is on estrogen?

A. Articles in newspapers and magazines often state that there is a 50 percent increase of breast cancer if a woman has been on estrogens for ten years or more.

Q. A 50 percent increase of breast cancer for women on HRT sounds frightening. What does that 50 percent increase really mean?

A. Between the ages of fifty and sixty, two women who are not on HRT out of a hundred will develop breast cancer over a ten-year period. If there is a 50 percent increase, three women out of a hundred will develop breast cancer. That translates into one out of a hundred who will develop breast cancer because she took estrogens. Now, that sounds a lot less worrisome than a 50 percent increase. It really means that a hundred women have to take estrogens for ten years to have one who might get breast cancer because of that hormone.

Q. What if a woman is that unfortunate one out of a hundred who develops breast cancer?

A. In general, women who are on estrogens tend to be much more likely to follow recommendations to have mammograms every year, so the cancer is usually diagnosed much earlier. The breast cancer is much less aggressive when it develops in a woman while she is on estrogen, so the death rate from breast cancer in a woman diagnosed while taking estrogens is substantially reduced. In a recent nurses' health study, women taking estrogen for less than ten years had a reduced risk of dying from breast cancer than women not taking estrogens. Women lived longer if taking estrogens even though a few developed breast cancer. This was because they were protected from heart disease.

Q. What do all those numbers say about estrogen causing death from breast cancer?
A. The information we have suggests that about one woman out of five hundred taking estrogens might get breast cancer because she is on estrogens and will not be cured by initial treatment. That's one out of five hundred women over a ten-year period. That's the worst-case scenario.

Q. How do the benefits of estrogen outweigh the risks, knowing that one out of five hundred women will get breast cancer because of estrogen therapy and not be cured by treatment?
A. Estrogens prevent death from heart disease. The benefits are that fifteen women out of five hundred will still be alive because they didn't die of heart disease. The benefits under those circumstances, even when you accept the worst case regarding breast cancer, well outweigh the risks.

Q. Is there a link between dietary fat and breast cancer?
A. The fat-in-the-diet issue comes up because there is a tremendous difference in the number of women who develop breast cancer in various countries. In Western countries, people have a higher-fat diet, a higher rate of obesity, and a higher incidence of breast cancer. In Asia, particularly Japan and China, the diet is very low in fat, obesity is uncommon, and the risk of breast cancer is much lower. Studies have shown that the incidence of breast cancer goes up dramatically in Japanese and Chinese women who move to Hawaii or to the mainland United States. It seems to be related to fat in the diet, but many other factors could be responsible. There have been no proper studies to test the fat hypothesis. The evidence is based merely on observation. It would take about $100 million to test the fat-in-the-diet hypothesis. There is no definitive information on this subject.

Q. What is the probable link between dietary fat and breast cancer?
A. A high-fat diet contains more calories than a low-fat diet and can lead to obesity. As a woman gets heavier, her body makes more estrogen. We know that estrogen is a cause of breast cancer.

Q. What do you recommend to women in terms of fat in the diet?
A. This is an area in which we say "Let's do things in moderation." Reduce fat in the diet, but do it in moderation. Obesity should be dealt with. By lowering fat in the diet, you lower the incidence of obesity, which makes you healthier overall and could reduce the risk of breast cancer.

Q. What about the alleged link between alcohol and breast cancer? What do you recommend in terms of alcohol in the diet?
A. The studies have been conflicting. Some show that alcohol can increase the risk of breast cancer. Others show no increased risk. A moderate amount of alcohol, in fact, prevents heart disease. There is no compelling evidence that moderate amounts of alcohol increase the risk of breast cancer. I think it's all right for women to drink a moderate amount of alcohol, which is generally equivalent to one to two drinks a day.

Q. Tell me about the link between cigarette smoking and breast cancer.
A. Most studies show that cigarette smoking does not increase the incidence of breast cancer. However, in a recent study some people seemed to have a genetic trait that caused them to handle the substances inhaled in cigarette smoke differently from other people. This genetic predisposition caused them to not break down certain substances as quickly as other people would. Those individuals showed an increased incidence of breast cancer from smoking. This is a complex issue; everybody is different.

Q. What other lifestyle decisions can affect a woman's risk of breast cancer?
A. Having babies at a younger age and breast feeding decrease the risk of breast cancer.

Q. How does lactation affect a woman's risk of breast cancer?
A. We really don't understand the scientific basis. The thought is that it's like an imprinting—pregnancy and lactation change the nature of the breast tissue. In animal studies, there are clear differences in the rate that breast cells grow in response to hormones, depending on whether the animal had been pregnant previously or not. We know that if a woman gets pregnant and breast-feeds at a younger age, she has as much as a one and a half to two times lower chance of developing breast cancer over her lifetime. The thought is that perhaps the milk-producing hormone prolactin somehow changed the nature of her breast tissue and makes it less susceptible to breast cancer later.

Q. What is the future of breast cancer prevention?
A. There are large ongoing studies on breast cancer prevention with a drug called tamoxifen (Nolvadex), which blocks the effect of estrogen in breast tissue. This drug was initially developed as a means to treat breast cancer. Early results of those studies show that in some individuals you can prevent breast cancer with tamoxifen. But it's a trade-off between the side effects of the drug and the prevention of breast cancer.

Q. What are the side effects of tamoxifen?
A. Although it doesn't occur commonly, tamoxifen can cause uterine cancer. About 2 women out of 1,000 who are on tamoxifen will develop uterine cancer each year. That is a major problem. Other minor side effects may be hot flashes or nausea. Tamoxifen otherwise is usually quite well tolerated. Newer drugs such as raloxifene, which are similar to tamoxifen in many ways but don't affect the uterus, are now being considered. An early study suggests that raloxifene might be better as a means to prevent breast cancer.

Q. Who is at increased risk for breast cancer?
A. Women with a family history of breast cancer, who are overweight, who became pregnant at an older age, who didn't breast-feed, who have had a late menopause, and in some cases who smoke.

Q. How does a physician determine risk?
A. Several factors are considered. Family history is important. If your mother had breast cancer, if she had breast cancer before age forty-five, if she had breast cancer in both breasts, or if you had a sister with breast cancer, then you are at high risk. Computer models take into account the other factors, such as early onset of menstrual periods, pregnancy, breast-feeding, and obesity with these familial factors. The computer model can predict one's risk of developing breast cancer.

Q. Are certain ethnic groups at higher risk for breast cancer?
A. Yes. We know now that the Ashkenazi Jewish population has an incidence of about 1 percent of mutations of the BRCA 1 (Breast Cancer 1 gene). This gene increases the risk of breast cancer substantially. It's really important for doctors to pay a lot of attention to that population.

Q. What would do you do if there's a high risk of breast cancer in a woman's family?
A. If the risk is great enough, I would test for the genes associated with breast cancer. It's exceedingly expensive—about $1,500. But many women who are at high risk would choose to do this. The problem is that if the result is positive, their insurance company might charge more for health insurance, although there's legislation now being developed to prevent that from happening.

Q. What percent of the population has a breast cancer gene?
A. There are two known breast cancer genes, Breast Cancer 1 gene (BRCA 1) and Breast Cancer 2 gene (BRCA 2). The BRCA 1 and 2 genes are found in only 5 percent of women with breast cancer or 1 in about 500 to 1,000 normal women.

Q. What should you do if you have one of these genes?
A. These genes increase the risk for cancer of both the breast and the ovary. Some physicians offer women who have these genes bilateral mastectomies—removal of both breasts. A recent study suggested that removing both breasts reduces the risk of breast cancer by about 90 percent.

Q. Why doesn't bilateral mastectomy reduce the risk of breast cancer by 100 percent?

A. Because it's almost impossible to get all the breast tissue out.

Q. Breast cancer studies often observe groups of people, but they're not scientifically rigorous. Many times the results are conflicting. How would you advise women to interpret studies in terms of what they should or should not do?

A. You have to take a balanced view. If you read that there is a 70 percent increase in risk of breast cancer for something that you do—perhaps you drink alcohol or the saturated fat in your diet is a little high—that doesn't mean you will have a 70 percent chance of getting breast cancer. It means that your risk over normal may be increased. But you have to know what that *absolute* risk is. Some things that give you an increased risk of developing breast cancer may have a marked effect of reducing your risk of dying of a heart attack. You have to put the results of these studies in perspective.

Q. Many women in their fifties have breast pain, especially if they're on hormones. What causes this pain?

A. Breast pain usually is caused by breast tissue responding to hormones such as estrogen and progesterone. Before menopause, estrogen is produced both in the early and the later parts of the menstrual cycle, causing some women breast pain. Progesterone is produced in the latter part of the cycle. After menopause, when these hormones are no longer made by the ovary, a woman's breast tissue atrophies or decreases in amount. Her breasts now are mainly fat with very little gland tissue remaining. However, if she goes on hormone-replacement therapy, the estrogen or the combination of estrogen and progesterone will maintain the breast tissue that was there prior to the menopause, and she may continue to experience breast pain.

Q. Many women have benign breast disease also known as lumpy breasts. What are those lumps and bumps? Why do they sometimes cause pain?

A. The breast contains ducts that allow the milk to come out of the breast into the nipple at the time of lactation. Those ducts are stimulated by estrogen. The area that connects to the ducts and makes milk (the milk factory) is called the alveola. Estrogens act with progesterone to stimulate the alveola. A partial blockage of the ducts will cause them to fill up with fluid. This is called a cyst.

In addition, the area around the ducts may undergo scarring. This is known as fibrous change. The combination of the two gives you fibrocystic—that is, fibrous and cystic—change. This consists of multiple lumps and cysts. If the estrogens are stimulating the duct tissue to grow, then there can be some swelling and pain. This is very active tissue that has been stimulated by hormones. Most experts believe that fibrocystic changes are within the range of normal for women. This process is called fibrocystic disease only when the changes become more severe and cause lumps requiring biopsy or pain requiring treatment.

Q. What percentage of women on estrogen have fibrocystic breast disease?
A. Postmenopausal women between the ages of fifty and sixty generally don't get fibrocystic breast changes unless they had fibrocystic changes prior to being on estrogen. It's natural to think that if hormones cause fibrocystic changes, hormone therapy will likely cause that process to continue.

Q. Should women with lumpy breasts perform monthly breast self-exams?
A. Generally we advise all women to do monthly breast self-exams. However, not all women with lumpy breasts should do monthly self-exams. The emotional distress from feeling these nodules each month and trying to figure out if they're bigger or smaller is not helpful to the patient or the physician. Many of these women examine their breasts every six months or they let the physician do it.

Q. Is there a higher incidence of cancer in women with fibrocystic breasts?
A. Fibrocystic change itself is not associated with a higher incidence of breast cancer. However, this is a complex issue because there is a whole range of benign breast disease conditions. Some of them have a

higher chance of developing into breast cancer later and some don't. In uncomplicated fibrocystic breast change, there is no increased rate of breast cancer compared with a normal individual. But with a lump in the breast that has cells that are growing too rapidly—this is called hyperplasia—there is a twofold increased risk of developing breast cancer, not in that lesion but in the breast itself. If the condition becomes atypical hyperplasia (see below), the chances of breast cancer are increased fourfold over normal. If there is a family history of breast cancer, there will be sixfold increased risk.

Q. What is hyperplasia?
A. Hyperplasia is when the gland tissue (not the fat tissue) in the breast is growing more rapidly than normally. For example, if it normally takes two weeks for two cells to become four cells, now it takes one week for two cells to become four cells because it's dividing more rapidly. A general theory about cancer says that every time a cell divides, there's a chance that there will be a mutation in that cell. The more rapidly cells divide, the greater the chance of a mutation and the greater the chance that the mutation will cause cancer. We think the risk of hyperplasia is just that the cells may be growing more rapidly and therefore will have a greater chance of ultimately developing into cancer. Hyperplasia is *not* a precancer.

Q. What is the significance of breast hyperplasia?
A. Hyperplasia tells you that a woman has a greater chance of getting breast cancer over her lifetime. This is really a warning sign of a higher risk of cancer than normal in either breast. If the hyperplasia area is in the left breast, the cancer might occur in the right breast. That has led a lot of people to say that a woman who has hyperplasia might have some underlying abnormality that would cause cancer in any area of the breast. That underlying abnormality is called a field effect, and it would suggest that there is something abnormal in that woman that may increase her risk of developing breast cancer.

Q. Is there any treatment for fibrocystic breasts?
A. For women on estrogen replacement therapy after menopause, the first step is to lower the estrogen and progesterone dosages. If a

woman is on 1.25 mg estrogen, we'll try to reduce her to 0.625 mg. If a woman is on progesterone, which most women are if they have a uterus, we want to also reduce the dose of progesterone. Most women are on 5 mg progesterone.

Q. Should women try to avoid caffeine and increase vitamin E to combat fibrocystic breast changes?
A. The evidence is based on testimonials from patients who feel that they've benefited in a dramatic way by stopping caffeine or taking vitamin E. We haven't done sufficient studies to prove that it really works. Reducing caffeine and taking vitamin E isn't harmful, and the results may be a dramatic improvement in some individuals.

Q. Is breast discharge a common problem? Is it serious?
A. Ten to 20 percent of women have breast discharge, including premenopausal women and those who have gone through menopause and are on estrogen. It can be perfectly normal but should be evaluated. If there is blood in the secretion, you need further evaluation. If there's no blood, the woman can be reassured that this is quite common. In some cases there may be milk discharge. That is a sign that prolactin, the milk-producing hormone, is high. Treatment is available for elevated prolactin. Elevated milk-producing hormone also can be due to benign tumors of the pituitary. These benign tumors can be treated too. Milk discharge can be a side effect of medication. Any medication that tends to block the adrenaline system can raise prolactin, including certain medications used to treat hypertension (high blood pressure) and those for depression or major psychiatric illness.

Q. What is the practical message that you're trying to tell women?
A. If breast cancer is diagnosed early, it can be cured. Screening mammography is really important. With this test, breast cancer can be detected in the curable stage. Small tumors can be taken out without removing the entire breast.

If your risk of getting breast cancer is high, you should see a breast specialist to guide you.

It's very important to think about your genes and your family history. If you have an increased risk of breast cancer because of a strong family history, you should go to an expert in genetics. Physicians are becoming more attuned to these special genetic clinics. The National Cancer Institute has begun to set up mechanisms for funding genetic screening programs for cancer centers. That makes a lot of sense because this is a new area in medicine. There's new testing and new information. Women at risk need specialists.

Q. What is your bottom-line advice to women?
A. If you discover a breast lump, discharge, or have breast pain, the chances that this is a sign of a malignancy are relatively low. A woman should not regard any of these symptoms as a death sentence. But they should be evaluated early on. There are treatments for most benign conditions. Even if it turns out to be cancer, the chances are very good that it's curable. The key is early evaluation.

6

Mammography and Breast Imaging

Ellen Shaw de Paredes, M.D.

Ellen Shaw de Paredes graduated from college in 1974 with a major in biology. She had envisioned her life as a biochemistry researcher but opted for a career in medicine and entered West Virginia University Medical School. After graduation she completed a radiology residency at the Medical College of Virginia in Richmond. She then joined a private radiology practice for one year. In 1983 she accepted the position of director of mammography at the University of Virginia School of Medicine in Charlottesville, where she eventually became vice chairman of the Department of Radiology. In 1994 Dr. De Paredes returned to the Medical College of Virginia as professor of radiology and director of breast imaging.

Q. What is the likelihood of any woman getting breast cancer?
A. The likelihood of a woman getting breast cancer in the United States overall in her lifetime is one in eight. That assumes a life expectancy of about eighty years. There are different ratios for each decade. The ratio is about one in fifty for women who are fifty to sixty years of age. It gradually increases with age to a final ratio of one in eight.

A fifty-year-old woman may hear this ratio and think that her risk of breast cancer is one in eight or that one out of eight of her friends will get breast cancer. That's not true for that year. It's true over her lifetime or that of her friends.

Q. What is the greatest risk of breast cancer?
A. The most significant risk for getting breast cancer is age. As a woman gets older, her likelihood of getting breast cancer increases.

Q. Does something suddenly happen at age fifty that increases a woman's risk of breast cancer?
A. No. It's a misconception that at age fifty a woman's risk of breast cancer suddenly goes way up. It is not true. The risk goes up with age. If you look decade by decade, the incidence of breast cancer is less for women in their forties than in their fifties, and less in their fifties than in their sixties.

Q. Do those previously dense breasts turn to fat at age fifty?
A. No. That's another misconception. Breast density is greater in younger women and gradually decreases with age. The breasts get more fat over time. But there's nothing magical at age fifty that makes that suddenly occur.

Q. Why are the overall numbers of breast cancers in women at ages fifty to sixty so high?
A. The overall numbers of breast cancers in fifty- to sixty-year-old women are high because there are more women in that age group compared to women in their seventies, for example.

Q. How often should women in their fifties get a screening mammogram?
A. Women in their fifties should get a screening mammogram every year. The most recent guidelines from the National Institutes of Health recommend annual mammograms for women over forty.

Q. What is mammography?
A. Mammography is an X-ray examination of the breast in which the breasts are compressed between a film holder and a plastic compres-

sion plate. An X-ray beam is then passed through the breast and information is captured on the film. A radiologist reads the film.

Mammography, an arm of the broader field of radiology, has become diversified in the past decade. It now includes sonography (another term for breast ultrasound), MRI (magnetic resonance imaging) of the breast, digital mammography as well as interventional procedures such as needle localizations, fine-needle aspirations, and stereotaxis or ultrasound guided breast biopsy.

Q. Tell me about screening mammograms.
A. In a screening mammogram, the radiologist looks for breast cancer in a woman who is asymptomatic. Screening mammograms are recommended for all women over a certain age and are performed on women who have no signs or symptoms of breast cancer.

Q. What is a diagnostic mammogram?
A. A diagnostic mammogram is a more comprehensive evaluation that works up an abnormality—a palpable lump (one that can be touched or felt), abnormal nipple discharge, or an abnormal finding on a screening mammogram. A diagnostic mammogram may include the same views as the screening mammogram (two of each breast), but different views may be added, including magnification views to analyze or identify an abnormality further. We also may use other modalities, such as ultrasound, to evaluate a breast mass.

Q. What is breast ultrasound? When is it used?
A. Breast ultrasound is an imaging technique that uses high-frequency sound waves passed through the tissue. A radiologist can tell if the tissue is fluid or nonfluid, based on the way the sound waves are reflected by the tissue. If the sound waves pass through the mass and show that it is a simple cyst (fluid-filled), we know that it's benign. If it shows that the mass is solid (nonfluid), it can be benign or malignant. In that case, the patient needs further evaluation.

Breast ultrasound is not a screening tool for asymptomatic women. It is used to diagnose a specific finding in certain scenarios.

If a patient or her doctor feels a breast lump, she will probably have a mammogram first. If the mass shows nonspecific features on the mammogram—that is, if it might be a cyst or a solid tumor—an ultrasound will be done to look at the internal characteristics of the mass.

Or if we find a mass on a screening mammogram that was not palpable, we often recommend a breast ultrasound. Again, we look for the same information—is it a benign cyst or a solid mass?

Q. Tell me about MRIs of the breast.
A. An MRI uses a magnetic field to create a three-dimensional image. It is not an X ray. During an MRI, the patient is put into a magnetic field. The movement of protons in the body's tissues creates an image in response to the magnetic field that tells us about the makeup of that tissue.

Q. When is MRI used for breast imaging?
A. MRI is used to evaluate specific abnormalities, such as complications of implants, including rupture, to determine if they are likely benign or malignant.

Q. What are the advantages of mammograms over MRIs or ultrasound?
A. No other modality has achieved the mammogram's high resolution that allows the radiologist to see very fine detail. Ultrasound doesn't and MRI doesn't.

For example, both breast cancers and some benign lesions can produce calcifications in the breast. A woman may receive a report of calcifications on her screening mammogram. A diagnostic mammogram will be recommended. That mammogram will include magnification views of the calcifications, which are very tiny—usually in the range of 100 to 200 to 300 microns in diameter. (We often call them microcalcifications because they're so small.) The fine detail of a mammogram allows the radiologist to see the shape of the calcifications, which tells whether they are the benign fibrocystic type of calcification or the more suspicious kind.

Q. Tell me more about breast calcifications.
A. Calcifications are calcium salts that have been secreted into the glands and ducts of the breast. They are commonly seen in women

who have fibrocystic breasts. The cells that line the milk ducts and lobules of the breast have the potential to produce calcium salts. If there are fibrocystic changes, which are overgrowths of the cells in the ducts and lobules of the breasts, calcifications can form. However, malignant cells also can produce calcium salts. That is why doctors might recommend that patients who have calcifications have a biopsy at some point.

In determining if calcifications are suspicious or not, two factors are considered—the shape of the calcifications and the distribution. If a woman's calcifications are scattered all over both breasts, they're probably fibrocystic and she would be monitored. But if there is one focal cluster of calcifications or a small group, that area has been active enough to produce the calcium. In that case, the level of suspicion goes up. It could be malignant. Those calcifications should be biopsied.

Q. What is in the future for breast imaging technology?
A. There is a great deal of research and development in digital mammography. As I explained before, in a traditional mammogram, the X-ray beam is passed through the breast and the information is captured on a piece of X-ray film enclosed in a cassette. The radiologist reads the films. Digital mammography uses the X-ray beam in the same kind of tube, but instead of acquiring the image on film, it is acquired on an electronic plate and the information is transferred through fiber-optic cables to a computer. The radiologist can read the image on a computer rather than on film.

Digital mammography has not been developed to the degree that it can be utilized for screening. It is currently used as a guide for interventional procedures. At this point, we can acquire digital images on small fields (part of a breast) but not the whole breast.

Digital mammography has the potential for allowing us to manipulate the image—to magnify or brighten or darken it—so that we could see even finer details, such as those calcifications. I think that ten years from now, we'll be routinely looking at mammograms in a digital form.

Q. In recent years, mammography has become more interventional. Tell me about interventional breast imaging procedures.
A. If you had written this chapter ten years ago, I would have described only two procedures. Today there are a number of interventional procedures. In terms of breast abnormalities, we divide lesions in two groups—palpable and nonpalpable. We divide the interventional procedures the same way.

If a woman comes in with a palpable breast lump, a fine-needle aspiration would be performed routinely, in which a thin needle is inserted into the mass. Cells or fluid are removed and sent to pathology. Depending on the pathology report, a further workup might include removal of the mass by a surgeon.

For lesions found on the mammogram that aren't palpable, a radiologist must either take a sample or guide the surgeon to its exact location, so that it can be biopsied or excised. In the latter event, a needle localization may be done, in which the radiologist inserts a tiny wire into the breast to mark the area. The surgeon uses that wire as a guide in taking out the tissue.

Q. Please discuss the new stereotactic technique for breast biopsy.
A. Stereotaxis for mammographic imaging is based on obtaining two fixed-angle views over the lesion. The two pictures allow the computer to calculate with a very high degree of accuracy the exact location of the lesion. It is similar to the technique used in Operation Desert Storm in which planes used two coordinates to calculate the distance of targeted missiles.

Stereotaxis is an outpatient procedure. The patient is awake but given a local anesthetic. She may lie prone on a table with her breast exposed through a hole. Or stereotaxis can be performed upright at a regular mammographic unit in which the breast is compressed, with a small opening over the area of interest, and the two fixed-angle pictures are taken. The computer then tells the radiologist exactly where to put the needle. We numb the skin, put a needle into the breast, and take samples. We use a variety of needle sizes.

Q. Tell me about stereotactic core biopsy.
A. Many women across the United States now undergo a new tech-

nique called stereotactic core biopsy, in which a larger 14-gauge needle takes out little cores of tissue that are sent to pathology. The radiologist makes a tiny nick on the skin, but there's no real incision, no stitching or suturing.

We also perform a core biopsy with ultrasound guidance if, based on the core's position, it will allow a better view of a mass. One big advantage of ultrasound is that it's in real time. As we look at the computer monitor, we see the exact movement of the needle. We can see the needle as it moves forward to take the core.

Q. How do you compare stereotactic and ultrasound biopsies to surgical biopsies?

A. Even though stereotactic and ultrasound biopsies are interventional procedures, they are less traumatic than a surgical procedure performed in the operating room. After we're done, the patient sits with ice on her breast for thirty minutes. Many of my patients go back to work the same day.

Q. What happens to the patient when an abnormality on the mammogram is found?

A. If the mammogram is abnormal, I tell the patient that she will need a biopsy. We consult with the referring physician and schedule the biopsy. We perform the biopsy, receive the pathology report, and get that information to the patient. If it's benign, we schedule another mammogram for her in six months that we will use as a new baseline. If it's malignant, she will be scheduled to see a surgeon. I take the patient to that point. Other radiologists may perform the biopsy procedure and have the referring clinician communicate with the patient. I prefer to complete the route with the patient and give her insights into what she might encounter next. A family physician does not often deal with breast abnormalities to the extent that we do.

Q. What do you advise women with lumpy breasts in terms of monthly self-exams?

A. Many women have fibrocystic breasts that feel lumpy all over. All too often they say "My breasts are so lumpy, I can't tell what's what, so I don't examine them." It's important that they examine their breasts not so much to differentiate what's benign from what's not benign but to tell the radiologist if there's a new lump. The woman who examines her breasts every month will know what's new or different. A new lump needs to be investigated. That lump isn't necessarily malignant. It might be a cyst or a benign solid mass. Women who perform monthly self-exams get to know their breasts much better than their physician can, who sees them only every six months or once a year.

Q. What should a woman do who has had a recent mammogram but finds a new lump?
A. She should not assume that the lump is benign because her mammogram three months ago was negative. She should go to her physician for further evaluation. A new mass can develop in three months or a mammogram can miss a mass that is present, particularly if the breasts are very dense.

Q. Tell me about the dangers of a mammogram.
A. The dangers of mammography are minimal. Several concerns have been raised over the years. One is the risk of radiation. Women should not be fearful that the radiation to their breasts from a mammogram will cause breast cancer. The amount of radiation needed to produce the mammographic image is extremely low. Thirty years ago mammograms used a totally different technique. The amount of radiation employed to create the image was much higher. In the last fifteen years the technology has developed so that the radiation is extremely low.

Another fear is of breast compression. Because the breasts are tightly compressed between the film holder and plastic compression plate in a mammogram, some women are afraid that the compression might bruise them, cause cancer, or damage their breasts in some way. The compression is not damaging. On rare occasions a woman may get a small bruise, but it doesn't cause cancer. The compression is an extremely important aspect of producing a high-quality mammographic image.

Q. The mammogram is considered the gold standard for evaluation of breast cancer. It's the best technology to find early breast cancer.

Mammograms reduce breast cancer deaths. Mammography usually works. But are tumors ever missed on mammography? Are breast cancers missed?
A. Yes. Mammography isn't 100 percent accurate. In a large study called the Breast Cancer Detection Demonstration Project, 280,000 women were screened. Mammography missed 8 to 10 percent of cancers.

Certain cancers may be missed for a variety of reasons. Very dense breast tissue with a lot of glandular tissue can cover up a breast tumor, especially if it's not one that has calcifications in it.

Breast cancers can be missed if they're in a position that's not included on the film. That's why it's extremely important that the technologist be very skilled at positioning the whole breast into the field of view. Too often the mammogram doesn't include enough of the posterior tissue. Although a woman might feel that the technologist is about to pull her breast off when she's trying to position her, it's very important that she gets all the tissue in.

The radiologist may not see the tumor because it is not obvious.

Another less frequent reason for missing a tumor is that the cancer may have features that make it look benign. The radiologist may see the tumor but, based on its features, may decide that it's benign and can be followed rather than deciding that it's suspicious and should be biopsied.

Q. How can a woman best evaluate the breast imaging facilities in her community?
A. Because of the FDA requirements in mammography, there has been a tremendous improvement in the quality of mammography in this country. It's the only radiological procedure that's regulated to that degree.

In 1992 Congress passed the Mammography Standards Act, which required all facilities in the United States performing mammography to go through a rigorous accreditation, certification, and inspection process under the auspices of the FDA. This act went into effect in the fall of 1994. It sets a minimum standard. Accreditation includes the film production, equipment used, physics testing, the technologists' training and certification, and the radiologists' training and certification. A current certificate should be hanging in the front office.

A woman should ask if the facility is FDA certified. She also should determine the radiologists' level of experience, how long they have been interpreting mammography, whether they are specialized in breast imaging, if they had fellowship training, and the level of continuing education they have obtained since training.

An academic institution will most likely have a specialist in breast imaging, as opposed to a smaller practice in which a general radiologist probably interprets mammograms. A university-affiliated facility is a good choice for a second opinion where a woman will see someone who has specialized in mammography.

Q. How can she find listings of FDA-certified facilities?
A. She can call the American Cancer Society or the American College of Radiology in Reston, Virginia. The FDA also has lists of FDA-certified facilities that are closest to her.

Q. Are radiologists' recommendations standardized?
A. Yes. Many radiologists use a format suggested by the American College of Radiology in terms of how we report and recommendations we give. If we think that the likelihood of a mass being benign is between 95 and 97 percent—a very small likelihood of malignancy—we put it into a six-month follow-up category. The patient will have a mammogram in six months and another six months later. If the likelihood of malignancy is greater than 3 to 5 percent, it goes into a suspicious category—it gets biopsied by the techniques that I described earlier.

Q. How do diet and nutrition affect breast health and breast cancer?
A. Breast cancer is more common in North American and European populations than in Third World countries. Some of that may be genetic. Some may be diet. It seems to be related either to obesity or to fat content in the diet. I think women should try to reduce their fat intake. Exercise is helpful in reducing the fat levels in the body.

Q. What about the issue of caffeine?
A. There have been several studies on caffeine and breast disease. There are different schools of thought. But there's no doubt that some women are more sensitive to caffeine. Caffeine can make breasts more tender, lumpy, or cystic. I advise women who have cystic changes, multiple cysts, and tenderness to decrease their caffeine intake. Many women who give up caffeine have symptomatic and mammographic improvement. Women should not have a lot of caffeine just before a mammogram, when they're going to be squeezed and compressed. Avoiding caffeine often decreases the discomfort of the mammogram.

Chocolate contains a lot of caffeine. Many women with fibrocystic breasts tend to be chocoholics and coffee drinkers.

Q. Do you have special advice for women who have breast implants?
A. Some women fear that a mammogram will break their implants. A properly done mammogram will not damage implants. It's very important that women who have implants have mammograms, unless they've had a mastectomy. The breast tissue around the implant must be imaged. Some women may have MRI to look for ruptures of their implants, but an MRI is not a screening for early breast cancer.

Q. What advice would you give women in their fifties regarding mammograms?
A. Few tests in medicine are as rigorously evaluated as mammograms. Screening mammography has been looked at from every direction and has been found to be of true benefit in reducing mortality from breast cancer.

One of the best gifts a woman can give herself is an annual mammogram. I diagnose many patients with breast cancer, and in some it has been several years since their last mammogram. They often feel very guilty and regret that they didn't come for an annual mammography. I tell them that there's no way to know if the cancer was there last year or the year before. There's no way of looking back and retrospectively trying to deal with it.

Have a mammogram every year after age fifty. Don't put it off.

7

Osteoporosis

Alan Dalkin, M.D.

Alan Dalkin graduated from college in 1980 with a degree in zoology and obtained his medical degree at the University of Michigan Medical School in 1984. He completed his internal medicine residency at the University of Chicago in 1987. He returned to the University of Michigan for subspecialty training in endocrinology and joined the faculty in 1990. Dr. Dalkin became assistant professor of internal medicine at the University of Virginia School of Medicine in 1991. He was promoted to associate professor in 1997.

Q. Tell me about bones.
A. Everybody gains bone until about age thirty. While there may be a period of time during which bone mass stays constant—perhaps five to fifteen years—thereafter everybody loses bone, from age thirty to forty until they die. Our bones remodel constantly. New bone is formed, old bone is taken away, new bone is formed, and old bone is taken away. After age thirty, this process is tipped in the favor of bone loss—more bone is taken away than formed. Most people maintain enough bone until death to preserve strength and prevent fractures and never have problems. But a subset of people lose a greater amount of bone, or something else affects the health of their bones, which predisposes them to osteoporosis.

Q. What is osteoporosis? What are the symptoms?
A. Bones give strength to our skeleton. As we lose bone, that strength

diminishes. Osteoporosis is a condition in which bone loss is extensive enough to cause fractures. The World Health Organization defines osteoporosis as having a bone mineral density that is equivalent to two and one-half standard deviations from the average at the time of peak bone mass, that is, at age thirty. The bone mass is measured at two sites, typically the hip and the spine.

Osteoporosis in itself is silent—until you fracture. Osteoporotic fractures can be very painful. Fracture doesn't usually occur until after the level of bone loss has been sufficient to diagnose a person with osteoporosis. In addition, fractures can change the shape of our bones. After a certain number of osteoporotic fractures, a person can develop osteoarthritis because the bone alignment becomes abnormal. Improper alignment of the back vertebrae or the hip joint can ultimately lead to osteoarthritis on top of osteoporosis.

Q. Tell me about women and osteoporosis.
A. Osteoporosis occurs much more commonly in women than in men. The loss of estrogen at the time of menopause hastens bone loss and in so doing predisposes women to fractures. By the time women have reached age seventy, 50 percent have lost sufficient bone to be at increased fracture risk.

Q. What percentage of women in their fifties have osteoporosis?
A. Close to 10 percent of women in their fifties have osteoporosis.

Q. How does osteoporosis correlate to menopause?
A. The earlier you enter menopause, the more likely you will be to have osteoporosis.

Q. So you're saying that there's a direct relationship between the loss of estrogen and osteoporosis.
A. Yes. The loss of estrogen accelerates the loss of bone.

Q. Why is bone loss directly related to a decrease in estrogen levels?
A. Nobody knows the exact reason. Estrogen appears to favor bone formation. When a woman loses estrogen, the amount of bone formation drops even further than it normally would as the process of re-

modeling takes place. The net effect is a greater loss of bone than if estrogens were present. But if estrogen is replaced, the precipitous bone loss can be prevented entirely—that is, if a woman takes estrogens from the time that her periods stop.

Q. Should all perimenopausal women take estrogen to prevent osteoporosis?
A. Yes, unless they have a reason not to, such as a personal history of breast cancer, family history of hormone-related cancer such as breast or uterine cancer, or a history of complications from estrogen treatments such as blood clots. In those circumstances, use of newer drugs such as raloxifene, which is like estrogen in some respects but does not increase the risk of breast cancer, may be indicated. In my opinion, a woman who takes estrogen should maintain bone mass just like a man—that is, she should be at a very low risk for osteoporosis.

Q. Why don't men get osteoporosis?
A. Men don't get osteoporosis because testosterone prevents bone loss. Although there is a decline in testosterone in aging men, it doesn't seem to get to a level at which the rate of loss of bone mass accelerates. In settings where men have very low testosterone, perhaps because of other medical conditions, they too lose bone. In that case, the same process happens in men or women.

Q. What dosage of estrogen is optimal in preventing osteoporosis in women?
A. In the United States, there are two commonly used preparations containing only estrogen(s). Premarin is conjugated equine estrogens and Estrace is ethinyl estradiol. Doses of 0.625 mg and 1 mg, respectively, are optimal in preventing osteoporosis. Larger doses don't provide further protection. Lower doses are being studied.

Q. What about estrogenlike compounds such as raloxifene?
A. Raloxifene works like estrogen on bone. It have been proven effective at preventing bone loss in perimenopausal women. It has not been tested in established osteoporosis. Whether raloxifene has helpful effects at other targets, such as preventing heart disease, is unknown.

Also, long-term estrogen use may be linked to breast cancer. Raloxifene has potential benefits in that this risk may not exist, although studies looking into that issue are under way.

Q. How do you know that poor diet and lack of exercise can cause osteoporosis?
A. Food and Drug Administration surveys have looked at the actual calcium intake of children and adults at various ages and concluded that there is a universal deficit in calcium intake in our country, especially in adolescent girls. Studies have shown that children with eating disorders, poor diets, and little exercise have less bone as adults.

Q. Will calcium and vitamin D restore bone at any age?
A. Calcium and vitamin D work very well to prevent bone loss while a woman produces her own estrogen. Dietary calcium and calcium supplements are a good idea at all ages. But calcium probably won't restore bone that's been lost. Thus the earlier you take it, the more effective it will be. It will give a cushion for later in life.

Q. What is the importance of vitamin D?
A. Vitamin D primarily helps the calcium be better absorbed through the intestine.

Q. Are calcium supplements as good as dietary calcium?
A. Nobody knows whether calcium tablets as the sole source of calcium are as good as calcium in milk and milk products. But most studies show that calcium is a necessary supplement.

Q. Why are calcium supplements usually recommended?
A. Supplementary calcium is a more reliable way of knowing how much calcium is ingested. If you take it in pill form, you know the minimum amount of calcium going into your body. However, the body loses calcium daily, and you can alter that daily loss. For example, high sodium intake will induce calcium loss. Thus factors other than intake also may be important.

Q. How do calcium supplements differ from one another?
A. Different supplements contain different calcium content. For instance, a calcium carbonate tablet contains 400 mg total calcium for every 1,000 mg total weight. A calcium citrate tablet has 250 mg calcium for every 1,000 mg weight. There's only 100 mg total calcium for every 1,000 mg in a calcium gluconate tablet. You need to correct for the amount of calcium in a tablet. Once you correct for elemental calcium, it doesn't matter whether you get it from calcium carbonate, calcium citrate, or calcium gluconate. They are all absorbed in the same way and do the same thing.

Q. What should we look for on the label?
A. You should look for elemental calcium, which is the true available calcium in each pill. Any label should list milligrams of elemental calcium.

Q. What forms of calcium supplement are effective and safe?
A. Calcium supplementation in any form—Tums, Oscal (calcium carbonate), Citracal (calcium citrate)—is safe in appropriate doses.

Q. Can calcium supplements cause side effects?
A. Calcium supplements can predispose some people to develop kidney stones. Some calcium is incorporated into bone but the rest is excreted in the urine. Usually 1,000 mg a day of calcium is not enough to cause kidney stones. But anyone at risk for developing such stones should take calcium under the supervision of a physician.

Q. Is bone density inherited?
A. There are genetic components that determine our bone density. A daughter or granddaughter of a woman who has had back or hip fractures is more likely to develop osteoporosis. Her family history is a risk factor for osteoporosis. Genetics may account for up to 75 percent of our peak bone mass.

Q. How do weight-bearing exercises and activities help our bones?
A. We don't know how they help, but it is clear that weight-bearing exercises and activity do help maintain bone density. Some people

think that electrical currents are set up through forced weight-bearing. Others question whether pressure on bone cells makes new bone. We do know that when someone is put on bed rest for an extended time because of an illness, bone mass starts to drop because this person is not bearing weight. What it is about bearing weight that makes bone form is not well understood.

Q. Can you overdo exercise as well as do too little?
A. Yes. Too much or too little exercise may be bad. There are women who overdo exercise. In the premenopausal age, excess exercise can reduce ovarian estrogen production, which in turn can cause bone loss.

Q. How much exercise is optimal?
A. Reasonable exercise—that is, twenty to thirty minutes—a few times a week is certainly good for cardiovascular health and probably helps bone density.

Q. Why are slim and small-framed women at risk for osteoporosis?
A. That's part of the genetic component. One's height and habitus (frame) are greatly influenced by genetics. Obesity seems to confer greater support on the spine. While there are numerous disadvantages to obesity, there is less osteoporosis in heavy individuals.

Q. If people who weigh 105 pounds could be made to weigh 205 pounds and still be the same height, they'd probably have less osteoporosis, but they'd probably have more heart disease.
A. Absolutely. Being overweight may be good for some things but not for others. It certainly has a potential to be good for osteoporosis. I rarely see women in my practice diagnosed with osteoporosis who are significantly overweight.

Q. What about ethnic risk factors?
A. There are clear differences among ethnic groups. Although there are some osteoporotic fractures in black women, African Americans appear less predisposed to developing osteoporosis. There is a higher incidence of osteoporosis in Caucasian women.

Q. Tell me about medications that cause bone loss.
A. Certain medications are associated with bone loss. Steroids that are used to treat inflammatory diseases (medications—such as prednisone, dexamethasone, and Solu-Medrol—called glucocorticoids) can cause thin bones. Too much thyroid hormone, either from pills or from a thyroid hormone condition, also can contribute to osteoporosis. Some medicines used to treat seizures may be bad for bones.

Q. What about smoking and alcohol as risk factors for osteoporosis?
A. Smoking and alcohol are both directly toxic to the formation of bone. The effects of smoking more than half a pack a day and drinking perhaps more than three alcoholic beverages daily over many years deplete the formation of new bone and increase the tendency to develop osteoporosis.

Q. Do you think that women with one or two risk factors should be screened for osteoporosis?
A. Any woman at risk—she does not necessarily have to have all of the risk factors I've discussed—but inheritance in particular, or body habitus, dietary problems, or medications—should be screened for osteoporosis.

Q. What is the screening process for osteoporosis?
A. The gold standard is the DEXA scan. These machines are very sensitive and specific in revealing the amount of bone density a person has. A DEXA scan should be done on all high-risk individuals.

Q. Physicians regularly identify people who are at risk for heart disease by checking their cholesterol. Why are they not doing the same for women who are at risk for osteoporosis?
A. Osteoporosis is like heart disease in many regards. In the early stages it is silent. An additional problem is that the machinery to detect osteoporosis is not universally available and may not be covered by insurance. Finally, time with a physician is usually quite limited and a discussion of osteoporosis is often omitted.

Q. What should women do about this?
A. Women should take the initiative—they should ask to be screened for osteoporosis or, at a minimum, they should identify their particular risk factors. Women who don't take estrogen or who have risks should insist on undergoing a screening test.

Q. Which women don't have to worry about bone loss and can skip the screening process?
A. If a woman is on estrogen replacement when she is perimenopausal, if she healthy and does not drink or smoke, has had normal calcium intake and has no family history of osteoporosis, she is not necessarily a candidate for screening.

Q. What if a woman is diagnosed with osteoporosis?
A. Luckily, there are a number of treatment options. The first line of treatment is estrogen, which has been shown to diminish the risk of fractures by up to 50 percent. Calcium and vitamin D supplements are also important. Two medications are available for women with established osteoporosis—alendronate and calcitonin.

Q. Tell me about alendronate and calcitonin.
A. Alendronate is also known as Fosamax. It is taken daily and has been shown actually to increase bone mass and reduce fracture rate. Fosamax has not been studied in conjunction with estrogen, but these two drugs work by separate mechanisms.

Calcitonin is a naturally occurring hormone in our bodies but is used in a higher level in the treatment of osteoporosis. Calcitonin has been shown to increase bone mass, but likely to a lesser degree than Fosamax. Calcitonin is available in a nasal spray. It also has not been tested in the presence of estrogen.

Q. What are the side effects of alendronate?
A. Alendronate can cause an upset stomach and diarrhea. It can cause some people to develop ulcers in the esophagus or the stomach. Therefore, Fosamax must be taken in the morning, on an empty stomach, and followed by a full glass of water to make sure that the pill doesn't stick in the esophagus or the upper part of the stomach. After

swallowing the tablet, the person must stay upright for thirty minutes. Also, foods and other drugs can inactivate Fosamax; hence, nothing can be taken orally for thirty minutes after a dose.

Q. What are the side effects of calcitonin?
A. Because calcitonin is a nasal spray, it can cause local irritation. It can also cause flushing and some dizziness. Calcitonin is usually very well tolerated after a short period of time. There are probably no long-term side effects.

Q. How long are people usually treated for osteoporosis?
A. Most people are treated for a minimum of two years. At that time we follow up to see if there has been a response. If bone mass has not improved, we might add another agent or change medications.

Q. Are there drugs that should not be combined with calcitonin or alendronate?
A. No medicines cannot be taken with alendronate or calcitonin. Nor would you need to adjust the dosages of any medications with calcitonin or alendronate. But as I said before, you must take alendronate thirty minutes before you take anything else.

Q. What if a woman who is diagnosed with osteoporosis does nothing?
A. A woman who does nothing about osteoporosis is unlikely to have a spontaneous improvement in bone mass. Women diagnosed with osteoporosis should be treated.

Q. What about a woman who has borderline bone loss, not enough to be classified as osteoporosis, though enough to be at a small but increased risk for fracture, with less bone than her age-matched peers?
A. That's a tougher question. I would recommend basic preventive care including estrogen and enough calcium and vitamin D to maintain the bone mass where it is. I would repeat the DEXA scan in a year or two to see if bone loss is continuing. In the future, other agents may be approved in the treatment of these borderline conditions.

Q. Can osteoporosis be cured? Can you ever build someone's bones up to a healthy level?
A. This question remains unanswered. While studies haven't been done over long periods of time, it appears that by increasing bone mass, we can repair or markedly reduce the risk of fracture. With Fosamax, we see marked reductions in new fractures and also significant reductions in recurrent fractures. That is, even bones that already have osteoporosis get better and stop breaking.

Q. Women who have osteoporosis often feel that their lives are forever changed and possibly ruined. They can no longer do things they used to enjoy. What can they do while they're being treated for osteoporosis?
A. If your bones are at risk of fracturing, there are bad things you can do and good things. High-impact activities are not a good idea until your bone mass has increased from the medications. Most women with mild osteoporosis can participate in moderate running and walking, which are good for cardiovascular health and important for personal satisfaction.

Q. What precautions should women with thin bones take? Can they ski? What can they do? What can they never do?
A. Precautions have to be taken. Proper footwear is a must. Avoid running in areas where there is a risk of falling. I would not recommend activities that present a high risk for breaking bones. Skiing may fall into that category. I would prefer activities that can be done in controlled, safe settings. People shouldn't try to push their limit. Swimming is completely safe and generally good for your heart and health. While swimming doesn't build up bone mass, I would be happy to see people swim because it causes no risk of fracture. Moreover, fracture prevention can begin at home. Loose carpeting should be avoided, and walkways should be wide and clear. Keep areas of walking well lit and avoid ice and snow.

Q. Should someone diagnosed with osteoporosis see a specialist?
A. Anyone who has osteoporosis should at one point or another see a physician who cares for osteoporotic patients on a regular basis, be it

an endocrinologist, an internist, an orthopedic surgeon, or a family practitioner. While the treatment regimens for osteoporosis are generally safe, they do have some pitfalls. Follow-up to see whether a treatment is working should be rigorous. As the medical community gets more familiar with these medicines, treatment may not require a specialist. But these medications are relatively new, as are the techniques for measuring bone mass.

Q. What is your overall advice in the prevention of osteoporosis?
A. The most important things are:

- Make sure that any medications that you take are safe for your bones. Ask your physician if your medicines could put you at risk for bone problems down the road.
- Proper diet is critical. Calcium is essential. Women who are on estrogen should take 1,000 milligrams of calcium per day. If you're not taking estrogen, the dose is 1,500 mg of calcium daily. In addition, women should take vitamin D—800 to 1,000 units per day.
- Exercise, especially weight-bearing activity, either walking or running, is critical in preventing problems, including heart disease and osteoporosis.
- All women should consider taking estrogen at the time of menopause. Even if you don't have osteoporosis, estrogen hormone-replacement therapy is the greatest single way to prevent it down the road.
- Ask your physician to determine if you are at risk for osteoporosis. I can't stress that enough. Tools are now available to detect a high risk of future fracture; and medicines that significantly improve bone health can be started.

SECTION II
Body Systems

8

Your Digestive System

Mark B. Pochapin, M.D.

Mark Pochapin graduated from college in 1984 with a major in biomedical engineering and a minor in material science. He attended Cornell University Medical School, where he also completed his internship and residency in internal medicine. In 1991 he did a two-year gastroenterology fellowship at Montefiore Medical Center in New York. He then became chief resident in internal medicine at The New York Hospital from 1993 to 1994; thereafter he was named associate program director for the internal medicine training program. In 1997 he was appointed associate chairman for educational affairs. Dr. Pochapin is an assistant professor of medicine at The New York Hospital–Cornell Medical Center, where he also has a private practice in gastroenterology.

Q. What is the gastrointestinal (GI) system?
A. The gastrointestinal system essentially consists of a hollow tube (the gastrointestinal tract) within the body that begins at the mouth and ends at the anus. It is comprised of the esophagus, stomach, and colon. In addition, there is a subset of organs that aid in digestion— the liver, gallbladder, and pancreas.

The GI system moves food and breaks it down so that it can be used for energy in other parts of the body. The digestive tract is essentially a biochemical warehouse, in which a variety of reactions take place. Proteins are broken down into amino acids and carbohydrates are made into simple sugars.

The colon does not digest food but works as a dehydrator by reabsorbing fluid and making solid stool from liquid matter. The stool is packaged and held in the rectum. The colon also houses abundant amounts of bacteria (normal flora), which help the colon to function and assist in the production and absorption of certain vitamins.

Q. What are common gastrointestinal conditions that develop as we age?
A. The most common GI conditions that develop with age are diverticulosis, diverticulitis, lactose intolerance, gallstones, colonic polyps, and colorectal cancer.

Diverticulosis is a condition in which small pockets form off the large intestine. The cause is usually a low-fiber, high-fat diet. Diverticulitis, an inflammation of these pockets, occurs when they become blocked and infected.

Lactose, the sugar in milk, is actually a baby food that adults don't need. With age, the enzyme that breaks down lactose disappears in some people, resulting in lactose intolerance. This condition is common in certain ethnic groups, including Asians and African Americans.

Q. Tell me about gallstones and gallbladder disease.
A. Ten percent of the population will develop gallstones, which are formed by the precipitation of insoluble materials, such as cholesterol and bile pigments, within the gallbladder. Two main types of stones can form—cholesterol stones or pigment stones. Cholesterol stones are more common.

Q. What are the risks of a woman developing gallstones?
A. Risk factors for gallstones include gender (females are at higher risk), obesity, age (over forty), increased number of pregnancies, certain cholesterol-lowering drugs, Crohn's disease, first-degree relatives (parents, siblings) with gallstones, and ingestion of female hormones.

We now see an increased incidence of gallstones in women in their fifties, possibly because they are postmenopausal and taking hormones. Estrogen is known to increase the risk of developing gallstones.

Q. What are the symptoms of gallstones?
A. The symptoms are pain after eating, usually on the right, upper side of the belly, sometimes accompanied by nausea.

Q. What if these symptoms are ignored?
A. One of those gallstones could drop into the plumbing system of the gallbladder and its connection to the intestine, known as the common bile duct. You could become jaundiced (turn yellow) and develop pancreatitis (an inflammatory condition of the pancreas), and cholangitis (an infection of the common bile duct).

Q. Tell me about polyps.
A. Polyps are small growths that form in the colon. There are two types of polyps—hyperplastic and adenomatous. They are both benign, but adenomatous polyps can turn into cancer.

Q. How common are polyps in women ages fifty to sixty?
A. Approximately 10 to 30 percent of women in this age group have polyps.

Q. Are polyps genetic?
A. Polyps are prevalent in certain families. If we find a large polyp or multiple polyps, we often screen other family members.

Q. How do polyps turn into cancer?
A. Colon cancers do not develop out of the blue. They must undergo change from a small polyp, to a large polyp, to a malignant polyp, to cancer that has grown through the polyp into the lining of the colon.

Adenomatous colon cancers take about ten years to grow. We have a huge time frame in which to interfere with the process.

Q. Is colon cancer the most prevalent cancer of the GI system?
A. Yes. It is the most common GI cancer we see.

Q. How common is colon cancer in women?
A. Colon cancer is the third most common cancer in women. The first is lung cancer and second is breast cancer.

Q. What are warning signs of colon cancer?
A. The hallmark of colon cancer is occult bleeding. "Occult" means unseen. In early colon cancer, a small amount of blood drips from the cancer into the stool. If the bleeding continues, the person can become iron deficient or anemic. This might be picked up during a routine blood test. Usually we don't worry about women who are still menstruating. But iron deficiency in postmenopausal woman or in a man may be an indication of occult blood loss.

Occult bleeding is sometimes diagnosed during a routine rectal exam. Blood might be found on a home stool guaiac test.

Q. What is a guaiac test?
A. A guaiac test is also known as a hemoccult. A stool sample is placed on a card in the doctor's office, or the physician may give it to patients to take home and mail back with three samples. Occult blood measured on this card may be a marker of bleeding in the GI tract.

Q. How accurate is the guaiac test?
A. The guaiac test is very inaccurate. A positive result indicates only about a 2 percent chance that the patient actually has cancer. Red meat or certain vegetables eaten the night before could activate the guaiac card. Inflammation around the rectum or hemorrhoids also can give false positive results. But it's the best we have, and it has the potential of saving a life.

Q. What if the guaiac test gives a positive result?
A. If the guaiac test is positive, the patient will be put into a higher risk group and screened for colon cancer with a barium enema and sigmoidoscopy or a colonoscopy.

Q. Tell me about sigmoidoscopy and colonoscopy, the screening tests for polyps and colon cancer.
A. Sigmoidoscopy and colonoscopy both involve guiding an endoscope (a tube with a light source at the end) up the rectum to get a direct visual image of the inside of the colon. The endoscope also has a long channel (the biopsy channel) through which various instruments can be passed to take biopsies, remove polyps, or cauterize

bleeding vessels. The sigmoidoscope is shorter than the colonoscope. Otherwise both instruments are the same.

Q. How far does the sigmoidoscope go?
A. The sigmoidoscope goes up to the sigmoid colon and sometimes as far as the descending colon.

Q. What about the length of the colonoscope?
A. The colonoscope goes through the entire colon.

Q. Why do most screening tests for colon cancer use the sigmoidoscope rather than a colonoscope?
A. Sigmoidoscopy is less invasive, patients don't need sedation, which involves some risk, and preparation is not as vigorous—preparation for sigmoidoscopy is a few enemas while colonoscopy involves very significant prep to wash out the colon. Also, sigmoidoscopy is cheaper and more likely to be covered by health insurance.

Q. Is sigmoidoscopy a sure test for colon cancer?
A. No. Sigmoidoscopy is only 60 to 70 percent accurate. An ongoing debate in the medical community concerns whether we should offer colonoscopy, a more invasive, riskier test, for screening that is more accurate and can give patients and their doctors peace of mind. My feeling is if there's any reason to do a colonoscopy, it should be done. I feel better knowing that the my patient's *entire* colon is free of disease and she doesn't have to worry about colon cancer.

I've seen patients whose cancers were missed on sigmoidoscopy. Their cancer was on the right side of the colon, which the sigmoidoscope doesn't reach. This is a rare event, but it happens.

Q. Should colonoscopy be performed on people in their fifties regardless of symptoms?
A. A colonoscopy at age fifty would clear a patient for about ten years. Some people are terribly worried about developing cancer. It would be very therapeutic for them if we could take one of those worries away.

Q. In this day of managed care, what excuse will get health insurance to pay for a colonoscopy?
A. Blood in the stool, a family history of colon cancer, a change in bowel habits, a change in the caliber of the stool, or a previous diagnosis of intestinal polyps.

Q. What if you find a polyp on sigmoidoscopy or colonoscopy?
A. We would remove the polyp and send it to pathology. Removal of all adenomatous polyps reduces and possibly eliminates the risk of colon cancer.

If we can't remove the polyp, we photograph, measure, and biopsy it. Large or cancerous polyps may need to be surgically removed in the operating room.

If the pathology report labels the polyp adenomatous, we place the patient in a surveillance program. If the patient only had a sigmoidoscopy, a colonoscopy would be performed. If there was just one polyp, we reevaluate the colon in three to five years. If we found multiple polyps, yearly evaluation would be more appropriate.

Q. What if the polyp is cancerous?
A. A cancer that is picked up early can be curable. If the cancer is confined to the colon and the lymph nodes are negative, a patient can be cured.

Q. Do people who develop colon cancer have radiation or chemotherapy too?
A. There are different stages of cancer. If the cancer has invaded through the colon wall, patients receive chemotherapy. Radiation sometimes is used for metastatic disease.

Q. What about survival rates for patients with colon cancer?
A. That depends on the extent of the cancer.

Q. Give me an example of a patient who should have a screening for colon cancer.
A. A fifty-three-year-old woman saw her physician for a routine medical evaluation. During her evaluation the previous year, the doctor

found microscopic blood in the stool during a rectal exam. Her guaiac test was positive, but other blood work was fine. Ninety-eight percent of the time a guaiac test gives a false positive result, but occasionally it is valid. That is why we use it as a screening test. It helps us decide on appropriate candidates for colonoscopy. This woman's physician discussed the test result with her. The patient decided not to have a colonoscopy.

Several months ago the woman felt okay but had become slightly constipated and noticed some alteration in her bowel habits. She visited her gastroenterologist. Her hemoccult was positive, for the second time in a year. Otherwise she seemed healthy. She finally consented to a colonoscopy.

The colonoscopy showed a large cancer in her sigmoid colon and a few polyps as well. As we previously discussed, polyps are the precursor lesions to cancer. The point to my story is, if this woman had undergone this evaluation a year ago, the cancer might have been just a large polyp. Even if it couldn't be excised by colonoscopy, it could have been surgically removed and curable.

The point is that people think a little blood in their stool can be ignored. They deny the possibility of cancer. Colon cancer can be cured if it's caught early.

Colonoscopy is a benign enough procedure and cancer is a serious enough disease that I would recommend the procedure for any valid reason. I rarely decide not to do colonoscopy when there's even a partial indication, unless the patient is elderly or ill, which could make the procedure riskier.

Q. How can women protect themselves from colon cancer?
A. They should be aware of the symptoms of colon cancer. Rectal bleeding, even if you have hemorrhoids, should be looked into. Alteration in bowel habits, such as diarrhea and/or constipation, can be a danger sign. Progressive constipation or change in the shape or caliber of the stool could result from a mechanical blockage in the colon, which should be evaluated.

Be aware of your genetic background. Be on guard if your brothers, sisters, parents, or even grandparents have had polyps or colon cancer.

Eat a high-fiber and low-fat diet. Fiber may decrease the risk of colon cancer. Conversely, a low-fiber, high-fat diet seems to increase the risk of colon cancer.

Q. Tell me about diarrhea.
A. Diarrhea is an increased frequency and decreased consistency of the stool. Sudden bouts of diarrhea are usually related to something ingested—a food intolerance or an infection. There are many infectious diarrheas. Diarrhea combined with abdominal pain and fever may be due to a bacterium such as *Salmonella*. When there is associated vomiting, the illness may be viral. Vomiting after eating might be caused by food poisoning. All those diarrheas usually stop in two to seven days.

Some diarrhea is associated with stress—before an exam or a stressful meeting. It also can come from a change in diet or environment.

Chronic diarrhea can be caused by a parasite called *Giardia*, which can be picked up from contaminated water. Someone who drinks river or well water can get *Giardia*. This can be treated with antibiotics.

Q. Tell me about constipation.
A. Constipation is the infrequent passage of stools. It is not caused by dehydration. Constipation can occur in a setting of stress or a change of environment. Many people become constipated when they go away from home. They may not have as much access to a bathroom, or they may change their diet and not get enough fiber, resulting in a harder stool that has less water and is more difficult to pass.

Constipation is usually best treated by increasing fiber in the diet. Some laxatives work by pulling water into the stool, softening it, and stimulating the colon to contract. Laxatives should be used only on a short-term basis. Chronic use of laxatives can make the colon sluggish. People can get hooked on laxatives. Increasing the amount of fiber is the best way to treat constipation.

Q. Tell me about psychological factors and the gastrointestinal system.
A. Stress and psychological factors can cause gastrointestinal illness.

Stress can be subtle—the person may have moved to a new house or a new job. Although she doesn't feel the stress, it may manifest itself in a GI problem. When we have no organic explanation of the gastrointestinal symptoms, we evaluate for stress.

Q. What is the connection between the emotions and the GI tract?
A. No one knows but I look at it this way: There are as many nerves in and around the intestine (the enteric nervous system) as there are in the spinal cord. The enteric nervous system is intimately connected with the central nervous system (the brain and the spinal cord). When stress/anxiety in the brain gets transmitted to the enteric nerves, it can cause queasiness, change the rate at which food moves through the bowel—things move too quickly (diarrhea) or too slowly (constipation)—and change the pain threshold.

Q. What is IBS, or irritable bowel syndrome?
A. The symptoms of irritable bowel syndrome (IBS) are abdominal pain related to food intake, bloating, and alteration in bowel habits, either diarrhea or constipation. Some people alternate back and forth. Patients with IBS often are told that there is nothing wrong with them. They may be tagged as hypochondriachal.

Forty percent of the problems in a busy GI practice relate in some way to irritable bowel syndrome. Gastroenterologists spend the most time on this disorder, although medical science has little hard data to offer.

IBS is a true disease. It has come under the heading of a functional bowel disorder—that is, the problem is with function and not with structure. A cancer blocking the bowel is a structural problem. A functional problem can be measured only by the way it works. With IBS, things work too fast or too slow. Patients with IBS usually have had lifelong bowel or stomach problems.

Irritable bowel syndrome usually is found in women of ages twenty to fifty. A fifty-year-old women first diagnosed with IBS would be unusual. This condition often diminishes by the late fifties.

The physician should reassure patients with IBS that this is a real disease, but most important, it doesn't lead to anything serious. It is not associated with cancers or any other GI condition. It is chronic, so you can't be completely cured, but there are ways of dealing with the symptoms.

Therapy revolves around a high-fiber diet. Fiber is beneficial at both ends of the spectrum—to patients with IBS who are prone to diarrhea and to those who are prone to constipation. Fiber also helps move products of digestion through the GI tract, which ultimately ameliorates gassy, bloating sensations.

Q. How does sleep affect the GI system?
A. Sleep is related to the GI system. Some people think that the GI tract helps to regulate the slow waves of sleep and that sleep helps to keep the bowel in proper regulation. Disruption of the sleep cycle also interferes with bowel motility—the movement from the top of the GI tract to the bottom.

Q. Why does the GI system have a certain regularity?
A. Regularity occurs because of the gastrocolic reflex ("gastro" means stomach; "colic" mean colon). When you eat, there must be room for the food in the intestine. You need to evacuate what's already there. Your distended stomach signals mobilization and evacuation from the colon.

Q. What causes intestinal gas?
A. Intestinal gas is either swallowed or produced by the body. People who drink carbonated beverages, or who swallow continuously because they're nervous, or who chew gum also swallow gas. Some of that gas comes up in a belch.

Other intestinal gas is produced by bacterial action on foods that are not well absorbed by the gastrointestinal tract. Beans are the prototype of a gassy food. Beans and other indigestible vegetables contain carbohydrates that the body does not handle well. When they get to the GI tract, bacteria start to metabolize these poorly digested by-products and produce gas in the process.

Q. Tell me about indigestion, heartburn, and acid reflux.
A. Indigestion is the sensation of feeling ill after eating. It is not a medical term. When patients complain of indigestion, we ask them to

break it down. Is it pain, is it acid coming up causing heartburn, is it nausea?

Heartburn is usually associated with acid reflux—acid coming from the stomach and going into the esophagus. The burning sensation is from acid injuring the lining of the esophagus.

Q. Tell me about hemorrhoids.
A. Hemorrhoids are small veins or blood vessels located at the bottom of the rectum. They are not pathologic. Most people have them. Hemorrhoids can be painful when a blood clot forms or if they become inflamed.

Q. What causes hemorrhoids?
A. No one really understands. Some scientists think that standing for long periods of time is a risk. People who are chronically constipated and strain a lot to move their bowels are more prone to hemorrhoids. Women who have had multiple pregnancies tend to have worse hemorrhoids.

A punctured hemorrhoid can cause copious bright-red rectal bleeding. People often become frightened at so much blood in the toilet. They think it might be from cancer. Actually, cancers don't usually bleed quite that much.

Q. How does cancer bleeding differ from hemorrhoidal bleeding?
A. Cancer bleeding and hemorrhoidal bleeding are very different. Cancer bleeding is usually more chronic and low grade. If the cancer is very close to the rectum, you might see some bright-red blood, but usually it is mixed within the stool. Blood from cancer is usually a darker color. You don't usually see it in the stool. Bleeding from cancer is very slow.

Q. What is the treatment for hemorrhoids?
A. The treatment for hemorrhoids is:

- Soak the hemorrhoids in a warm bath. This actually shrinks them.
- Don't use regular toilet paper, which is very abrasive. Use baby wipes, which are moist and soothing.

- Often anti-inflammatory creams that contain a small amount of steroid are prescribed. Nonprescription ointments are also available.
- Sometimes over-the-counter stool softeners or fiber laxatives are recommended.

Q. What about surgical procedures to treat hemorrhoids?
A. Hemorrhoids usually don't require surgery. If a hemorrhoid is very large or bleeds persistently, it can be taken off with a rubber band that is attached until the hemorrhoid falls off, a laser can burn it off, or it can be surgically removed.

Q. How can hemorrhoids be prevented?
A. A good way to prevent hemorrhoids is a high-fiber diet, which allows easier passage of bowel movements, less constipation, and ultimately less trauma to the anus.

Q. Tell me about hiatal hernia.
A. Hiatal hernia is a laxity in the diaphragm that allows the connection between the esophagus and the stomach to move into the chest. When someone with a hiatal hernia takes in a breath, the diaphragm may contract, causing negative pressure. Because the mechanical barrier between the esophagus and the stomach is gone, acid moves up into the chest. Some people with hiatal hernias have no symptoms. If symptoms are severe, surgery is an option.

Q. Tell me about ulcers.
A. Ulcers are a very common problem. An ulcer is a defect in the lining of the stomach or duodenum (the first part of the small intestine). Once the lining is damaged, acid exacerbates the damage and causes a craterlike sore. Large inflamed ulcers are painful. If an ulcer erodes into a blood vessel, it can cause life-threatening bleeding. If it gets too deep, it can perforate the stomach, the small intestine, and even involve the pancreas.

Initially an ulcer was thought to be due to lifestyle and stress. Now it seems to be an infectious disease caused by a bacterium called

Helicobacter pylori. This bacterium is very prevalent. You don't necessarily have an ulcer if you have the bacterium.

When patients have symptoms of an ulcer such as pain related to eating, we give them acid-suppression treatment and possibly antibiotics to eradicate the *H. pylori* bacterium.

Q. What are Crohn's disease and ulcerative colitis?
A. Crohn's disease and ulcerative colitis are inflammatory bowel diseases. They are very common in certain ethnic groups, such as Ashkenazi Jews.

Crohn's is a disease in which the bowel is chronically inflamed and the body can't turn off the inflammatory response. It seems to hit specific areas of the bowel. Crohn's can affect the small bowel and/or the large intestine but has a predisposition for the terminal ileum, where the small intestine joins the large intestine. It also can affect the colon. Some areas can be normal while others are diseased.

That contrasts with ulcerative colitis, which starts from the anal canal and moves up through the colon. Ulcerative colitis doesn't involve the small intestine and doesn't skip areas. This disease moves up to a certain point, stops, and the rest of the bowel is normal. The symptoms of colitis are frequent bowel movements, loose stool, and possible bloody diarrhea.

The symptoms of Crohn's disease are pain, diarrhea, rectal bleeding, weight loss, certain vitamin deficiencies, and malabsorption. The pain can be diffuse or localized to the right lower side.

Q. What is the treatment for Crohn's?
A. Steroids are used intermittently to decrease the active inflammation. We don't like to keep patients on long-term steroids.

There are useful medications such as Pentasa (mesalamine) and Asacol (mesalamine). Dipentum (olsalazine) and Azulfidine (sulfasalazine) are useful only if the colon is involved. They are derivatives of aspirin that do not get absorbed into the intestine. Most of the active ingredient stays in the intestine and acts at the surface.

Another medication, called an immunomodulator, puts brakes on the immune system and decreases the amount of inflammation. This medication can keep patients in remission. Crohn's is probably an immune-system disease. This medication gets closer to the etiology of the disease.

Q. Is Crohn's disease seen in women in their fifties?
A. Crohn's is seen and occasionally develops in women in their fifties, but it is more common in either younger or older age groups.

Q. Tell me about stomach and esophageal cancer.
A. Chronic and long-term ingestion of alcohol, salt, and nitrates as well as smoking may increase the risk for these cancers.

Helicobacter pylori is implicated in stomach cancer. One particular type, the mucosa-associated lymphoid tissue (MALT) lymphoma is caused by the *Helicobacter* bacterium. Adenocarcinoma, a common cancer of the stomach, also may be related to this bacterium. If we eradicate this bacterium and the risk of ulcers, we also may reduce the risk of cancer.

Q. What are the symptoms of these cancers?
A. They are very much like those of ulcers. Stomach cancers may be malignant ulcers. The symptoms are abdominal pain, weight loss, and early satiety or feeling full just after you start to eat.

Dysphagia, a feeling that food is stuck, is symptomatic of esophageal cancer. Other symptoms may be burning or chest pain.

Q. Is there any good news about these cancers?
A. There's good news and bad news. Gastric (stomach) cancer is on the decline. But the incidence of gastroesophageal cancer, which is at the junction of the esophagus and the stomach, is increasing. Some people think that the use of acid inhibitors (over-the-counter antacids) is a possible cause. However, the overall consensus is that these medications are safe.

Q. How can someone know when belly pain is a danger sign?
A. When the belly pain is severe.

Q. Tell me about danger signs that are emergencies.
A. Severe abdominal pain, which may or may not be accompanied by

fever, could be from a perforated intestine, a perforated ulcer, a perforated appendix, or a hernia that has twisted off. Someone with this type of severe pain should be taken to an emergency room.

Persistent nausea and vomiting with abdominal pain could be from a bacterial or viral infection called gastroenteritis, but it also could be from an intestinal blockage and should be seen by a physician. Finally, black, maroon, or red blood in the stool may indicate significant blood loss and should be evaluated by a physician.

Q. Do you believe that certain foods can prevent cancer?
A. Yes and no. I don't believe that certain foods prevent cancer. But eating a healthful, low-fat, high-fiber diet is important. Antioxidants may play a role in cancer prevention. Fruits and vegetables are high in antioxidants. They won't hurt and may possibly help reduce the risk of cancer. I don't think that what you eat will totally prevent cancer.

Q. Do you have words of advice for women in their fifties who want to keep their GI system healthy?
A.
- Eat a healthful, high-fiber diet.
- Participate in some type of physical activity. Exercise helps bowel motility. Movement can push food through the intestine more quickly. Constipation and diarrhea seem to be less of a problem for people who are physically active.
- Don't smoke.
- Avoid chronic or heavy use of alcohol. An occasional drink is okay, but heavy use can cause ulceration and injury to the lining of the gastrointestinal tract and is a risk for esophageal and gastric cancer.
- Be aware of your own body, of your family history, and of your genetic makeup.

With proper screening and surveillance, you can have a major impact on your own health.

Colon cancer is preventable and curable. I can't stress that enough.

9

Backs, Bones, Tendons, and Joints: Your Musculoskeletal System

Hansen A. Yuan, M.D.

Hansen Yuan was born in Burma and moved to the United States after high school. He attended a small college in Michigan with plans to do graduate work in oceanography. At the urging of his father, he opted for a career in medicine and entered the University of Michigan Medical School. After graduation in 1969, he did a one-year rotating internship and a five-year orthopedics residency at Upstate Medical Center in Syracuse. He then went to Long Beach Memorial Hospital in California on a fellowship in spine surgery. He returned to Syracuse in 1974 to join the faculty of the Upstate Medical Center, where he created a multidisciplinary spine care program and served as chairman of orthopedics from 1986 to 1990. Dr. Yuan is currently professor of orthopedics and neurosurgery and chief of the Division of Spine Care in the Department of Orthopedics and Neuro-Surgery at the State University of New York Health Science Center at Syracuse.

Q. What is the major cause of backaches?
A. Sitting causes most backaches because it places the spine in an abnormal contour and puts a tremendous load on the disks.

Q. Do back problems worsen with age?

A. Unfortunately, they do. The back has many joints and disks. We wear out those joints and disks as we age.

Q. What is a disk?

A. A disk is a soft-tissue spacer located between two vertebrae. (The vertebrae are the bony segments that make up the spinal column.) The center of a healthy disk is gelatinous and full of fluid. This jellylike material serves as a cushion between the adjacent vertebrae and helps to maintain motion. The peripheral rim of the disk is like a radial tire fiber that holds one body to the other.

Q. The human body has the capacity to heal from injury. Do back problems also cure themselves?

A. The back has a healing capability. But if the back is injured beyond a certain limit, that healing capability will not bring it back to normal.

Q. When is it okay to ignore back pain?

A. We all experience strained back muscles. If you have pulled a muscle but feel better in a day or two and you don't have a recurrence two or three times a year, you probably don't need professional care.

Q. When is it time to seek professional care?

A. You should seek care if you have frequent recurrence of back pain, extremity pain and/or weakness, or bladder and/or bowel symptoms. You could be experiencing symptoms of a nerve injury from a ruptured disk.

Q. Is a ruptured disk the same as a herniated disk?

A. Yes.

Q. How are herniated and ruptured disks different from bulging disks?

A. Herniated and ruptured disks are the same. They are both more significant protusions than bulges.

Q. Why do disks cause back problems?
A. Disks cause problems because we sit too much, we overload them, we don't take care of our bodies, and disks gradually tear as we get older. Disks get brittle and rupture. A disk that ruptures in the wrong direction can hit a nerve and cause pain that may include sciatic pain or sciatica.

Q. What is sciatica?
A. Sciatica is pain (often experienced in the back of the thigh) caused by compression against the nerve root. In terms of low back, sciatica can be caused by a disk, a spur, or a fracture—anything that impinges against the sciatic nerve.

Q. Do most patients with ruptured disks need surgery?
A. No. Ninety percent of disk ruptures do not need surgery. They will do well treated aggressively but nonoperatively.

Q. What are the nonsurgical treatment options for a ruptured disk?
A. Nonsurgical options include a day or two of bed rest, medication for comfort, and active rehabilitation with physical therapy or chiropractic treatment.

If the symptoms of a herniated disk don't improve and the patient still has peripheral leg pain, we might ease the discomfort with an epidural nerve block, which is an injection of local anesthetic and steroids. This decreases the nerve inflammation, allowing the patient a faster recovery.

Q. When should surgery be considered for a herniated disk?
A. Surgery should be considered only when someone has had a very aggressive trial of nonoperative care for eight weeks to three months. A very small percentage of patients may need surgery either because the herniation is too large or because of its location.

Q. What happens to the two adjacent vertebrae when a disk is removed?
A. When a disk is removed, the two adjacent vertebrae come closer together and the disk space narrows. The window where the nerve

route extends also narrows. The loss of that cushion sometimes causes the patient to become shorter.

Q. What is the success rate of surgery for a herniated disk?
A. The success rate for surgery on a large herniated disk is about 85 percent.

Q. Will leg pain recur after surgery?
A. The recurrence is about 10 percent; pain usually occurs only if another disk ruptures from that level or disk space. Bad track records after back surgery are usually due to spine degeneration at adjacent levels.

Q. How can back problems be prevented?
A. By protecting the back and slowing down the wear and tear.

Q. How can we protect our backs?
A. Avoid lifting heavy objects by straining. Good body mechanics are essential.

Don't sit for long periods of time. Sit in an upright chair, maintaining a good lumbar lordosis (an exaggerated forward position of the spinal column) that protects your back. Proper posture is very helpful.

Q. How can we slow down the wear and tear?
A. Three major ways: Stay in shape. Keep your weight down. Strengthen and tone the abdominal muscles that support your spine.

The spine essentially consists of little blocks piled on top of each other. The muscles around these blocks support your back. If you develop muscle tone and keep your weight down, you'll decrease wear and tear of the disks.

Q. Will certain types of exercise strengthen the back?
A. Yes. Exercises that increase motion and flexibility are good. Motion is especially important because disks are not supplied with blood. Nutrients must cross a bone barrier. Motion allows the nutrients to enter the disk to keep it alive and viable.

Q. Is it true that heavy laborers who have back injuries don't usually have disk problems?
A. Yes. Heavy laborers don't have disk problems because they keep in motion, they are on their feet, and their back muscles have excellent tone. If they injure their backs, the disks may degenerate, but to a limit.

Q. Give me an example of an exercise program that will strengthen backs.
A. Swimming combined with NordicTrak and partial situps would be good. Repetition of these exercises will build up tone and permit motion while maintaining posture.

Q. Is weight-lifting good for backs?
A. Light weight-lifting with a lot of repetition is good for your back. Heavy overhead weight-lifting is very bad. Bench presses can strain your back.

Q. Does being overweight contribute to back problems?
A. You're not necessarily at risk for injuring your back just because you're overweight, but it does contribute to the problem. Losing weight may slow down the disks' wear and tear, but it won't help a bad disk get better.

Q. What is the major orthopedic problem of women in their fifties?
A. Osteoporosis is the biggest problem facing women in their fifties. When a woman goes through menopause, she loses estrogen, one of the major components of bone support. Exercise, proper nutrition, and estrogen supplements can help her maintain bone density. That's important because once her bone density drops, nothing may help.

Q. Doesn't alendronate build bone density that was lost?
A. We don't know about alendronate on a long-term basis. It's too new. We believe that alendronate can help some women, but it may not help everybody.

Q. Tell me about other back problems of fifty- to sixty-year-old women.

A. About 25 percent of women in their fifties have a condition called degenerative spondylolisthesis, in which the spine at the L (lumbar)-4 and L-5 level begins to slip, causing back and leg pain and in some cases the inability to stand and walk any distance.

Q. What causes degenerative spondylolisthesis?

A. Degenerative spondylolisthesis is a condition seen mostly in women who have had babies. During pregnancy, their big bellies stressed the L-4 and -5 levels that are at the pelvic brim. The load caused this level to ultimately degenerate.

Q. What is kyphosis?

A. Kyphosis is a condition seen in women beginning in the last half of their fifties. It is due to disk degeneration. The spine flattens out and the joints become arthritic, resulting in spinal stenosis (closing). When the spinal canal narrows, these patients tend to hunch over and sink in height.

Q. Why do women with kyphosis hunch over?

A. When these women try to stand straight, they pinch off the spinal canals. When they hunch over, the spinal canals open. These patients are fine sitting, but they can't stand for long periods of time or walk very far. When they stand, they slowly begin to sink down and curve over, to as much as 90 degrees.

Q. How can kyphosis be prevented?

A. By keeping flexible and straight. Stretching and extension exercises will help.

Q. Tell me about knee and hip problems.

A. Knee and hip arthritis are fairly common problems. There are two kinds of arthritis—degenerative and traumatic.

About 25 percent of people in their fifties develop degenerative arthritis, which is a gradual wear and tear of joints over time. It sometimes runs in families.

Traumatic arthritis usually is due to an injury that occurred in a patient's younger days. One traumatic injury to a joint can cause it to degenerate over time.

Q. Tell me about joint replacement surgery.
A. We get good results with hip and knee replacement surgery. Shoulder replacements are not as successful. Elbow and ankle replacements don't yield good results.

Q. Why are hip and knee replacements successful while other joint replacements are not?
A. A hip is a ball and socket. It's straightforward. A knee is more like a hinge. People have had more problems with knees and hips so we've worked on these joints for a long time. We're improving our success with shoulder replacements, but not with elbow and ankles. Elbow and ankle joints move multidirectionally, which makes them difficult to replace. The ankle is the most difficult because it is a major weight-bearing joint, it's small, and technology has not taken us to the point of getting a good replacement.

Q. Tell me about hip replacement surgery.
A. In hip replacement surgery, we cut out the hip bone and replace it with either metal or a polyethylene against ceramic. We replace the two surfaces of the joint. Ceramic is very strong under pressure. A ceramic hip is the best hip you can buy today. We also use vitalium and titanium.

Q. Do you use the same materials for knee replacements?
A. Yes.

Q. How long do hip and knee replacements last?
A. We've seen total hip and total knee replacements last twenty-five to thirty years.

Q. How long do hip and knee replacements last on average?
A. In general, they will last fifteen to twenty years, although they can last as long as twenty-five to thirty years.

Q. Is tennis elbow a particular problem for women in their fifties?
A. Yes. Tennis elbow commonly occurs in the fifty- to sixty-year age group. As women go through menopause, their ligaments tighten because of hormone changes, making them more prone to tennis elbow and carpal tunnel syndrome. Their ligaments are no longer as yielding as when they were younger. They also tend to shorten, scar down, and cause irritation and therefore pain.

Q. What is carpal tunnel syndrome?
A. Carpal tunnel syndrome is pain, burning, and/or tingling across the palm side of your wrists, thumb, index, middle finger, and half of the ring finger caused by a compressed nerve. The transverse ligament compresses against the median nerve, resulting in these symptoms.

Q. How do you treat carpal tunnel syndrome?
A. We sometimes inject steroids to cut down the inflammation. Restricting certain motions can help. Or we can surgically release the ligament, freeing the nerve. That can be done by open surgery or endoscopically.

Q. How does jogging affect joints and backs?
A. Jogging is good for cardiovascular health and bone density, but it's not good for your joints or your disks. Jogging and running should be done in moderation. People who run marathons can really hurt their bodies.

Jogging in good shoes on a nice track or turf for a mile or two every other day is fine for most people. But if you experience back, leg, or joint pains, you should stop jogging to see if the symptoms disappear.

Q. What do you advise women in their fifties who want to prevent back, joint, and other orthopedic problems?
A. People must understand that their bodies are not machines. They are living organisms that need protection, maintenance, and care.

We can protect our backs, joints, and overall skeletal system by using good body mechanics and keeping our muscles toned.

Maintenance and care consists of a balanced exercise program of aerobics, joint movement exercises, low-impact exercises, and exercises that provide total body motion.

As we get older, we don't get better. Couch potatoes are at worst risk for back, joint, and other orthopedic problems.

10

Healthy Feet

Lawrence G. Lazar, D.P.M., D.A.B.P.S.

Lawrence Lazar's college major was biopsychology. After graduation in 1984, he taught high school chemistry for one year. He then attended the Pennsylvania College of Podiatric Medicine and did a two-year residency in reconstructive and traumatological surgery of the foot and ankle at St. Joseph's Hospital in Philadelphia. After a year in private practice, he moved to Cleveland to become assistant professor of surgery at the Ohio College of Podiatric Medicine. In 1996 he joined a private podiatric practice in Washington, D.C. Dr. Lazar is assistant clinical professor at George Washington University Hospital and a clinical attending physician at the Sibley Memorial Hospital in Washington. He is a diplomate of the American Board of Podiatric Surgery.

Q. What is a podiatrist?
A. A podiatrist is a physician who specializes in the foot and ankle. Podiatric training is equivalent to allopathic or osteopathic except that candidates attend single-track medical schools and specialize in care of the foot and ankle. Podiatrists who have gone through residencies are qualified to perform extensive foot surgery. Other podiatrists can do only minor surgical procedures, such as toenail and hammer toe surgery.

Q. What happens to our feet as we get older?
A. As we get older, our feet wear down. Our skin, tendons, ligaments,

and muscles begin to age, thereby losing elastic properties they once had. Our bones also lose density.

Q. What are the common foot problems of women in their fifties?
A. There are two classes—nail and skin problems and musculoskeletal problems.

Nail problems in women in their fifties include ingrown toenails and fungused toenails. Skin conditions range from athlete's foot and bromhidrosis (smelly feet) to foot fissures (cracks), corns and calluses, plantar warts, blisters, neuromas, and skin cancers.

The most common musculoskeletal foot problems in women of this age group are digital deformities, including hammer toes, claw toes, bunions, as well as heel pain.

Q. Tell me about ingrown toenails.
A. Certain people are prone to developing ingrown toenails. The shape of their nail matrix and bone causes the nail to grow in a curved fashion, impinging on the flesh. The improper cutting of toenails does not cause ingrown toenails, as many people think. However, tight shoes can aggravate this condition. If left untreated, an ingrown toenail could develop into an infection that might ultimately lead to a bone infection.

Q. What is the treatment for an ingrown toenail?
A. We first remove the corner nail spicule (a piece of nail impinging on flesh). If the ingrown toenail recurs or causes an infection, a permanent procedure can be performed, in which the root in the corner of the nail is burned out. After that, the risk of developing another ingrown toenail is negligible.

Q. Tell me about toenail fungus.
A. Fungus is present all over our skin. It may or may not be a pathogen. Minor trauma to the toenail, such as the pressure of tight shoes, can cause a small break in the nail of the first or fifth toes, which receive the most trauma from the sides of the shoe, and allow the fungus to penetrate. The fungus slowly invades the nail and, over a number of years, causes breakdown of the intrinsic nature of the nail,

leading to color changes, brittleness, and thickening of the nail plate. When nails thicken, they can become painful and difficult to cut.

The surgical treatment is total nail removal with two options. We can burn out the root and not allow the nail to grow back, leaving a hardened area of skin. Or the nail can be removed but allowed to grow back. In that case, when the nail is taken off, we aggressively treat the nail bed with topical antifungals, hoping to penetrate the matrix from which it grows.

New oral antifungals have become a popular form of treatment because they are safer for the liver than older drugs were. However, they still may have potential toxic effects on the liver. We always get a liver function test before treating patients with these medications. People who have had liver disease, such as hepatitis, would not be candidates for these drugs.

I recommend that patients with toenail fungus use an antifungal powder to decontaminate their shoes. People neglect their shoes. Socks get clean in the wash, but shoes don't. If the shoe is very old, the fungus may be deep into the leather. Discarding the shoe would then be the best option.

Q. Why treat toenail fungus if it is not life threatening?
A. Toenail fungus is not life or limb threatening, but it can be socially debilitating to the point where many sufferers won't take their shoes and socks off in public.

If left untreated, the nails can become very thick and painful. The fungus may spread to other toenails, to fingernails, and possibly to family members. A fungused toenail can cause an ingrown toenail because it may grow very thick in the corner and impinge on the flesh.

Q. Tell me about athlete's foot.
A. Athlete's foot is a fungus infection that occurs between the toes as well as on the sole of the foot. It is easily treated with topical antifungal creams or solutions. People with athlete's foot should use an antifungal powder in their shoes. More serious cases may require an oral antifungal.

Q. What is bromhidrosis?

A. Bromhidrosis, sometimes referred to as smelly feet, is due to excessive sweating that causes foot odor. It can be related to anxiety or just to having a high number of sweat glands that are very active in the feet. Often bromhidrosis is accompanied by sweaty hands.

This condition can be offensive and socially demoralizing. The treatment is to keep the feet dry. The better drying agents contain a 10 percent formalin solution. Again, you must address the shoes and decontaminate them with an antifungal powder.

Q. Tell me about foot fissures.

A. Fissures and dry skin are related. Very dry skin can fissure and cause a crack. This is common at the heels. Certain people are more likely to develop dry skin based on the number of sebaceous glands and moisture in their skin. Dry skin is worsened by hot showers and dry air. Skin is drier in the winter. I recommend cooler showers and the application of a strong emollient cream once or twice a day.

If dry skin causes a deep fissure, you should seek professional help. Cracks in the skin can become infected. Our treatment is to sand down the cracks and remove the harder tissue, or we may close off the fissure with a small bandage. Over-the-counter emollients can be used then. If those don't work we prescribe more powerful emollients that contain mild acids.

Q. What are calluses and corns?

A. Calluses and corns are areas of epidermis—the outer layer of the skin—that have thickened in response to pressure or friction. A callus is diffuse whereas a corn is more nucleated with a core of hard tissue.

As people hit fifty, the fat in the ball of the foot begins to thin. This fat is a natural padding. When bony prominences in the foot cause pressure on the skin on one side and a hard shoe presses against the skin on the other side, the skin thickens to prevent breakdown or ulceration, resulting in a hard area, the callus. That skin is dead and not painful. But walking on it is like stepping on a pebble—it compresses nerves and causes pain.

Shoes can aggravate this problem. A soft shoe will retard the growth of calluses and corns but not prevent them completely.

Corns can develop on the top of contracted toes (hammer toes) and can be very painful. Corns can be treated by removal of the hard tissue, using protective padding, and in some cases, surgery to straighten the crooked toe.

Surgical removal of a callus can relieve pain on the bottom of the foot.

Q. Tell me about plantar warts.
A. Plantar warts, found on the sole of the foot, are caused by a virus. They can be identified by their little black pepper spots. Plantar warts are more common in women than men. Some people are naturally immune to this virus. When plantar warts are located on a weight-bearing area, they can be excruciating.

These viruses are difficult. After removal, they can grow back. If left untreated, they may spread to other areas.

A variety of methods are used to remove a plantar wart. We can use acid, freezing or cryosurgery, surgical excision, or laser. The new pulsed-dye laser's wave length targets the color red and therefore destroys the wart's blood supply. This new method of wart removal is less invasive than surgical excision.

Q. Tell me about blisters.
A. Blisters often occur in runners who go over five miles or wear improperly fitted running shoes. They show up in high-friction areas of the foot. Long-distance walking often produces blistering. The fluid in the blister can be drained or left to dissipate on its own. Well-fitted and properly cushioned shoes are our best defense against blisters. Keeping feet dry with socks that absorb moisture or the use of foot powder also helps eliminate blisters.

Q. What is a neuroma?
A. A neuroma is an inflammation of the digital nerve that causes pain, numbness, or burning. The first sign is the need to take off one's shoe and rub the foot to ease the discomfort. Some people believe that neuromas are caused by metatarsals (the long bones of the foot that connect the toes) that are spaced too closely impinging on the nerve.

Others believe that tight shoes are the villain. Tight-fitting shoes certainly can exacerbate a neuroma.

Treatment consists of cortisone injections and the use of orthopedic pads or orthotics. (Orthotics are custom-molded arch supports that improve the weight distribution as we walk, by better aligning our foot bones and joints.) Surgical excision allows pain relief. An area of residual numbness will result.

Q. Do you see skin cancer on the foot?
A. Yes, but less than on other areas of the body that are more sun-exposed.

Q. How do you differentiate skin cancers of the foot from benign lesions?
A. Many people have small colored spots on their feet. These can be freckles, moles, or birthmarks. A change in a dark spot could be a warning sign worthy of a physician visit.

Skin cancers usually have irregular borders. Melanomas, for example, are also dark or hyperpigmented. Anyone who finds a new dark lesion should seek immediate professional care.

Q. Tell me about hammer toes.
A. This is a condition in which the toe curls up and the knuckle becomes very prominent. The raised knuckle can press against the inside of the shoe causing irritation and the development of a corn. Hammer toes are caused by a muscular imbalance that may be inborn, developmental, or the result of diabetes.

Treatment options include the use of protective padding, wearing shoes with high toe boxes, or surgical straightening of the toe.

Q. What is a claw toe?
A. A claw toe refers to the contracture at the tip of the last knuckle. It is similar to a hammer toe.

Q. Please talk about bunions.
A. Another term for a bunion is hallux valgus. There are two kinds of

bunions—those that develop in juveniles and developmental bunions that occur more commonly in women beginning at age forty.

A bunion is a large bump on the inside of the foot in which the big toe turns toward the other toes. It is really a type of arthritis of the great toe joint. Bunions can be very painful and are irritated by tight shoes. Bunion surgery is one of the most common surgical foot procedures.

Q. Tell me about bunion surgery. Do bunions recur after excision?
A. Given that there are different types of bunions and varying amounts of joint arthritis, if the appropriate procedure is selected, the recurrence rate is low (less than 3 percent) and patient satisfaction is high. Patients should be sure that the doctor has performed this procedure frequently.

Q. Tell me about heel pain.
A. Heel pain occurs when a band of tissue on the bottom of the foot begins to shorten as a result of normal aging and causes tugging on the heel bone. This may or may not produce a heel spur (bony protuberance).

Q. How are women different from men in terms of their feet?
A. When the day is over, the first thing women do is take their shoes off. Men don't usually do that. That tells you something about fashion and fashionable shoes.

Q. A good segue to talk about shoes. What's your advice?
A. Wear shoes that fit the feet more than they fit the eye.

Q. Many women won't accept that.
A. I know. My female patients won't accept that. But styles are changing. Shoes are becoming more sensible.

Q. What's a sensible shoe?
A. A shoe that fits the foot well.

Q. Please talk about high versus low heels.
A. High heels are bad because they throw all the weight to the front of the foot and don't allow the Achilles' tendon to stretch. Because of the shortened Achilles' tendon, the foot is no longer in a position to handle the pressures of walking.

Low heels are acceptable these days. Women will wear high heels, but they should not walk very far in them and the shoes should be worn in moderation.

Q. Which fashionable shoes can best protect the feet?
A. Shoes with cushioning and softer side materials that will allow room for expansion as the day goes on.

Q. Tell me about exercise shoes.
A. The technology available now in running and other exercise shoes is phenomenal. It's difficult to find a really bad athletic shoe.

Shoes used for exercise wear out fast and need frequent replacement. The average running shoe provides maximal function for about 275 to 300 miles. I see people who run fifteen to twenty miles a week who have worn the same shoe for two to three years. That's too many miles for one shoe.

Q. Tell me about flat feet.
A. Flat feet are not bad feet as long as they are flexible. We used to think that all flat feet were problems. Men with flat feet were not allowed into the military.

Q. When should someone use an arch support?
A. Most people do not need arch supports. They should be used only when recommended by a professional.

Q. What is pronation?
A. Pronation occurs when the arch rolls in and the heel turns outward; as a result, the foot cannot function properly when walking. This can result in bunions, hammer toes, and pain in the arch. An orthotic or arch support may be indicated.

Q. What is supination?
A. Supination, the opposite of pronation, occurs when the arch height increases. It's not a problem. People who supinate often have uneven shoe wear on the outside of their shoes. They are more likely to develop ankle sprains. "High-top" exercise shoes may be helpful.

Q. Should people exercise their feet?
A. No. Normal walking is sufficient foot exercise. If there has been a problem, a professional may prescribe special exercises to increase strength and flexibility.

Q. Does excess weight cause foot problems?
A. Yes. Excess weight can cause heel pain. When you're heavy, there's too much force going through the foot with each step, which can result in a variety of foot problems.

Q. When is it time to seek professional help for your feet?
A. When you experience pain that doesn't go away or if you notice a lesion.

Q. What are the worst things that women do to their feet?
A. Wear high heels and tight stockings. Tight stockings cause pressure on the toes.

Q. What is your overall advice to women in their fifties?
A. Take care of your feet. Wear sensible shoes that feel good on the foot as well as on the eye. Get a checkup from a professional. Check for problems. Seek care if you see something worrisome, such as a liquid drainage from the corner of a toenail with pain and redness, or if you normally walk two miles each day for exercise and then suddenly you develop foot pain after the first half mile.

When tires wear out on our cars, we buy new tires. We can't replace our feet.

11

Healthy Skin, Hair, and Nails

Michael H. Gold, M.D.

Michael H. Gold graduated from college in 1981 with a degree in biology. He attended the Chicago Medical School and did his internal medicine internship at Emory University School of Medicine in Atlanta. In 1989 he completed his dermatology residency at Northwestern University School of Medicine in Chicago. He then moved to Nashville, where he joined an established dermatology practice. After eight months Dr. Gold founded the Gold Skin Care Center in Nashville.

The Skin

Q. Tell me about the skin of a woman in her fifties.
A. The skin of a woman in her fifties is thinner and more translucent than it was in her youth. Her face may have the beginnings of fine lines and wrinkles. She might have more pronounced nasal-labial folds between the nose and mouth and crow's feet around her eyes. Her ears and earlobes are probably longer than they were in her twenties.

Q. What is the effect of gravity on a woman's face as she ages?
A. Gravity pushes everything down. A ratio of 1 to 1 to 1 describes her face when it was young—the forehead, middle, and bottom third of her face were approximately equal in size. As she ages, that ratio

changes to 2 to 1 to 1. The forces of gravity cause the lower two-thirds of the face to push downward. The forehead actually appears to elongate over time.

Q. Why do lines and wrinkles develop as we age?
A. Some facial lines and wrinkles are attributable to expression and are part of the natural aging process, but most skin damage is due to photoaging, another word for sun damage.

Q. What other skin problems are caused by the sun?
A. Sun is the principal cause of skin cancers as well as broken blood vessels that develop under the skin.

Q. When was most of the damage done?
A. Eighty percent of skin damage that develops later in life occurs because of what people did before age twenty.

Q. What did women in their fifties do when they were teenagers to cause skin damage? Why did they do it?
A. When the generation of women who are now in their fifties were young, they didn't know and weren't taught that sun was damaging to their skin. They played or worked in the sun without taking any precautions. They would drive to the beach or pool, preferably in a convertible automobile with the top down. They never applied sunscreen but used baby oil and reflectors. Their skin would become red and blistery. They tried to get as dark and tan as possible. In the winter, they sat under sun lamps and lay on tanning beds.

Only in recent years have we begun to understand the problems caused by sun exposure.

Q. Tell me about skin cancers.
A. There are three types of skin cancer—basal cell, squamous cell, and melanoma.

Q. How common are skin cancers?
A. Approximately one in six people will develop a basal cell carcinoma at some point in their lives. One in fifty people will be diag-

nosed with a squamous cell carcinoma. Although there are other risk factors for malignant melanoma, it is known that people who have numerous moles are at greater risk of getting a melanoma if they go in the sun and constantly sunburn.

Q. Are melanomas more common in the United States today?
A. Absolutely. The incidence of melanoma was one in one thousand twenty years ago. Today one in one hundred people will develop a malignant melanoma at some time in his or her life.

Q. Are there sex differences?
A. Yes. Melanoma occurs more in women than in men because women are more apt to be in the sun. Women, because they are more conscious of their bodies, are more likely to identify these skin lesions earlier than men.

Q. What are actinic keratoses and solar keratoses?
A. Actinic keratoses and solar keratoses are scaly growths that develop on the skin. They are known as sun keratoses. Actinic and solar keratoses are caused by sun exposure and are very common as people get older. They are considered to be precancerous. They may develop into basal cell or squamous cell carcinomas.

Q. How are sun keratoses treated?
A. They should be treated aggressively because approximately 40 percent could turn into skin cancer later in life. They can be removed surgically, with a chemotherapeutic agent, or with the application of liquid nitrogen.

Q. What is rosacea?
A. Rosacea is a type of "acne" that fifty-year-olds can develop. This condition may be genetically predetermined; some think there may be a hormonal imbalance or a change in skin bacteria. The etiology remains unknown. Rosacea shows up as tiny broken blood vessels on the nose and cheeks and is sometimes accompanied by pimples. Rosacea is easily controlled and treated with oral antibiotics like tetracycline or a topical antibiotic called Metrogel. Lasers can eradicate the vascular

lesions or resistant blood vessels associated with rosacea. Rosacea often is made worse by ingestion of coffee, chocolate, spicy foods, or alcohol.

Q. Does diet otherwise affect the skin?
A. It really does not. Several glasses of water a day are probably helpful in keeping the body, and thus the skin, hydrated.

Q. What is the best way to prevent skin damage and slow the aging process of the skin?
A. Applying sunscreen daily is the best protection and may prevent increased sun damage. Other medicines are now being evaluated for skin protection.

Q. What SPF (sun protection factor) is most protective?
A. The SPF should at least 15. Sunscreen should be applied twenty to thirty minutes before going in the sun and should be reapplied after swimming or excessive perspiration.

Hair

Q. Why does hair turn gray as we get older?
A. Hair turns gray because it loses pigment. This is a hormonal process and a normal part of aging. Genetics also plays an important role.

Q. Are hair dyes safe?
A. Hair dyes are usually safe, but some people can't tolerate them. Allergic reactions may occur as well as a burn of the scalp.

Q. Does a woman's hair normally get thinner as she ages?
A. A woman's hair does get thinner, but unlike a man, she should never go totally bald. There are very few completely bald women, unless they have diseases, such as alopecia totalis or universalis. Many women don't understand that it's normal to lose hair as they age. Some will lose a little while others may be able to see their scalp.

Q. Are certain kinds of hair loss in women abnormal?
A. Yes. Certain diseases or hormone abnormalities can cause women to lose hair. It is assumed that a man with hair loss has male pattern balding. If a woman develops sudden hair loss, blood tests and skin biopsies of the scalp often are done to rule out certain medical problems.

Q. Which medical conditions cause hair loss?
A. Collagen vascular diseases, such as lupus erythematosus, which are prevalent in women, can cause hair loss. Certain hormonal defects, such as a deficiency of testosterone or estrogens, and thyroid abnormalities also can cause the hair to fall out. Many of those conditions are treatable and, when effectively treated, the hair loss may stop.

Q. Do some women have genetically thin hair?
A. Yes, just as men do. But their hair probably has been thin for years. These women don't suddenly go to a dermatologist at age fifty because of thinning hair.

Q. What is your opinion of Minoxidil as a treatment for thin hair?
A. There is no reason someone concerned about thinning hair should not try Minoxidil. The topical application has no appreciable side effects. Minoxidil is sold over the counter and is not extremely expensive. Ninety percent of people who use Minoxidil stop losing hair. That is part one of the battle. Twenty percent of men and 30 percent of women (of the 90 percent who stop losing hair) who use this product regrow some hair.

Q. Are new treatments being developed to treat hair loss?
A. Yes. Another treatment now available is called Propecia. This is the same medicine taken by men to lower prostate hypertrophy. Propecia is prescribed at a lower dose to treat thinning hair. This is the first pill ever developed for hair loss. Time will tell whether this will be a useful medicine for hair loss.

Q. Is excess hair a problem for women as they get older?
A. Facial hair can be a problem for some women. It can be caused by

hormones and/or genetics. Dermatologists can eradicate facial hair with lasers and light sources. Other treatments include shaving, waxing, depilatories, and electrolysis.

Q. What is your prescription for healthy, beautiful hair.
A. Good genes.

Fingernails

Q. What happens to our fingernails as we get older?
A. As we get older our fingernails can crack, peel, and get thinner.

Q. Tell me about medical conditions that can be diagnosed by looking at fingernails.
A. Two examples are endocarditis, which causes fingernails to form blood vessels at the cuticles, and psoriasis, in which pits may form in the nails.

Q. Tell me about fungus infections in the nails.
A. Topical treatments do not cure fungal infections, but certain oral treatments, such as Sporanox and Lamisil, have been successful in 80 to 90 percent of patients. Although these medications seem to be safe, Sporanox may cause drug interactions in people who take other medications.

Q. Can anything be done to improve our fingernails?
A. There is very little that can be done to improve the fingernails. Nail strength and growth are inherited.

Q. What do you advise women in their fifties who want to keep their skin healthy and to look as good as they feel?
A.
- Do the smart things that you didn't do as a kid.
- Avoid the sun, especially in the peak hours, which are 10:00 A.M. to 2:00 P.M.
- If you must be outdoors, wear sun lotion with an SPF of at least 15 and reapply it occasionally during the day. Wear a hat with a wide brim and long sleeves.

12

Your Eyes

Reay H. Brown, M.D.

Reay Brown's college major was government. After graduation in 1972, he attended the University of Michigan Medical School and did his ophthalmology training at the Johns Hopkins School of Medicine in Baltimore. He specializes in the treatment of glaucoma and has developed instruments for glaucoma surgery. Dr. Brown is the Pamela Firman Professor of Ophthalmology at Emory University School of Medicine.

Q. Tell me about the eye.
A. The eye is a sensory organ that works like a camera. The cornea, a clear substance that makes up the front of the eye, and the intraocular (inside of the eye) lens focus light on the retina, which sends visual information to the brain, by way of the optic nerve, and creates a visual image.

As an optical system, the eye is designed so that the light focused by the cornea and lens gives 20/20 sight without a glasses correction.

Q. What is 20/20 vision?
A. Normal vision is 20/20. The first, or upper number refers to the distance to the test object and the second, or lower, number refers to the size of the test object. From a practical standpoint, the lower number refers to how far from the specific test object a person with "normal" (20/20) vision can see the object clearly. The upper number is how close the person needs to move to the test object in order to

see it clearly. For example, if your vision is 20/40, it means that what a normal person can see clearly at 40 feet is clear to you only at 20 feet.

Q. What is hyperopia?
A. Hyperopia is farsightedness. With hyperopia, the eyeball is too short. Farsighted people do not see anything up close in focus.

Q. What is myopia?
A. Myopia is nearsightedness. Myopia occurs when the eyeball is abnormally long. Nearsighted people see objects clearly up close but those in the distance are blurred.

Q. What are the treatments for myopia and hyperopia?
A. Eyeglasses can completely correct both myopia and hyperopia. Refractive surgery is becoming an increasingly popular option to correct even a high degree of nearsightedness as well as farsightedness.

Q. What is astigmatism?
A. Astigmatism is an eye condition in which the cornea is not completely round and smooth. Vision may be blurred. Astigmatism also can be corrected with eyeglasses or refractive surgery.

Q. How does the eye move around?
A. Each eye has six extraocular muscles. These keep the eyes straight and move them sideways, up and down, or in a rotary fashion.

Q. Tell me about tears and the lacrimal gland.
A. The tears are part of the lacrimal system, which is located in the eyelids. This is not part of the eyeball. Your tears flow from the lid.

Q. What is presbyopia?
A. Presbyopia, a loss of the ability to focus up close, is the most common eye problem of those in their fifties. Most people begin to experience presbyopia in their forties. Women who didn't need glasses when they were younger now can't read without them.

Q. Tell me about dry eyes.
A. Dry eyes are a bothersome problem that can develop with age. They are caused by a lack of tears or by a change in the composition of the tears. This is a common condition, as reflected by the profusion of over-the-counter tear supplements in drugstores and supermarkets.

Q. What is a cataract?
A. A cataract is an opacity in the lens. Unfortunately, cataracts are an inevitable part of the aging process. If a person lives long enough, she will develop cataracts. But some people won't develop cataracts until eighty or ninety years of age.

Q. Can the onset of cataracts be delayed?
A. There's no definite evidence that cataracts can be delayed.

Q. What are the symptoms of cataracts?
A. The symptoms are blurred vision or problems with glare from sunlight or automobile headlights.

Q. Tell me about surgery for cataracts.
A. Cataract surgery is an example of technology that has soared to incredible heights of success. When I was in training, cataract surgery required a large incision. The patient stayed in the hospital for five days. Today the operation is performed with a very small incision that doesn't require any stitches. In many cases, only topical anesthetic is applied. Patients usually see very well immediately after the surgery or by the next day. The recovery is extremely rapid and the patient can resume normal activities almost immediately.

Q. Tell me about glaucoma.
A. Glaucoma is a very serious condition affecting two to three million people in the United States. Only half of those people know that they have the disease. Glaucoma is seen in 1 to 2 percent of people in their fifties. It affects black women eight times more commonly than Caucasians.

Glaucoma is essentially a plumbing problem of the eye. It is partially caused by a wearing out in the eye's drainage system, which loses its capacity to process fluid.

Fluid is made inside the eye and flows out of a natural drain in front of the iris, the colored part of the eye. The balance between the amount of fluid made and its outflow determines the pressure on the inside of the eye. Too much pressure inside the eyeball can eventually damage the optic nerve, resulting in the blindness of glaucoma.

Q. What are the symptoms of glaucoma?
A. There are no symptoms until glaucoma is very advanced. One day you discover that you've lost a large part of your side vision.

Q. How do you measure eye pressure in glaucoma?
A. Eye pressure for glaucoma is measured similarly to the way you check air pressure in a basketball—you press on it. If it indents easily, the pressure is low. If it doesn't indent, the pressure is high. We do this with a sophisticated device applied to the eye surface that accurately measures eye pressure.

Q. Does the risk of glaucoma increase with age?
A. Yes.

Q. Tell me about the treatment for glaucoma.
A. The most common treatment for glaucoma is beta-blocker eyedrops. The patient applies them in each eye once or twice a day. The drops decrease the amount of fluid made in the eye.

Q. What are the side effects that result from using these eyedrops?
A. They can cause the heart rate to slow and breathing difficulties in people with asthma. There can be increased depression and sexual dysfunction.

Q. Does lifestyle or anything we do affect the development of glaucoma?
A. No.

Q. Does glaucoma run in families?
A. Glaucoma does run in families.

Q. What is your hope for glaucoma?
A. A surgical approach to the treatment of glaucoma needs to be developed. Glaucoma drops are expensive and have too many side effects.

Q. What is macular degeneration?
A. Macular degeneration is an eye disease that affects a small part of the retina. (The macula is located in the middle of the retina and controls central vision.) Macular degeneration can develop as early as the fifties.

The main symptom is blurred central vision, which can become progressively worse and ultimately lead to the inability to read. People with macular degeneration rarely become completely blind.

Q. Is macular degeneration familial?
A. Yes, but it's not inherited in as predictable a way as eye color. Most people whose parents have macular degeneration *will not* develop the disease.

Q. Tell me about floaters.
A. Floaters are debris in the vitreous humor (the clear gel in the eyeball) that appear as floating spots. They are very common, especially in people who are highly nearsighted. Most people have them if they look carefully.

Q. What about floaters are indicative of a retinal detachment?
A. Floaters can indicate the presence of a retinal detachment. A sudden shower of floaters, flashing lights, or loss of vision in a discrete area of your visual field could indicate a retinal detachment.

Q. Is detached retina age-related?
A. A detached retina can occur at any time, but it is age-related. It is more likely to develop when you're sixty than when you are twenty.

Q. What is strabismus?
A. Strabismus is a condition in which the eyes don't move together. The eyes may turn in or out or one may be higher than the other.

Q. What is amblyopia?
A. Amblyopia is diminished sight in one eye with no apparent physical abnormalities. This problem develops during childhood. For example, if someone was born with strabismus and the two eyes weren't moving together, the brain would choose to look through one eye and ignore the other. The ignored eye doesn't develop the same visual capability and probably will see 20/200 at best, which is a tenth the vision of a 20/20 eye. This condition is called lazy eye.

Q. What is retinitis pigmentosa?
A. Retinitis pigmentosa is a rare inherited disease affecting the retina, which may manifest itself at first as night blindness. It can cause blindness. Retinitis pigmentosa usually develops before the fifties.

Q. Tell me about sties.
A. Sties are very common. Tear ducts produce fats and mucous material. When these ducts become clogged, an abscess or sty can develop. Sties often clear up without treatment. However, hot compresses at frequent intervals can be very helpful in speeding up the recovery process. A topical antibiotic and steroid combination also can be effective.

Q. Tell me about conjunctivitis (pink eye), which women in their fifties may be exposed to from their grandchildren.
A. Conjunctivitis can be extremely contagious. People who develop conjunctivitis should be very careful about washing their hands frequently, not sharing towels, and avoiding any contact that may spread the infection. It is best for those with conjunctivitis to stay home from work or school to keep away from other people. It can spread very fast. The highly contagious "pink eye" is caused by a virus; therefore, topical antibiotics are not effective. Conjunctivitis causes only a red and irritated eye; it usually doesn't cause lasting problems.

Q. What about other eye infections?
A. Eye infections usually are self-limited and get better on their own.

Q. Tell me about eye melanoma.
A. Melanomas of the eye occur when pigment cells underneath the retina develop into a malignant tumor. They are rare.

Q. Tell me about diabetic retinopathy.
A. In people with diabetes, the small blood vessels of the eye may become abnormal and bleed inside the eye. Often laser treatment can prevent this bleeding. Anyone who has diabetes should have her eyes examined by an ophthalmologist regularly. While a woman may have learned just a year ago that she had diabetes, the problem may have been present for ten years. Problems can develop in the eyes at any time.

Q. Is night myopia a problem of older adults?
A. Night myopia is a problem for many people, including older adults. At night, the pupil dilates, which exposes more of the outer portion of the lens to light, causing spherical aberrations. In addition, the light at night has shorter wavelengths. Together, these nighttime changes cause objects to appear less well focused.

These patients have problems driving when it is dark. The problems becomes worse in the rain.

Q. Tell me about nutritional supplements, diet, and their effect on eyes.
A. High levels of vitamin C and beta carotene (a relative of vitamin A) have been associated with a reduced risk of degenerative eye disease such as cataracts and macular degeneration. Research in this area is very active, and studies are under way to see whether the vitamins and minerals such as manganese, selenium, zinc, copper, glutathione, niacinamide, and riboflavin can help prevent deterioration of the eye. This is a very complex area, and it will be many years before we have definitive answers. Because people greatly fear eye disease, there is potential for abuse by the nutritional supplement industry. I tell pa-

tients to eat a diet rich in fruits and vegetables and that taking vitamins probably won't hurt them.

Q. So all that advice our mothers gave us about eating carrots wasn't just an old wives' tale?
A. No. Carrots contain vitamin A, so they may well be helpful in keeping the eyes healthy.

Q. Can lifestyle changes help our eyes?
A. A healthy diet and lifestyle are good for the eyes, as they are for the rest of the body. I don't specifically ask my patients to stop smoking, lose weight, or decrease excessive alcohol consumption as a way to prevent eye diseases because the effects are so indirect. However, blood vessel disease can cause small strokes that may be confined to the eye and could cause blindness in one eye. The risk is probably reduced if a person doesn't smoke, has a healthy diet, and otherwise maintains a healthy lifestyle.

Q. Why and how often should women have their eyes examined?
A. Women should have their eyes checked every two years to guard against glaucoma, diabetic retinopathy, and other conditions that can be diagnosed by looking in the eye.

Q. What are worrisome eye symptoms that would warrant immediate attention?
A. Worrisome symptoms are blurred vision, pain, or redness in the eyes.

Q. What is the future of ophthalmology?
A. Refractive surgery will improve to the point that few people will wear glasses.

Glaucoma will be the next frontier of surgical success.

The future in retinal treatments may be transplantable retinal tissues that could treat macular degeneration.

Genetic advances will dominate all medical and surgical improvements in ophthalmology. We will do genetic testing to determine which eye diseases a patient might be predisposed to or may have developed already. Genetic engineering probably will come later and revolutionize all our treatments or preventions.

Q. What advice would you give women in their fifties who want to take good care of their eyes?
A. Enjoy your eyes. You can't wear them out. Most eye diseases can be prevented or treated effectively, so have a regular eye exam to detect any problems as soon as possible.

The eyes are more resistant to aging than almost any other part of the body. With routine eye exams, and a little luck, most people should be able to see 20/20, some with help from either glasses or cataract surgery, all their lives.

13

Your Hearing

Robert Dobie, M.D.

Robert Dobie graduated from college in 1967 with a bachelor's degree in biology. He attended Stanford University Medical School, completing a surgical internship as well as a residency and fellowship in otolaryngology. In 1975 he joined the faculty of the Department of Otolaryngology at the University of Washington School of Medicine in Seattle, where he rose from assistant professor to professor of otolaryngology. Dr. Dobie has been chairman of the Department of Otolaryngology at the University of Texas Health Sciences Center at San Antonio since 1990.

Q. Tell me about the basic anatomy of the ear.
A. The ear is composed of three major parts—the outer ear, the middle ear, and the inner ear.

Q. What is the function of the outer ear?
A. The outer ear is mostly decorative, but it passively boosts and decreases certain sound frequencies.

Q. What is the middle ear and how does it transmit sound?
A. The middle ear is actually an outpouching of the sinuses and nasal cavity. It is lined with mucous membrane and subject to the same problems that affect the nose and sinuses, such as allergies and colds.

The eardrum (also called the tympanic membrane) is located between the outer and the middle ear and contains a chain of three bones: the malleus (or hammer), incus (or anvil), and stapes (or stirrup).

The middle ear ensures that airborne sound does not get deflected away. Without a working middle ear, sound energy that entered the ear canal would bounce off the eardrum and return to the air.

Q. What is the purpose of the inner ear?
A. The inner ear functions in hearing and balance.

Q. How does the inner ear allow us to hear?
A. The cochlea, a spiral organ in the inner ear (the word literally means snail), is made up of a set of hair cells. Hair cells at the apex of the cochlea are attached to a floppy, massive membrane and respond to low-frequency sounds. Those at the base of the cochlea are attached to a stiffer, smaller membrane and react to high-pitched tones. When sound reaches the inner ear, fluids vibrate and stimulate hair cells that are connected to the auditory nerve, and ultimately it reaches the auditory centers of the brain.

Q. How does the inner ear control eye coordination and balance?
A. The inner ear contains five balance organs that are similar in structure and function to those that serve hearing.

Three of these organs are located inside the semicircular canals, which are actually full circles arranged at right angles to one another. The major purpose of the semicircular canals is to enable us to keep a stable image on our retinas when we move our head. These doughnut-like circles are filled with fluid that sloshes around when we shake or rotate our head. For example, if you stare at a clock on the wall and move your head back and forth, the clock stays stable in your gaze because your inner ear balance organs are also moving.

A secondary goal of the inner ear is to assist with balance and functions to keep us upright. Two otolith organs control balance. When you tilt your head, the otolith organs tell the brain which way the head is moving as well as its position.

Q. Is the inner ear the only body part that controls balance?
A. No. Your balance is controlled by your eyes, the inner ear organs as well as input from your skin, joints, and other parts of your body.

Q. What happens to hearing as people get older?
A. As people age, they lose hair cells in the inner ear, most commonly at the base of the cochlea, which affects hearing high-frequency sounds.

Because people are not engineered to last forever, everything wears out over time. People have differing rates of decline, but every organ eventually deteriorates. This is certainly true of the hair cells in the inner ear.

Q. When does hearing loss begin?
A. Hearing loss begins in the teenage years. Young adults normally lose ultra–high-frequency sounds, such as the squeal from a television set, which are not important and usually go unnoticed.

Q. Do most people lose hearing at the same time?
A. No. Hearing loss due to aging is highly variable. Some people have very good hearing in their seventies, while for others progressive hearing loss starts in their forties.

Q. Is hearing loss due to aging a gradual or a quick process?
A. It's a gradual deterioration.

Q. How is our hearing damaged?
A. Hair cells at the basal end of the cochlea that are susceptible to loss from aging are also damaged by excessive noise, head injury, and certain drugs. Drug-related hearing loss is uncommon because medications that cause permanent hearing loss are almost always given intravenously in a hospital setting, usually for life-threatening conditions. High doses of aspirin, between eight and twelve tablets a day, can cause temporary hearing loss, but hearing almost always returns when the aspirin is discontinued.

Q. How would you describe the hearing of people in their fifties?
A. The fifties is not a particularly vulnerable decade for hearing loss. Most common hearing disorders begin earlier in life and become apparent in later decades. The fifties is merely a decade when specific hearing problems get worse.

Q. What percentage of women in their fifties will have hearing loss great enough to warrant a hearing aid?
A. About 10 percent of women in their fifties will have hearing loss that is significant enough to warrant a hearing aid. Although that is a fairly high number, most of those women knew they had a hearing problem before they hit fifty.

Q. Tell me about some of the hearing problems that people may face in their fifties.

A.
Conductive Hearing Loss
In conductive hearing loss, the outer ear or the middle ear or both are blocked, so that the sound can't get into the inner ear. Conductive hearing loss could be due to earwax plugging the ear canal, a hole in the eardrum, a dislocation or fixation of one of the ossicles, the brittle bones of the ear, or fluid filling the middle ear because of allergy or infection. Most conductive hearing losses can be corrected by medical or surgical means.

Sensorineural Hearing Loss
Sensorineural losses are inner ear hearing losses that, with only a few exceptions, cannot be corrected. The majority of people with this problem will either put up with impaired hearing or get a hearing aid.

Earwax
Earwax is a combination of dead skin and a greasy secretion that is produced by the cerumen glands. Earwax normally migrates out of the ear canal and falls out of the ear onto a pillow or shirt. Wax can become impacted in the ears of people who have excessive hair in the canal, which blocks the migration. Probing into the ear with a bobby pin, paper clip, or Q-tip also can pack the wax in.

Ear Pain

Ear pain usually is caused either by infections or temporomandibular joint syndrome (TMJ). The pain of TMJ is often felt in the ear but actually is radiated from a nearby structure.

Otosclerosis

Otosclerosis is a hereditary middle ear disease that affects some women in their fifties. People with otosclerosis almost always have some hearing loss before they turn fifty.

Otosclerosis usually affects both ears, one more than the other. The stapes—the smallest of the three bones in the middle ear—becomes jammed with excessive bone growth, which keeps sound from entering the inner ear. When it becomes severe, it can be treated surgically by removing the stapes or by drilling a hole through it, allowing sound to get into the inner ear.

Meniere's Disease

Meniere's disease is a condition in which the inner ear fluids periodically become distended. Patients experience bouts of hearing loss in the affected ear as well as episodes of vertigo accompanied by nausea and vomiting. The hearing returns to normal, but after a number of episodes, patients may suffer some permanent hearing loss. Meniere's disease can be controlled with a low-salt diet, avoidance of nicotine, stress management, and diuretics (water pills). Five to 10 percent of patients with this condition undergo surgery to stop the spells of vertigo.

Tinnitus

Tinnitus is described as a ringing, buzzing, chirping, humming or cricketlike noise in the ears. These are common descriptions, but patients usually use *one* of these words. Ten percent of people over fifty have tinnitus. For most people, tinnitus becomes a background noise that they are unaware of. They have become acclimated to the sounds.

Tinnitus in both ears or alternating between the ears is rarely of any medical significance, but if it is present just in one ear, we become concerned. Unilateral tinnitus is a red flag for a small, benign tumor on the balance nerve—we think of this possibility and do more tests, but fewer than 5 percent of people with unilateral tinnitus actually have a tumor. Pulsatile tinnitus (synchronous with your pulse) demands some degree of workup because it can be an indication of artery and vein problems, including narrowed carotid arteries, or certain tumors.

Q. What are symptoms of hearing problems that should be treated as red flags?
A. The number-one symptom is pain. The second is discharge or bleeding. Number three is a sudden or progressive hearing loss—this is usually due to a viral infection, but it could be the result of a tumor. Another is unequal hearing between the ears or noise just in one ear. If either of these symptoms persists, it should be checked out. If caught early, many ear disorders are easy to treat.

Vertigo is another red flag. It is relatively common in the fifty- to sixty-year-old age group. Vertigo is a hallucination of movement experienced when the balance part of the inner ear goes awry. Vertigo is felt as a spinning sensation, usually accompanied by nausea or vomiting. Several ear disorders cause fluctuating vertigo.

Another kind of dizziness that originates in the inner ear is disequilibrium, which means poor balance. People with episodes of vertigo or disequilibrium should be checked for an inner ear disorder. More than half of patients who present to otolaryngologists with vertigo have Meniere's disease or benign positional vertigo. The most common cause of vertigo seen in the primary care physician's office is probably labyrinthitis (also called vestibular neuronitis). This usually gets better by itself.

Q. What are early signs of hearing loss?
A. People who are developing significant hearing loss have trouble understanding conversations when there is a noisy background. As the hearing loss progresses, they begin to misunderstand words in a quiet setting. Patients often say, "I hear but I don't understand." At that level of hearing loss, people have no trouble hearing a word spoken, but they misunderstand the word. They ask for repeats and rely more on vision than they used to.

Q. When is it time to do something about hearing loss?
A. I would strongly urge patients to get a hearing test when they

avoid social activities or have job problems because of their poor hearing. I also recommend a hearing test whenever poor hearing interferes with *any* activities of daily life—usually this means speech comprehension. When these people are fitted with a hearing aid, their mood and quality of life usually improve.

Q. Tell me about hearing aids.
A. A hearing aid is essentially a fancy amplifier with a little microphone that picks up sound. The tuning circuits in the amplifier boost frequencies that you can't hear and present them deep inside the ear canal.

Hearing aids have improved in recent years. Higher fidelity and better circuitry boost low-intensity sounds to be heard but don't increase high-intensity sounds to an unbearable level. Newer hearing aids are available in microminiature versions that literally disappear inside the ear. They are so tiny that a half-inch length of clear plastic line must attached for extraction from the ear.

Q. How much do hearing aids cost?
A. The top-of-the-line, programmable, completely-in-the-canal disappearing-type of hearing aid costs about $4,500 for two. Garden-variety, good-quality hearing aids that fit outside of the ear canal run $600 to $700 each.

Q. Are hearing aids covered by insurance?
A. Only a few private health insurance companies cover hearing aids.

Q. Should women in their fifties have regular hearing checkups?
A. Probably not. In most cases people know when they have hearing loss. But it's important to seek professional help if you have symptoms that I listed as red flags.

Q. What do you advise women who want to maintain their hearing?
A.
• Avoid excessive noise exposure.
• If you have a noisy occupation, wear hearing protection. If you

must shout to be heard in a normal conversation, the noise level is probably above the line for hazard.

- Wear hearing protection if you participate in noisy hobbies, such as hunting and shooting—that includes any gun bigger than a .22.
- Avoid habitual exposure to loud noises at rock concerts that cause temporary hearing loss, ringing, buzzing, or a muffled feeling in the ears. Eventually these noises cause permanent hearing loss. The problem can be circumvented by wearing high-fidelity ear plugs that protect hearing without distorting the music. Many rock musicians use them regularly.
- Avoid head injury. Wear your seat belt in an automobile or a helmet if you ride a horse or a bicycle. Head injury is not only a major cause of brain injury, it can also cause hearing loss.

14

Healthy Teeth and Gums

Eugene T. Giannini, D.D.S.

Eugene Giannini completed a combined degree program in dental education at New York University, earning a bachelor of arts, and a doctor of dental surgery degree from Georgetown University School of Dentistry in Washington, D.C., in 1988. He then completed a one-year general practice residency in dentistry at Westchester County Medical Center north of New York City. In 1989 he joined a multidisciplinary dental practice in Fairfield County, Connecticut. In 1990 he returned to Washington, where he joined a dental practice partnership. Dr. Giannini currently practices general dentistry in Washington with an emphasis on periodontal disease prevention, dental reconstruction, and cosmetics.

Q. What happens to teeth and gums as we get older?
A. As we get older, teeth and gums are subject to wear and tear. Old restorations (fillings, crowns) may require replacement as they fatigue from daily use. Various medical conditions and medications can change the oral environment (the mouth), making the teeth more susceptible to decay and the gums subject to periodontal disease (gum disease).

Q. Can dental problems found in older adults be prevented or reversed?
A. Most dental problems can be prevented or minimized with good

oral hygiene techniques, the use of fluoride, proper nutrition, and regular dental exams.

Decayed teeth can be restored, but they can never be returned to the way they were. Gum disease can be halted and health maintained from that point on.

Q. What characterizes the oral health of women in their fifties?
A. The oral health of women in this age group depends on their genetic makeup, personal habits, nutrition, and the health care they have received over the years. Major problems that I see include tooth decay, periodontal disease, xerostomia (dry mouth), and worn restorations.

Q. Tell me about tooth decay.
A. Contrary to the popular belief that cavities are for kids, the adult population is at equal or greater risk for cavities. Exposed root surfaces, which occur as gums recede, lack the protective enamel covering found on the crown of the tooth. The root surfaces are prone to attack by plaque, which can result in dental decay, and are called root caries. According to the American Dental Association, the majority of people over age fifty have some tooth-root decay.

Q. Tell me about plaque and tartar.
A. Dental plaque is a sticky yellowish material that adheres to the teeth. It is made up of bacteria enclosed in a matrix of proteins and sugars. Plaque must be mechanically removed from the tooth, using a variety of oral hygiene instruments—picks, brush, and floss.

Tartar (sometimes called calculus) is dead, calcified plaque. On its own, tartar is not harmful, but due to its irregular and rough surface, it is an ideal place for bacteria to thrive, which can be harmful to the gums.

Within minutes of brushing the teeth, a layer of protein called pellicle forms on the clean tooth surfaces. Pellicle serves as a host on which bacteria can grow. Certain conditions can favor the accumulation of these deposits—crowded teeth, existing calculus, rough or irregular surfaces on fillings, dental restorations, and mouth breathing, which dries out the oral cavity, making the plaque more tenacious.

Q. Tell me about the latest techniques in drilling and filling cavities.
A. The high-speed rotary dental handpiece (drill), which was introduced over thirty-five years ago, is the standard device used in modern dentistry. Recent advances have been made in this air-abrasive technology that promise pain-free removal of decayed tooth structure without the drill noise. Lasers promise to make this process even quieter and more comfortable.

Q. What is the expected lifetime of a filling or restoration?
A. Many factors contribute to the life of a restoration—the patient's habits (ice chewing, tooth grinding), medical conditions, and plaque control.

Amalgam (silver) fillings can be expected to last five to fifteen years; posterior composites, which are tooth-colored plastic-type fillings, can last five to eight years; gold inlays, five to twenty years; porcelain/ceramic inlays/crowns, five to fifteen years; and posterior ceramic and metal crowns, five to fifteen years.

Q. Tell me about gum disease.
A. Gum disease, or periodontal disease, is one of the most widespread afflictions in human beings. It affects three out of four adults at some stage in their lives.

Q. What causes gums to bleed?
A. Bleeding gums can be a warning sign of periodontal disease. Bacterial dental plaque may have accumulated at or beneath the gum line. Bleeding gums also can signify serious medical conditions such as vitamin deficiencies, diabetes, and leukemias.

Some hormonal contraceptives as well as anticoagulants such as Coumadin can cause the gums to bleed.

Q. What is gingivitis?
A. Gingivitis is an inflammatory disease limited to the gingivae, or gum tissues. It is caused by an accumulation of bacterial plaque and may be aggravated/exacerbated by hormonal changes and some medications. With proper treatment it is reversible and causes no long-term effects.

Some menopausal and postmenopausal women suffer from a rare type of gingivitis called gingivitis climacterica, which causes changes in the appearance of the gum tissue with smooth, shiny areas. Some patients report a dry mouth and a burning sensation. Symptoms may be relieved with estrogen therapy.

Q. What is periodontitis?
A. Periodontitis is the result of untreated gingivitis. However, not all cases of gingivitis lead to periodontitis.

The symptoms of periodontitis can include some or all of the following: gums that bleed during brushing; pus between the teeth and gums; red, swollen, or painful gums; loose teeth; receded gums; and bad breath.

When the inflammatory response extends to the supporting alveolar (jaw) or jaw bone, it is called periodontitis. Many factors play a role in the development of this condition, ranging from the types of bacteria present and the nutritional status of the patient to the patient's immune system. Periodontitis can be prevented with proper oral hygiene. It progresses slowly or rapidly depending the patient's immune system, home care, whether he or she smokes or is diabetic.

Q. What is the treatment for periodontitis?
A. The initial therapy consists of removing plaque and proper home care. Removing plaque is usually done with a dental scaling or cleaning. When deep pockets exist under the gum line, the dentist may recommend a root planing and curettage. The hard deposits of calculus and plaque are removed from the tooth and root surface, resulting in a clean root surface free of toxins. Usually this is done with local anesthetic. Initial therapy usually resolves gingivitis and mild periodontitis.

Advanced cases of periodontitis, characterized by more bone destruction and breakdown of the gum tissue's attachment to the tooth root (loss of gingival attachment), usually require more involved surgical intervention.

Q. What could result if inflamed gums are not treated?
A. If left untreated, inflammation can spread to the supporting tissues

of the teeth. Bone can be destroyed, resulting in tooth mobility and eventual tooth loss.

Q. What type of dentist specializes in gum disease?
A. A periodontist is a dentist who receives additional training to specialize in the treatment of the teeth and their supporting structures, the gums and bone.

Q. What are the latest treatments for gum disease?
A. Guided tissue regeneration (GTR) allows bone to grow back in some situations. It can be used in combination with dental implants.

Antibiotic therapies combined with periodontal procedures improve the success rate in curing periodontitis.

Q. What is a dental implant?
A. A dental implant is a man-made artificial tooth root upon which a dental crown or cap can be attached. Implants usually are made of titanium, the same material used for artificial hips and knees. The dentist, periodontist, or oral surgeon places the artificial tooth root into the jawbone. Over a period of time, usually about six months, the jaw bone fuses to and integrates with the implant. Function and esthetics can be thus restored to patients who have lost teeth because of disease or trauma.

Q. What is xerostomia (dry mouth)?
A. Dry mouth can be caused by medical disorders or by medications such as antihistamines, decongestants, diuretics, and painkillers. When there is a decrease in saliva, food debris can remain on the teeth along with plaque. Saliva also functions to buffer or neutralize acids produced by plaque. With a decrease in the quantity and quality of saliva, decay can thrive.

Q. How does osteoporosis affect women's teeth?
A. Studies have shown that postmenopausal women with osteoporosis are more likely to have dentures by age sixty. Estrogen replacement after menopause seems to be useful in preventing osteoporosis, but no

definitive link has been established between decreased estrogen and gum disease.

Q. How does nutrition affect the teeth and gums?
A. A balanced diet contributes to overall health. That includes oral health. Vitamin C deficiencies can result in diminished wound healing and gum inflammation. An inability to absorb vitamin B-12 also can result in burning tongue syndrome.

Q. What causes tooth pain?
A. Tooth pain can be cause by decay in the tooth, thermal changes (hot or cold), trauma, or cracking in the tooth structure. All these factors inflame the dental pulp (nerve) and result in pain.

Q. Is it okay to ignore tooth pain?
A. It is never a good idea to ignore tooth pain. If the problem is diagnosed and treated early, chances are that the treatment and costs will be minimal. However, if ignored, pain can lead to more serious problems, even if it goes away.

Q. Why are some teeth sensitive to hot and cold?
A. Teeth can be sensitive to thermal changes for several reasons. Gum recession and periodontal disease can expose root surfaces, making it easier to stimulate the nerve in the tooth, which makes it more sensitive to changes in temperature. Amalgam fillings are sometimes sensitive to thermal changes. Recently placed or deep fillings can result in transient hypersensitivity to cold because of nerve inflammation.

Q. Do certain foods cause teeth to ache?
A. Teeth are sometimes sensitive to sweets or acidic items, especially if there is dental decay, a broken or leaking filling, or exposed dentin on root surfaces.

Q. Is pain from a sinus infection felt in the teeth?
A. Yes. Sinus infections can result in tooth pain. The roots of the maxillary molars (molars on the upper jaw) are in close proximity to the maxillary sinuses (the sinuses above your upper jaw) and can be

stimulated, causing a toothache. Usually this pain involves a quadrant of teeth rather than a single tooth.

Q. Is tooth pain ever indicative of a serious medical problem?
A. Yes. A warning sign of a heart attack can be pain that radiates to the jaw.

Q. Can dental problems, such as cavities and abscesses, cause other aches in the head?
A. Yes, in cases of pulpal damage, some affected nerves can feel as if the pain is radiating to the ear, sinuses, or opposing jaw.

Q. What is a root canal?
A. Root canals are performed on injured or diseased nerves of the tooth. When the tooth pulp (nerve) is injured, it dies. The body's immune system attacks the dead tissue, resulting in an abscess. A root canal consists of the removal of the dental pulp. The inner area of the tooth is cleaned and sterilized. The space is filled and sealed. This allows the tooth to be maintained in the jaw bone.

Q. Who performs root canals?
A. Root canals are performed by general dentists or by specialists known as endodontists.

Q. What is a crown restoration?
A. A crown is a type of dental restoration that covers the tooth and is visible in the mouth, allowing renewed function and strength. The tooth is ground down to accommodate the thickness of the crown material. A crown can be made of ceramic or metal. The color of the ceramic or porcelain crown can vary to match the shade of adjacent teeth.

Q. When and why are crowns (or caps) indicated?
A. Crowns (caps) are placed in order to restore a broken or cracked tooth or to change the appearance of a tooth, that is, to make it bigger, smaller, straighter, or whiter.

The goal of most crowns is to make the tooth stronger and less likely to split or break.

Q. Do some dentists specialize in crown fabrication and restoration?
A. Some dentists take continued training to become prosthodontists. These specialists usually excel in complex cosmetic or restorative cases involving crowns, bridges, and dentures. There is no specialty devoted solely to the fabrication of crowns.

Q. What are partials?
A. A "partial" is short for removable partial denture. These are dental appliances that restore the function and appearance of missing teeth. Usually these dentures have clasps to secure them to the remaining natural or crowned teeth. They can be made of metal or a combination of plastic and metal.

Q. When and why are orthodontic procedures prescribed for women in their fifties?
A. Orthodontic procedures function to improve the appearance and health of teeth. Adults increasingly find themselves interested in improving the crowded appearance of their smile. While orthodontics results in a beautiful and straight smile, it also can place the teeth in a relationship to better maintain periodontal health. Teeth that are not crowded are easier to clean and less likely to build up calculus and experience inflammation, which can result in periodontal bone loss.

Q. Tell me about dentures.
A. Dentures function to replace missing teeth and/or the supporting tissues of the teeth. They restore function for eating and speech as well as restore appearance for individuals who have lost their teeth due to disease or trauma. Many times dentures are viewed as an interim step in the reconstruction of an implant-retained smile. Dentists today can utilize implants (artificial tooth roots made of titanium) to better anchor and stabilize dentures. Once patients are fitted for dentures, it is important that they regularly visit the dentist as part of a preventive maintenance program—even if they have no teeth! Dentists need to examine for the presence of oral cancers and other pathology such as

infection as well as verify the fit and stability of the dentures. The oral tissues under the dentures are subject to change, and modifications may be required to ensure a proper and comfortable fit.

Q. Why do teeth yellow with age?
A. The outer layer of tooth visible in the mouth, the enamel, is composed of a porous crystal structure that is visible microscopically. Over the years, deposits from products such as coffee, tea, or tobacco can impregnate this surface and become embedded in this microscopic structure. In addition, over time the enamel is likely to crack and chip. These cracks attract stain and deliver them deeper in the tooth.

Q. Tell me about teeth-whitening procedures.
A. There are several ways to change the color of teeth.

Surface stains from coffee, tea, and tobacco can be polished away during a cleaning in the dentist's office.

Bleaching is the most common method used today to change the color of teeth. Bleaching solutions deliver oxygen into the tooth surface and remove stains that have penetrated the tooth surface. The teeth become brighter and whiter without the removal of any tooth structure.

Bonding covers the entire discolored tooth surface with a plastic or composite material.

Veneers cover the entire surface of a tooth with a ceramic material. This is similar to applying a fake fingernail—it is cemented over the tooth. Veneers are used when color and tooth shape are to be changed. They are also used when stains do not respond to simpler, less invasive techniques.

Crowns also change the color of severely stained teeth.

Q. Tell me about bleaching teeth. What about these kits I see for sale in stores?
A. Patients should avoid over-the-counter products for whitening teeth. Use of oxygenation products when there is dental decay or a defective filling could result in irritation of the dental pulp and could lead to nerve death.

Q. What is cosmetic dentistry?
A. Cosmetic dentistry includes all dental procedures that function to restore or enhance the appearance of the smile. It can range from the replacement of a discolored filling to placements of crowns or veneers, to tooth bleaching, orthodontic treatment, periodontal surgery, and combinations of all these treatments.

Q. What qualifies a dentist to perform cosmetic procedures?
A. Most dentists have received basic training in some cosmetic procedures. With their continued educational training, their artistic skill, and experience, some dentists can deliver different levels of cosmetic procedures.

Q. What should a woman consider before she decides on cosmetic dental work?
A. She should consider what she likes or dislikes about her current smile. Is it the color of her teeth or a single tooth that bothers her, or is it the size or shape of her teeth or their crowding? Is it the lack of teeth and an inability to function properly without discomfort? She should know the qualifications of the dentist to whom she is entrusting herself. What experience does that dentist have in treating similar cases? What is the cost of the total treatment, in time and dollars? What does she hope to achieve by having this work done?

Q. Tell me about preventive dental care.
A. Preventive dental care is the basis of all dentistry. The goal of preventive dentistry is the instilling of good habits to support the health of the teeth and gums. This includes home plaque control (brushing and flossing), proper diet and nutrition, and routine dental visits. With early detection of dental problems, simple solutions can be carried out, eliminating or limiting more involved treatment, which is usually more expensive.

Q. How often is it optimal to have dental checkups?
A. Usually twice a year, but this can vary, depending on the oral health of the patient. Patients with periodontal disease may need to be seen at intervals ranging from every few weeks to every six months.

For patients undergoing chemotherapy or those with disorders affecting oral health, more frequent visits usually are recommended and prescribed both by their dentist and physician.

Q. Why brush teeth?
A. Brushing removes the sticky bacterial plaque along with food debris from the teeth. Done properly, brushing also stimulates the gingival tissue. It reduces the risk of dental cavities, thus increasing the longevity of restorations and eliminating the risk of periodontal disease.

Q. What are the best methods of brushing teeth?
A. The best brushing method is to place a *soft* nylon bristle brush at a 45-degree angle where the tooth meets the gum. You should feel the bristles under the gum line. Then gently agitate in a back-and-forth motion. Pay attention to the cheek, tongue, and biting surfaces.

Q. Should the tongue be brushed as well?
A. Yes. You should brush your tongue routinely to remove bacteria that can grow in the numerous irregularities on its surface.

Q. When should we brush our teeth?
A. After each meal and at bedtime.

Q. How often should a toothbrush be replaced?
A. When the bristles show signs of fraying, usually every three months, and after a respiratory or throat infection.

Q. What about electric toothbrushes?
A. An electric toothbrush can be more effective in removing plaque than a regular toothbrush, used in the same amount of time. The bristles should be soft and polished, whether you're using an electric or a manual toothbrush.

Q. Are some toothpastes better than other?
A. Yes. Those containing fluoride are better because they decrease the risk of dental decay.

Q. What about dental floss?

A. Flossing is essential for healthy teeth and gums. Floss removes the sticky bacterial plaque from tooth surfaces at and beneath the gum line. Only floss can remove plaque from the tight areas between the teeth. Flossing should be done daily and whenever food lodges between your teeth.

Q. Are fluoride rinses good?

A. Fluoride rinses decrease the risk of dental decay when used in combination with brushing and flossing. They should be used daily.

Q. What about dental irrigators?

A. Dental irrigators remove plaque and food debris from between the teeth and under fixed bridgework. They are not a replacement for brushing.

Q. How does the food we eat affect our teeth?

A. The food we eat and how we eat it can affect our teeth. Sugar in the diet is likely to result in dental decay. Acids are formed by bacterial plaque breaking down sugars. It's a matter of time—the time that the teeth are exposed to the sugary food. Tacky, sticky foods that are usually high in sugar, such as taffy, caramels, and chewing gum, are especially bad.

Foods that fit into an overall balanced diet are good for teeth. Detergent foods, such as apples, celery, and carrots, stimulate saliva production and work to remove plaque by being chewed and rubbed against the teeth.

Q. How has dentistry changed in the past decade?

A. Dentistry has become more consumer driven. Now a greater selection of dentists and techniques is available to patients. The profession of dentistry has sought to make dental experiences more comfortable and preventive. Advances in infection control have made the dental office safer than ever. Newer technologies offer cosmetic and implant dentistry to more people while maintaining cost and reducing risk.

Q. What do you advise women in their fifties who want beautiful, healthy, pain-free teeth?
A. Eat a balanced diet, practice proper oral hygiene, and seek periodic dental examinations and cleanings.

Q. What is the future of dentistry in this country?
A. The future of dentistry will reveal a generation of patients with fewer fillings and dentures.

Laser technology will offer alternatives to traditional dental drills.

Advances in anesthesia will eliminate the need for injections.

Increased computerization will allow patients to have dental restorations fabricated chairside.

Gene therapy will enable dentists to regenerate a missing or decayed tooth. This is an exciting area. Dentists will truly be able to restore teeth.

SECTION III

Brain, Mind, and Psyche

15

Headaches

Raymond Coll, M.D.

Raymond Coll was born and educated in South Africa. He graduated from Witwatersrand University Medical School in 1961 and completed his internship in medicine and surgery at Baragwanath and Coronation hospitals in South Africa. He emigrated to the United States in 1968 and completed a residency in neurology at The New York Hospital–Cornell Medical Center. In 1971 he opened his neurology practice in New York City. Dr. Coll is associate clinical professor of neurology at The New York Hospital–Cornell Medical Center.

Q. Why do heads ache?
A. Pain-sensitive structures in the head cause heads to ache. When those structures are stimulated for any reason, the response is pain.

Some headaches are associated with serious disease, such as strokes, brain hemorrhage, brain tumors, inflammatory processes, and trauma. Most headaches are not associated with organic disease. Usually they are related to stress or other environmental factors.

Q. What is the mechanism that causes headaches?
A. We don't understand the basic mechanism that causes headaches other than the fact that pain-sensitive structures are stimulated.

Q. How can someone know when her headache indicates a serious illness?
A. Her head pain may indicate something serious if it is intensely

severe, prolonged, or has occurred abruptly, especially if she is not prone to headaches. In that event, she should seek immediate medical attention.

Q. Tell me about migraine headaches.
A. Migraines, also known as vascular headaches, are one of the most common types of headache in which dilation of arteries in the scalp is thought to produce the pain.

Migraine is known as a young person's headache, but it can begin later in life. It can occur in both sexes but is more common to women.

Q. What percentage of women suffer from migraine headaches?
A. Thirteen to 17 percent of women suffer from migraine headaches.

Q. Tell me about the different types of migraine headache.
A. One type is the classical migraine in which the throbbing, pounding, pulsating headache is preceded by an aura that consists of neurological symptoms, such as blurred vision or the perception of jagged lines or stars.

In a common migraine, the second type, the pain is not preceded by neurological symptoms. Common migraine is five times more frequent than the classical type.

The third category, ocular migraine, is one in which the visual component—blurred vision or jagged lines—is experienced but the headache does not follow. Diagnosis of ocular migraine can be difficult. The physician must rule out other causes of blurred vision, such as vascular insufficiency to the retina.

A cluster headache, the last type of vascular headache, is a severe one-sided ache around the eye—behind the eye or over the forehead or eyebrows. Often it is associated with tearing from the eye and a blocked nostril on the same side as the pain. Cluster headaches usually begin suddenly, last an hour or two, and often wake people from sleep. Patients describe them as the worst headaches they ever had in their lives. Cluster headaches are uncommon in women. They are called cluster headaches because they tend to occur in clusters, that is, for several weeks at a time.

Q. Please describe the pain of a migraine headache.
A. A migraine headache is characterized by throbbing, pounding, pulsating pain in a localized area of the head—the front, back, side, or sometimes over the eye. The pain does not often encompass the entire head.

Q. What are accompanying symptoms of migraines?
A. Migraines frequently are accompanied by nausea and vomiting plus light and sound sensitivity. Diarrhea is sometimes experienced. After the headache subsides, patients may complain of tenderness in the scalp.

Q. What are common causes of migraine?
A. They are caused by a variety of environmental factors, such as stress, hunger, or lack of sleep. Alcohol, especially red wine, monosodium glutamate, nitrates, chocolate, and aged yellow cheeses can also trigger migraines.

Q. Tell me about treatments for migraine headache.
A. Once the physician is satisfied the pain is due to migraine, the treatment may be multifaceted. We can prescribe medications to deal with the pain, but the underlying problem should be addressed. Whatever is causing the headache—stress, anxiety, depression, lack of sleep, or poor dietary habits—should be dealt with.

Q. Tell me about medications for migraines?
A. Sumatriptan, a very effective treatment of acute migraine, is prescribed in tablet form or by injection and recently has been made available as a nasal spray. Although it is contraindicated in people who have cardiac disease, who are sulfonamide-sensitive, or during pregnancy, it is well tolerated by most patients. Sumatriptan is a very expensive medication—the major drawback.

A second effective migraine treatment is based on ergot, a vasoconstrictor. As a vasoconstrictor medication, ergot constricts blood vessels and thus relieves the pain of migraine. It should be avoided if the patient is pregnant or suffers from cardiovascular disease. Ergot is a pharmacological substance that can be taken orally, by injection, rectally as a suppository, or placed under the tongue. A nasal spray is also available. It is best absorbed intravenously or rectally. Ergot preparations are best used to treat an attack if taken early on, but are not effective as a preventive measure.

Other drug options are combination treatments, such as Tylenol with a short-acting barbiturate and caffeine. Some migraines respond to aspirin alone.

For patients whose headaches are prolonged (more than twenty-four hours) and unresponsive to standard medications, we may prescribe a cortisone preparation called prednisone for a twenty-four-hour period.

Beta blockers may be taken as daily preventive treatments for patients who suffer frequent, debilitating migraine headaches (three to four headaches a month to three to four a week). Beta blockers are medications that block the normal action of beta receptors in blood vessels, which is to dilate vessels. So beta blockers will lead to constriction of a blood vessel.

We sometimes give mild antidepressants or tranquilizers to headache sufferers.

Q. Why do migraines diminish for many women around the time of menopause?
A. This is probably related to decreased estrogen production. Some factors that contribute to the development of headaches, such as the stresses of raising a young family and the intensity of professional life, diminish with increased age and decreased responsibility.

Q. Is estrogen the reason women suffer with more migraine headaches than men?
A. Yes, but estrogen is not the only cause. Figures that compare women's migraines to those of men show that they are three to four times as common among women. Men produce very little estrogen, but they do get migraine headaches.

Q. Tell me about the correlation between migraine headaches and hormones.
A. There is a strong relationship between migraine headaches and

hormones. Women get migraines during ovulation, menstruation, or when they're on birth control pills. Postmenopausal women may suffer with these headaches when they take estrogen. Women who were never previously bothered by headaches sometimes get vascular headaches with hormone-replacement therapy. We think estrogen is the cause.

Q. Tell me about tension headaches.
A. The physical cause of tension headaches is the contraction of scalp muscles, which extend from the eyebrows back to the end of the hairline. Like other muscles, the scalp has the capacity to constrict involuntarily. When that happens, a bandlike pain develops. Tension headaches are often described as a feeling similar to that of a too-tight bathing cap.

Q. What are the environmental causes of tension headaches?
A. Tension headaches usually are caused by stress. When we treat patients with tension headaches, we address their stresses.

Q. How are tension headaches different from migraines?
A. Tension headaches don't have the neurological components or the throbbing, pounding, pulsating pain of migraine, and they're usually not associated with secondary problems such as vomiting. A tension headache is a more diffuse, bandlike, all-encompassing headache that seems to overtake the entire head.

Q. Tell me about treatments for tension headache.
A. We choose treatment based on the individual. Many people are unaware of stress, don't realize that it is a pattern in their life, and deny or don't want to talk about stress because it's too personal.

Several medications benefit people with tension headaches, including Valium, Xanax, and Elavil. In treating tension headaches, it is essential to ensure a successful night's sleep and deal effectively with stress. If this doesn't work, we might send patients to a psychiatrist or psychologist for biofeedback therapy. We sometimes advise people to change their pace of life or their careers—a major life change can be critical to people suffering from headaches.

Q. What about headaches that are due to depression?
A. Headaches are a common manifestation of depression. They are described as dull and nonspecific and are dealt with by alleviating the depression.

Q. Tell me about medications that cause headaches.
A. Many medications may cause headaches. Those include nitroglycerin preparations, Zoloft, Prozac, birth control pills, and estrogen. The patient's medical history is critical in this situation because she could stop taking her medications temporarily to see if her headaches improve.

Q. Please describe sinus headaches.
A. Sinus headache often is associated with a cold or postnasal drip but may occur in chronic sinusitis. The classical sinus headache causes severe, constant, and pressurelike pain in front of the face, over the forehead, below the eyes, or on the cheeks that is aggravated by bending forward, blowing the nose, or sneezing. On examination, the patient feels tenderness when tapped over the sinus. A medical history will help the physician determine if the patient suffers from frequent sinusitis. In some cases, we order a CT (computed tomography) scan of the head to confirm the presence of sinusitis.

Q. How do you treat sinus headaches?
A. Sinus headaches are an infectious or allergic syndrome. We treat with antibiotics or decongestants and antihistamines.

Q. Tell me about sex-related headaches.
A. A small number of patients get headaches during intercourse. The sudden increase in intracranial pressure during orgasm provokes the headache.

Q. Tell me about posttraumatic headaches.
A. Posttraumatic headaches, caused by a physical blow to the head, can be prolonged. The more severe the trauma, the more likely that the headache will drag on. One must be certain that the injury did not cause bleeding into the skull or brain.

Q. Can eye problems cause headaches?
A. Yes. Endogenous problems of the eye, such as glaucoma, can cause headaches, as will minor problems, such as inadequate eyeglass lenses.

Q. Are headaches sometimes psychologically influenced?
A. Unequivocally yes. A headache can be both caused and aggravated by emotional factors such as depression, anger, or maladjustment to one's life. In fact, most headaches have an emotional component.

Q. Can dental problems, such as cavities or abscesses, cause headaches?
A. Dental problems may cause radiated pain, but the primary source of pain is the tooth.

Q. When is it time to see a physician for headaches?
A. When there is an acute onset of a very severe headache, particularly in someone who is not prone to headaches, or when a headache persists. A persistent headache is one that continues for more than several hours, especially if severe.

Q. Why should someone go to a neurologist rather than a primary care physician?
A. A neurologist has more experience in treating headaches. Most well-trained general physicians can diagnose the common varieties of headaches and will, it is hoped, refer the patient to a neurologist if they can't diagnose the headache or successfully treat it.

Q. Does exercise help headaches?
A. If a person needs to relax and reduce stress, exercise can help. No one knows whether endorphins (natural opioids released during exercise) are effective against headaches.

Q. Can exercise cause headaches?
A. Yes. Strenuous exercise can increase intracranial pressure, causing headaches. These are called exercise headaches.

Q. What is the worst thing women can do in terms of headache?
A. The worst thing they can do is neglect a headache that might be a precursor of something serious. A severe headache could be secondary to a hemorrhage, due to a blood clot that is a manifestation of a stroke, or symptomatic of a brain tumor or infection—problems that must be treated by a physician.

Q. What do you advise women in their fifties who want to prevent, palliate, and cure their tension or migraine headaches?
A. For tension or migraine headaches, with the guidance of her physician, a woman should try to figure out if they're stress related, food related, or due to lack of sleep or some other identifiable factor, such as medications. Then they should work out a plan to cure or prevent these headaches.

Q. What is your key piece of advice regarding headaches?
A. Don't fool around with headaches or self-medicate. You don't fool around with chest pain. You don't fool around with other bodily symptoms. If you have a bothersome headache, seek help. This is not the time to medicate yourself with aspirin. Get yourself to a doctor. This is a symptom that must be taken seriously.

16

Chronic Pain

Kathleen M. Foley, M.D.

Kathleen Foley graduated from college in 1965 with a bachelor's degree in biology. After graduation, she attended Cornell University Medical College, then did a one-year medical internship at New York Hospital, followed by a year of genetics research. She began her three-year neurology residency in 1971 at The New York Hospital–Cornell Medical Center. In 1974 she moved across the street to study pain in cancer patients at Memorial-Sloan Kettering Cancer Center, where she is currently a professor of neurology. Dr. Foley has served as chief of the Pain and Palliative Care Service at Memorial-Sloan Kettering Cancer Center since 1981.

Q. What is pain?
A. Pain is a sensory perception that has physical and psychological components.

Q. What are the different classifications of pain?
A. There are three classifications of pain—acute pain, recurring pain, and chronic pain. The different mechanisms of pain are referred to as somatic, neuropathic, and visceral.

Q. Give me an example of somatic pain.
A. An example of somatic pain is a superficial cut or a pulled muscle

in which tissue has been injured but will heal. Postoperative pain fits into that category.

Q. What is neuropathic pain?
A. Neuropathic pain is caused by a cut or injury to a nerve, which gives rise to burning or tingling sensations. Loss of sensation in the peripheral nerves—to the hands and feet—is commonly associated with this type of pain.

Q. Tell me about visceral pain.
A. Visceral pain is exemplified by pain from an ovarian cyst, endometriosis, gallbladder pain, or abdominal pain. This can be acute and chronic pain. And the pain often is referred to another site, such as the shoulder in gallbladder or ovarian disease.

Q. Why is it important to categorize pain?
A. Because the treatments are different, depending on the type of pain. Some pains are dangerous, in which case the pain is a signal. And some pains are part of life.

Q. What are the hallmarks of serious pain?
A. An acute pain, which you've never experienced before, should be evaluated quickly. Sudden onset of severe chest pain or the worst headache of your life could be serious, even life-threatening, and requires a trip to an emergency room or a physician's office.

Q. What about aching pains that are there one day and gone the next?
A. Those may become chronic pains, such as aches in the knee or shoulder. Although the implications could be serious, there isn't the immediate threat to your life.

You should try to figure out the components of your pain and its underlying cause. Did you pull a muscle or strain your knee? Does your thumb or hand hurt after gardening for five hours?

Q. How does pain hurt?
A. When a stimulus causes pain, receptors in the peripheral nervous

system, specific pathways in the central nervous system, and very specific neurotransmitters and peptides modulate the pain, which your brain then interprets.

Q. Do people have different pain thresholds?
A. Most people's threshold for pain is the same. It's their tolerance that's different, which is a complicated phenomenon. Tolerance includes the meaning of the pain and the degree of that person's control over it.

Q. How does suffering differ from pain?
A. Suffering includes both the physical and emotional symptoms of pain. Suffering is defined as a threat to one's integrity.

Q. Can pain that is part of life impede a person's normal functioning?
A. Yes. If you believe that your pain causes harm or injury, then it will impede your functional status. For example, you may think that every time you use your painful knee, you'll harm it. So you won't use it and you lose function. That's a major problem for chronic pain patients.

Q. Tell me about chronic pain.
A. Chronic pain, as defined by the International Association of the Study of Pain, is pain that lasts longer than three months. That's an arbitrary time limit and doesn't define any particular type of pain.

Q. Does chronic pain itself cause problems?
A. Yes. Chronic pain can wear away at one's personality. It can keep sufferers from participating in activities of daily living and interactions with family and friends. Pain can cause people to withdraw and ultimately become isolated. Pain is demoralizing and can lead to depression and a complex downward cycle of pain, demoralization, depression, pain, demoralization, depression, and so on.

Q. Tell me about the psychological effects of chronic pain.
A. When patients receive persistent negative stimuli with no way to

escape, the secondary consequences can be demoralization and depression. There are people with chronic pain who function at a high level. Some patients, however, are more susceptible to the psychological aspects of pain. We don't know why. They may have lower levels of endogenous peptides, a different opioid receptor system, or different neurotransmitters. (Peptides are the substances that serve as the messengers between nerve cells. Opioids are endogenous substances, as well as drugs, that provide pain relief through specific receptors in the brain and nerves.)

Scientists believe that people may differ in the hard-wiring of their opiate receptors and the neuropathways. Recognizing that difference is important; it respects the patient's chronic pain rather than viewing her as a complainer or a malingerer.

Q. How can someone suffering with chronic pain find relief?
A. That depends on the type of pain. Disease-related strategies can cure certain types of pain. For example, someone with painful hip arthritis could get a hip replacement, or a knee replacement might restore a painful knee.

Otherwise, the armamentarium available for treating chronic pain includes drug therapy, physical therapy, and cognitive and behavioral therapy.

Q. Tell me about medications used to treat pain.
A. The World Health Organization (WHO) has published the *WHO Analgesic Ladder* that lists steps for treating pain. Step I, for mild pain, is treatment with aspirin or acetamenophen; step II, for moderate to severe pain (such as pain after a tooth extraction), is drugs like codeine combined with aspirin or Tylenol; and step III, for severe pain (postoperative pain, for cancer patients, or pain of acute trauma), is drugs like morphine or strong opioids. This stepwise ladder allows patients to move to a stronger drug based on the intensity of the pain and the mechanism of the pain.

Q. What about side effects of painkillers?
A. These drugs do have short-term and long-term side effects. Be-

cause of current U.S. drug policy and the concern of drug addiction, there's a great deal of negativity toward opioids. However, scientific data show that aspirin and the nonsteroidal anti-inflammatory drugs are potentially more dangerous than opioids.

Q. How does the danger of over-the-counter analgesics compare to that of opiates?
A. The enzyme systems that nonsteroidal anti-inflammatory drugs impact on cause gastric ulceration and renal injury, whereas opioids do not harm your stomach and kidneys. These over-the-counter drugs are potentially dangerous, particularly to the elderly, and should be used carefully.

Q. How does physical activity affect pain?
A. The new "wellness construct" is appropriate to people with pain. That is, you'll have more pain if you're immobile, more pain if you are stiff, more pain if you haven't continued to use your muscles. It's very important that pain patients keep active.

Q. Does psychological or psychiatric counseling help people who suffer from chronic pain?
A. Yes. People who suffer with chronic pain need to change the way they live their lives. Rather than constantly searching for something to eradicate their pain, they must develop a strategy for living with it. Cognitive-behavioral therapy helps patients address the meaning of the pain and its role in their lives. Behavioral approaches to pain control may include biofeedback and relaxation techniques, deep breathing, and imagery.

Q. What is the first thing someone who is suffering with diffuse pain should do?
A. The first thing is to try to figure out the pain—what causes it, what makes it worse, and what makes it better. Ask yourself these questions: Do simple analgesics make it better? Is the pain related to activity, to eating or drinking? Try to have a sense of the components of the pain. Then take that information to a doctor. The patient's thinking about

the pain in advance will help the physician sort out potential causes so that he or she can pursue the next level of strategy.

Q. Why do some physicians underestimate pain that the patient is experiencing?
A. Pain isn't something that we can measure. Some physicians may categorize a patient as a whiner or a complainer. This is especially true for female patients.

Q. Why do women have the stigma of being complainers?
A. Perhaps because women are more willing to talk about their pain than are men.

Q. Are there any data regarding this gender issue?
A. Yes. We've studied cancer patients and have not observed that women experienced more pain problems than men. That helps to erase the gender issue.

Q. What types of physicians specialize in the treatment of pain?
A. Rheumatologists, anesthesiologists, neurologists, psychiatrists, oncologists, internists, and physiatrists.

Q. What if the cause of the pain can't be found?
A. After we've done all the appropriate tests and can't find the answers, we wait and watch.

Patients should develop a degree of advocacy and ask, What do I do next? What would work? You haven't helped me so what's the next step?

Q. What are common causes of pain suffered by women in their fifties?
A. One common cause of pain in women in their fifties is menopausal headache. There are also diffuse musculoskeletal pains, such as joint pains of the knees and/or shoulders and strains and aches from shin splints, tennis elbow, or bursitis. Arthritis is a leading cause of pain in this age group. There may be an escalation in pain secondary to osteoporosis.

Q. Is some pain related to hormones?
A. Changes in hormone levels, particularly at menopause, can increase musculoskeletal pain.

Q. What is referred pain?
A. The nervous system usually functions by having the pain exactly where the nerve is located. With referred pain, however, there's an intertwining of pain pathways. Nerves at a spinal cord level, for example, may cause you to feel pain in your abdomen, when, in fact, the pain comes from your leg. Another example of referred pain is from the gallbladder. You might not hurt at your diseased gallbladder, but that pain is felt in your shoulder. Ovarian or uterine pain also is commonly referred to the shoulder.

Q. What is fibromyalgia?
A. Fibromyalgia, a syndrome that affects a large group of patients, causes diffuse pain throughout the body and the muscles. Its cause is unclear. We don't understand the mechanism of the pain.

Q. What is temporomandibular joint (TMJ) disorder?
A. Temporomandibular joint disorder is a syndrome associated with pain in the face, neck, and jaw that is made worse by jaw movement and better by rest. Sometimes it is related to a malalignment of the jaw. TMJ is more common in women and sometimes is associated with psychological symptoms. This chronic pain syndrome usually affects younger women but can continue to cause pain in women in their fifties.

Q. What about the pain of migraine headaches?
A. Migraines are most common in the twenty- to forty-year-old age range. The incidence and prevalence decrease with menopause, but some women in their fifties suffer migraine headaches.

Q. What are trigger points?
A. They are areas in the muscle that are focally tender. If one presses on the area, the patient will report pain at that site. Injections of saline or local anesthetics may reduce the pain.

Q. Tell me about nerve blocks.

A. A nerve block is a local anesthetic infiltrated around a nerve that impedes conduction, therefore reducing or eliminating pain. When your dentist anesthetizes a tooth, you're getting a nerve block.

Nerve blocks also are used as a mode of therapy to temporarily interrupt pain.

Q. What is transcutaneous electrical nerve stimulation (TENS)?

A. A transistor radiolike device with electrodes is attached to an area of skin and produces electrical stimuli to the site of pain. The pulsation and electrical activity enters into the spinal cord, goes to the brain, then back down, and blocks the pain by activating large-diameter nerve fibers. This is used predominantly on patients with mild musculoskeletal or nerve injury pain. It is not a very potent system.

Q. What's the worst thing people do when they experience pain?

A. They give in to the pain and become withdrawn, unable to function or care for themselves and their families.

Or they get so caught up with their pain that they seek inappropriate therapies.

Q. What is the best thing to do when experiencing pain?

A. Find a doctor who believes that you are in pain. Listen to that doctor and follow his or her instructions. Read about your problem. Find out as much as possible about your pain. Join a support group, such as the American Chronic Pain Association.

Q. Can all pain be completely cured?

A. Not all pain can be completely cured. I have enormous respect for patients with chronic pain who continue to live their lives. We physicians are good at dealing with some aspects of pain, but we have a long way to go.

Q. What is the future of pain control?

A. Extraordinary research is taking place that already has increased our understanding of the mechanisms of all types of pain as well as the interplay between pain perception and the psychological aspects.

The use of drug combinations already allows us to safely expand the role of opioid drugs, for example. There will be new knowledge about receptors, leading to development of receptor-selective drugs. Science eventually will make a major difference in pain therapies.

Q. What is your advice to people who are in pain?
A. Chronic pain can cause profound depression. People must recognize the psychological consequences and do something about it.

Have an open mind regarding the appropriate therapies for chronic pain, whether it is drug therapy or cognitive-behavioral therapy. Balance treatment approaches to your quality of life.

If you have pain, don't think you're crazy. Pain could save you in a serious illness.

17

Memory and Memory Loss

Norman R. Relkin, M.D., Ph.D.

Norman Relkin majored in molecular biochemistry and biophysics in college. After graduation in 1979, he spent a year at the National Institutes of Mental Health in the Laboratory of Cerebral Metabolism, where he was introduced to brain-mapping techniques. He earned his M.D. and Ph.D. degrees at the Albert Einstein College of Medicine in New York. In 1987 he continued his medical training at The New York Hospital–Cornell Medical Center. He completed a one-year internship in internal medicine, a residency in neurology that included a year as chief resident, and a fellowship in behavioral neurology and neurophysiology. In 1991 he and his colleagues created the Cornell Neurobehavior Evaluation Program, which deals with clinical problems on the interface of neurology and psychiatry. Dr. Relkin subsequently has focused his research and clinical practice on Alzheimer's disease and disorders of aging. Dr. Relkin has been director of the Cornell Memory Disorders Program since 1993 and is currently associate professor of clinical neurology and neuroscience at The New York Hospital–Cornell Medical Center.

Q. Tell me about the memory status of people in their fifties.
A. The fifties represent a transition from the early years of life, when memory is rarely impaired, to later years, when memory disturbances become increasingly prevalent.

People in their fifties normally experience a subtle decline in memory and may begin to question their memories, but their occasional lapses do not usually have a major impact on their daily lives. When tested, an average fifty- to sixty-year-old can remember a seven-digit telephone number after hearing it once or twice. (Unfortunately, we now have to remember area codes too, and less than a quarter of us at this age can remember ten digits heard once.)

Memory problems in this age group can be caused or exacerbated by stresses, both biological and societal. For women, these might include the symptoms of menopause, the so-called empty nest, early retirement, the death of parents, or the loss of a spouse.

Q. Why do people in their fifties have trouble recalling names?
A. You certainly don't have to be in your fifties to have that problem! Naming difficulties are a common complaint with advancing age for a variety of reasons. When we're introduced to someone new, we have to focus our attention on the name to retain it, and dividing our attention often becomes more difficult with advancing years. While we generally retain our ability to learn as we get older, we tend to process information more slowly. This makes it more difficult to take in new information, particularly when it is coming in at uncontrolled real-world speeds. Most of us would have no problem remembering a name that we had five minutes to rehearse, but the fleeting exposure provided by a handshake and casual introduction affords much less of an opportunity to commit things to memory. In addition, as we age it is not uncommon to get more self-conscious about our memory and worry more about losing it. This anxiety itself actually can worsen naming performance. Most people become less fluent in calling up the names of objects and other words with the passing years. This may reflect a greater susceptibility of involved areas of the brain to age-related and disease-related impairment.

Q. Do we increasingly lose memory as we age?
A. The likelihood of experiencing memory loss (and other forms of cognitive impairment) increases with advancing years. If one compares the memory of fifty- to sixty-year-olds with that of twenty- to thirty-year-olds, one sees decreased ability to recall words and events in the

older group. Not everyone declines significantly, but a subgroup of individuals does bring the average down.

Q. Why do we gradually lose memory as we get older?
A. Certain areas of the brain essential to memory shrink with age. A variety of processes, such as free-radical damage, loss of hormonal influences, programmed cell death, and other factors, may cause this shrinkage. Aging-related loss of neurons (brain cells) has been shown to affect the hippocampus, situated in the temporal lobes of the brain, which is believed to be important in the recall process.

Q. Tell me about memory.
A. In the general sense, a memory is any trace of the past. The brain is home to many different types of memory, stored and mediated by different structures and processes. These different forms of memory are not all equally vulnerable to the effects of age and disease. Complete memory loss is rarely seen, except in conditions such as the persistent vegetative state. More commonly, memory loss is partial, and follows certain rules.

For example, you almost never forget your own name, despite what television and movie depictions of amnesia lead us to believe. Autobiographic memory can be lost, but even in diseases such as Alzheimer's that devastate the memory systems of the brain, knowledge of one's personal past often is retained until late in the disease process.

Other types of memory are relatively immune to all but the most severe forms of brain injury. For example, you probably have heard the cliché "It's like riding a bicycle." This expresses the view that some things, once learned, are rarely forgotten. Indeed, the skills involved in riding a bicycle or playing a piano concerto are laid down in what our procedural memory stores. Procedural memory is the type required to retain the sequences of movements involved in carrying out almost all of our daily activities. Memory of this kind is not readily available to our conscious thoughts but nevertheless can be invoked at will. Once we learn a skill to the point that it is automatic, it becomes very easy to relearn that skill in the future.

Remembering names, dates, places, and events involves a different set of structures and processes in the brain from procedural memory. This general type of memory, sometimes called declarative memory, permits us to bring factual information into our consciousness. It is this type of memory that is affected first in Alzheimer's disease, as well as other brain diseases. It also may be among the first manifestations of the effects of age on the brain.

To complicate matters, the various forms of memory I've mentioned so far all have different stages to their acquisition and retention. We now use phrases like "short-term memory" and "long-term memory" in common parlance. These actually correspond to very different systems within the brain, and again, these systems have different degrees of vulnerability to disease. Short-term recall tends to get lost more frequently than long-term recall, although conditions like head trauma and alcohol-related deficiencies can lead to long-term memory loss as well.

One further point: Forgetting is not usually a disease but a very important part of the memory process. While arguably it might be desirable to remember everything we experience, it would tax the processing ability of the brain and threaten our survival if we didn't have the ability to selectively remove memories from our consciousness so that we can attend to the matters at hand. Anyone who has had a tragic event in his or her life knows that forgetting is not only normal, it's essential at times.

Q. Are women more at risk for Alzheimer's disease?
A. For the forms of Alzheimer's disease that begin after age sixty, the risk is slightly greater for women than for men.

Q. Do memory problems run in families?
A. Yes, to the extent that certain families have more frequent occurrence of Alzheimer's disease or other forms of dementia. Whether certain families show a greater degree of age-related memory decline outside the context of dementia has not been conclusively established.

Q. Tell me about the relationship between estrogen and memory.
A. There is emerging evidence that estrogen may play a positive role in normal memory function and that estrogen-replacement therapy in

the postmenopausal period may decrease the risk of Alzheimer's disease. These effects have yet to be fully confirmed, but they are entirely plausible based on the known effects of estrogen on the brain and the mechanisms of memory loss in aging and dementia.

Q. Should women take estrogen to reduce their risk of Alzheimer's disease?
A. I believe that ongoing studies ultimately will demonstrate some beneficial effects of estrogen-replacement therapy on the aging brain, but there are still a lot of unanswered questions. It will be some time before we know whether currently prescribed doses of estrogen are the most effective, or which forms of estrogen are best, or whether progesterone combined with estrogen (hormone-replacement therapy) actually may be counterproductive. There are also worries about side effects of estrogen. The risk of breast cancer appears to increase the longer one receives estrogen-replacement therapy, which is a real concern for a woman in her fifties whose average life expectancy extends for an additional thirty years. However, for someone who has been diagnosed with a condition like Alzheimer's, which on average proceeds from initial symptoms to death in about a decade, this may not be as great a concern. Newer agents called selective estrogen receptor modulators may sidestep the adverse effects of estrogen on the uterus and breast while maintaining beneficial influences on other organs. It will be some years before such agents become generally available and their value in relation to memory is confirmed.

Q. How does estrogen lower the risk of Alzheimer's disease?
A. No one knows for certain, but several mechanisms have been proposed. Estrogen may reduce the production and/or deposition of the beta-amyloid protein in the brain, which is one of the contributing causes of Alzheimer's disease. Other research has found that estrogen can act as a kind of growth factor in the brain and promote the development of increased connections between neurons. Estrogen also appears to have antioxidant properties that fight the harmful effects of free radicals. It also may boost the activity of the neurotransmitter acetylcholine, an important mediator of memory functions. There may be other benefits that remain to be discovered.

Although from the current perspective, it may seem as if estrogen is a virtual panacea for the brain, the realities are probably less positive. I believe that estrogen has some very beneficial effects on the brain, but its usefulness as a memory enhancer or an Alzheimer preventive will require further study.

Q. Tell me about Alzheimer's disease.
A. Alzheimer's disease is a neurodegenerative disorder that causes a progressive loss of self, by impairment of memory and then of other cognitive functions. It arises from a complex interaction of genetic factors and life exposures. It is age-related to the extent that the older one gets, the greater the risk of developing Alzheimer's disease becomes. Several lines of evidence suggest that it may begin with the deposition of the protein called beta-amyloid in the brain.

The idea that people with Alzheimer's disease remember details of their childhood with great exactitude but can't remember what happened that morning is to some extent true. Memories that are laid down more recently (short-term memory) are more likely to be lost as a result of amnesia (a generic medical term for memory loss), whether it is due to Alzheimer's, head trauma, stroke, or other processes.

Alzheimer's disease is not an inevitable concomitant of aging. Many people who live past one hundred show no signs of cognitive impairment. There appears to be a plateauing of the risk of Alzheimer's disease after ninety, but at that age nearly one of every two persons already suffers from dementia.

Q. Can someone as young as fifty get Alzheimer's?
A. The incidence of dementia in the fifties is less than 1 percent. There have been documented cases of Alzheimer's in individuals as young as twenty-nine, but such cases are exclusively among individuals with a rare early-onset familial form of the disease. Although clinical symptoms of Alzheimer's may not be a common problem in this age group, there is increasing evidence that this disease can take root twenty to thirty years prior to the time that it is diagnosed, which encompasses and includes the decade of the fifties.

Q. What is dementia?
A. Dementia is a generic, all-encompassing term for a loss of cognitive ability that persists for at least six months, involves memory and at least one other area of thinking and is sufficiently severe to interfere with a person's daily activities. There are many different types of dementia. Alzheimer's disease is the leading cause of dementia among the elderly.

Q. Tell me about people who carry the APOE-ε4 (Alzheimer's) gene?
A. The full name of the gene is apolipoprotein E. This gene has three common forms—ε2, ε3, and ε4. About 25 percent of the population possesses APOE-ε4. People who carry either one or two copies of this gene are at increased risk for Alzheimer's as well as for some forms of heart disease. They also seem to be at increased risk of developing long-term cognitive and neurological deficits after head trauma and for an age-related disorder that can lead to bleeding in the brain.

Q. Can anything be done for people who carry the APOE-ε4 gene?
A. There are no established interventions for APOE-ε4 carriers at this time. Gene therapy has been proposed as a possible future treatment. To the extent that APOE-ε4 fosters earlier onset of Alzheimer's, and ε2 is associated with later onset, treatment of ε4 carriers by giving them the ε2 gene or gene product may have beneficial effects in delaying Alzheimer's symptoms.

Q. Should people get tested for this gene?
A. Currently we test only certain people as an adjunct to diagnosis if they have signs or symptoms of dementia, because finding APOE-ε4 can increase the certainty that the cause is Alzheimer's. When preventive treatments become available, genetic screening may be carried out to identify those at highest risk for the disease.

Q. Can the deterioration of Alzheimer's disease be slowed?
A. Estrogen, antioxidants, and anti-inflammatories may help, but we do not yet know appropriate doses, nor are we certain of the specific benefits. Each of these interventions also carries risks of side effects.

Many new treatments are under development that may slow the underlying disease process, including drugs that target the amyloid deposits in the brain.

The symptoms of Alzheimer's may be relieved temporarily by FDA-approved treatments such as Aricept. Aricept boosts the function of brain cells that use acetylcholine, a neurotransmitter that is decreased early in the course of the disease.

Q. Are memory lapses symptomatic of other medical conditions?
A. They certainly can be. The memory system is both intricate and delicate. A variety of processes can affect it detrimentally, such as vitamin deficiencies; infectious diseases such as Lyme, AIDS, and syphilis; autoimmune disorders like lupus; as well as diseases of the liver, kidneys, and even the heart. Excess fluid around the brain, a condition called hydrocephalus, can affect memory. Brain tumors can cause memory loss, but isolated forgetfulness is not usually a sign of a tumor.

Strokes and transient ischemic attacks can cause memory loss. I have even seen people who had lapses in memory in whom the problem was a heart arrhythmia interrupting the flow of blood to their brain. They appeared to be in early stages of Alzheimer's when what they really needed was a pacemaker.

Q. Tell me about emotional problems as they affect memory.
A. Depression is one of the leading culprits in causing memory problems. Anxiety disorders, insomnia, psychosis, and a variety of other psychiatric problems also can be associated with memory loss. Memory and attention are very closely linked. Patients suffering from depression often have trouble concentrating and encoding new information, and this may impart the impression that they have a primary memory problem. There is sometimes selectivity to their recollections, with a tendency to recall the negative and forget the positive. Usually memory problems related to depression resolve when the depression is treated, but if they fail to, it is sometimes an indication of an underlying neurologic disorder.

Q. Can memory loss itself be the cause of emotional problems such as depression?

A. Loss of memory, like the loss of anything near and dear, can leave a major void in the individual's life and may precipitate depressive reactions.

Q. What about the effect of medications on memory?
A. Psychoactive drugs, such as anxiolytics (antianxiety medications) and some antidepressants, beta blockers (to treat hypertension), antiglaucoma drugs, and many other medications can adversely affect memory. Medications are among the first thing a physician should ask about when a patient complains of a memory disturbance, since the offending agent often can be replaced or eliminated with subsequent improvement in recall.

Q. Tell me about general nutritional status and memory problems.
A. Certainly this is an area where there is a pressing need for more research. Poor nutrition can have secondary effects on memory. People who abuse alcohol may get most of their calories from alcoholic beverages and develop vitamin deficiencies that lead to memory loss. Other causes of vitamin deficiency, ranging from disorders such as bulimia to gastrointestinal conditions causing malabsorption, can affect memory.

Q. How do head injuries affect memory?
A. Head injuries can affect memory in the immediate aftermath or in the long run. A head injury that occurred in the last thirty years can have implications for memory loss in later life, particularly in individuals who have a genetic susceptibility, such as the APOE-ε4 gene. A blow to the head can physically damage the fibers connecting different regions, a condition called diffuse axonal injury, or damage parts of the cerebral cortex that are closest to the skull. This frequently impairs attention as well as short-term recall.

Q. What is the link between thyroid and memory problems?
A. Either hypothyroidism (decreased thyroid function) or hyperthyroidism (excessive or "overactive" thyroid function) can affect cognition. Hypothyroidism is encountered more frequently and is treated

with thyroid hormone supplements. It is rarely the cause of an isolated memory problem but can be a contributing factor.

Q. Can exercising the mind slow memory loss?
A. This is a controversial area. I believe to some extent that this is so, and I believe that failure to exercise the mind can weaken our recall ability. A variety of evidence supports the idea that mental stimulation can help. Studies have shown that connections between certain neurons become denser in animals that are raised in a stimulating environment. Observational studies have shown a lower incidence of disease such as Alzheimer's among individuals who have pursued advanced degrees and remain intellectually active into their later years, although there is some reason for skepticism that this is due to actual protective effects of learning on the brain. Whatever the ultimate truth of the matter may be, I think it is good advice for women in their fifties (or at any age) to stay mentally active.

Q. Do mind exercises help people experiencing memory problems?
A. That depends on the processes that are causing them to lose their memory. In Alzheimer's disease, for example, attempts at exercising memory beyond the early stages are relatively futile, leading mostly to greater frustration. On the other hand, rehearsal and memory retraining exercises may temporarily improve daily function for someone who is having age-associated memory impairment. A program of memory retraining can increase the confidence of such individuals, reducing the adverse effects of anxiety on recall and having a more lasting effect on their memory performance.

Q. Give me an example of exercises that can improve memory.
A. A program for memory retraining typically begins with a discussion of the nature of memory and how it is mediated by the brain. A variety of techniques intended to improve recall are then reviewed and specific exercises are given to entrain these strategies. For an individual whose spontaneous recall is impaired but recognition memory is preserved, self-cueing and mnemonics may be helpful. For the person with "executive" dysfunction, who has trouble organizing information and formulating recall strategies, the latter skills need to be targeted.

Whatever the problem, the individual needs to rehearse the techniques until they can be performed effortlessly and automatically. It is also important to instill in the individual a sense of self-confidence about the memory. A physician or psychologist can help a great deal by providing reassurance that the problem being experienced is not symptomatic of a progressive or fatal process, as is often the fear of those experiencing memory loss.

Q. When it is time to seek professional help for serious memory problems?
A. People who are suffering from the most dreaded form of memory loss—Alzheimer's disease—are quite frequently unaware that there is a problem. In fact, their family or friends bring them to medical attention more often than they come on their own.

That is in contrast to what often occurs with conditions such as depression. People with clinical depression often seek the help of a physician, sometimes thinking that their memory loss is caused by early Alzheimer's disease, when in fact a mood disorder is causing the problem.

Any memory problem significant enough to interfere with daily life or to cause daily anxiety should be brought to medical attention.

Q. What advice do you have for women who feel that their symptoms are worse than those of other people their age or that their symptoms represent a dramatic change for them?
A. Bring your symptoms to the attention of your doctor and insist that they be evaluated thoroughly. Too often a busy physician will dismiss a woman in her fifties who complains of a memory disorder out of the mistaken impression that diseases that cause memory loss never begin in that age group, or that psychological problems might be responsible and therefore can be ignored. In fact, depression is every bit as much of an illness and as demanding of treatment as Alzheimer's disease. There are also a variety of other treatable conditions that can contribute to memory loss, and the first step is to recognize that a memory problem exists and evaluate it appropriately.

Q. What type of physician should someone with memory problems see?
A. In the United States, the internist or primary care physician is usually the first recourse. An advantage to the system is that the primary care physician often has known this person over time and may be in a good position to judge whether the memory complaints are significant relative to the person's age and other medical conditions. However, once a determination has been made that a cognitive problem exists, or if the nature of the problem remains unclear, consultation with a neurologist, psychiatrist, or psychologist may be most appropriate.

Q. What is the future of medicine for people who suffer from memory disorders?
A. In the near future, medications that forestall the progression of Alzheimer's disease by a few years are likely to be found. The value of treatments such as hormonal therapy, antioxidant therapy, and anti-inflammatory drugs and other emerging therapies may be confirmed. As we look to the more distant future, we hope not simply to ameliorate symptoms, which is the current mainstay of therapy for Alzheimer's disease, but to prevent decline and replace lost function.

We are now seeing the early stages of research for regrowth and redifferentiating neurons. There are also emerging classes of pharmaceuticals that appear to be more specific in their effects on the memory system of the brain. I expect that eventually it will become possible to augment memory abilities of the brain, even in the absence of disease.

Q. What do you advise people who have Alzheimer's in their family, have the gene, or fear that they are at risk?
A. People tend to base their actions on their perception of risk rather than objective statistics. Knowledge of one's genetic predisposition may be beneficial in deciding which of many possible diseases a person should work hardest to prevent, but it also may motivate them to try as yet unproven interventions that carry their own inherent risks. Part of making an informed decision is understanding risk-benefit ratios. Knowledgeable genetic counseling is probably of equal or greater

benefit than genetic testing for the majority of people at the present time. I advise those concerned about Alzheimer's risk to consult with a genetic counselor or another suitably trained health professional.

Q. What do you advise women in their fifties who experience forget-fulness or memory lapses?
A. If you are concerned, bring your concerns to your physician. Be reassured that, in many cases, memory lapses in the fifties can be reversed and do not necessarily portend future decline.

18

A Good Night's Sleep: Controlling and Curing Insomnia

Donald Bliwise, Ph.D.

Donald Bliwise was a psychology major in college. After he earned his Ph.D. at the University of Chicago in 1981, he moved to Stanford University, where he did research in sleep as it relates to aging. In 1992 Dr. Bliwise moved to Atlanta, where he became associate professor of neurology and director of the Sleep Disorders Clinic at Emory University Medical School, positions he now holds.

Q. Tell me about sleep and the stages of sleep.
A. Sleep is divided into four non-REM (rapid-eye-movement) sleep stages, which eventually lead to REM sleep.

Stage 1 is the lightest period of sleep. If sleep is uninterrupted, the person will descend into stages 2, 3, and 4, and remain in those non-REM stages for approximately seventy to ninety minutes. She will then revert to stage 2 sleep and enter the first REM period.

Q. What is REM?
A. REM is an acronym for rapid eye movement. REM sleep is characterized by a variety of physiologic changes, the most notable of which is movement of the eyes, which rapidly dart back and forth. People usually dream during this stage.

Other bodily changes during REM sleep include increased breathing and heart rates, an absence of muscle tone, particularly in jaw and chin, and in males, penile tumescence. Certain areas of the brain are intensely active during REM sleep.

Q. Do we need to go through all four stages of sleep to accomplish complete restorative processes in the brain and body?
A. Not necessarily. Continuity of sleep is probably more important than going through all four stages. External or internal interruptions are very disruptive and can ruin the restorative properties of sleep.

Q. Do sleep requirements vary for different people?
A. Yes, but within limits. One person may define herself as an insomniac while another accepts her identical sleep patterns as normal.

Most people need between six and nine hours of sleep. There are slight individual differences. When subjects in sleep studies spent several days in a time-isolation environment (shielded from time cues, such as light and dark) and were allowed to wake and sleep when they chose, most people slept about one-third of their "day," even if the "day" exceeded twenty-four hours. The internal timing mechanism of most adults results in approximately eight hours of sleep each night.

Q. What about people who claim they need only five hours of sleep?
A. These people usually will experience a cumulative sleep debt. This deprivation builds up after a few weeks. If allowed to sleep longer, they will make up for the lack of sleep, although not on an hour-for-hour basis.

Q. What are the consequences of sleep deprivation?
A. The most predictable consequence is sleepiness the following day, manifested as inattention, yawning, distractibility, unintended sleep episodes, irritability, and even depression.

Q. Why do people have insomnia?
A. Many factors contribute to poor sleep or insomnia. Age and illness may contribute to poor sleep. Psychiatric problems, such as depression and anxiety, are associated with sleep problems. Shift work, travel

across time zones, and altered schedules also can disrupt sleep and cause insomnia. Menopause is another cause of poor sleep.

Q. Do sleep problems get progressively worse as we age?
A. The quality of sleep decreases as we age. Stages 3 and 4 decline, length of sleep becomes shorter, and major sleep disorders, such as periodic leg movements and sleep apnea, tend to increase.

Q. Do people who can't sleep get caught up in a state of anxiety and fear of not falling asleep?
A. Yes, many people get into a vicious cycle. When they go to bed at night and can't sleep, a subtle conditioning process occurs. Lying in bed, unable to sleep, becomes associated with a performance anxiety syndrome. They begin to dread going to bed, because they won't be able to sleep. This can lead to associated conditioning—you're in bed, you can't sleep, which leads to further insomnia.

Q. How can this cycle of insomnia and anxiety be stopped?
A. The worst thing to do is lie in bed. You should get up and go into another room. Read, crotchet, knit, or watch TV to take your mind off sleep. After thirty minutes or an hour try again. If you can't sleep after twenty minutes, get out of bed. Lying there trying to fall asleep merely compounds the problem.

Q. Does chronic lack of sleep cause mental or physical problems?
A. Some studies have shown that illness happens to people who don't sleep very much. At the most dramatic levels, mortality rates are higher.

Other studies show that people who don't sleep well over a long period of time may develop clinical depression. We always have known that depression can cause sleep problems, but now there is evidence that lack of sleep can cause depression.

Q. Is poor sleep genetically linked? Do sleep problems run in families?
A. Like many other physiologic functions, sleep can be genetically determined. There is a tendency for poor sleep as well as for major

sleep disorders to run in families. Environmental factors are also re-sponsible for some sleep problems.

Q. Why do women have more sleep problems at the time of meno-pause?
A. If poor sleep began with menopause, the endocrine system is prob-ably involved. Some long-standing sleep problems become exagger-ated at menopause, which is caused by a number of different factors. Women who gain significant weight or complain of fatigue and snor-ing during the night may be experiencing sleep apnea, which increases after menopause.

Q. Does estrogen replacement reduce insomnia in menopausal and postmenopausal women?
A. Very few studies have studied the effect of estrogen replacement on sleep. We don't know whether estrogen replacement will help women with sleep disturbances.

Q. Should we accept poor sleep as we get older?
A. No. You can improve your sleep.

Q. What can we do to improve our sleep, without taking drugs?
A. Regular activity is important. Many studies have shown that exer-cise promotes deep sleep (stages 3 and 4). A sedentary lifestyle is a negative as far as sleep is concerned.

You may need to change certain habits. Caffeine intake causes sleep difficulties for many people. Alcohol can be another problem. Wine at dinner can make you relaxed and sleepy, but alcohol has a very short half-life and its sleep-induction effects wear off quickly as it is metabolized in the body. When its effect wears off, you can experi-ence a middle-of-the-night insomnia. Smoking is also associated with insomnia.

A predictable schedule is important for good sleep. We encourage people to have a regular bedtime and wake-up time. Although sleep is induced by an internal drive, it also responds to external stimuli. Vari-ance in schedule can be disruptive to sleep.

Daytime naps should be prohibited if you can't sleep at night. You'll be less likely to fall asleep at night, if you sleep during the day.

Bright light is a very powerful stimulus that affects the quality of sleep. Sunlight and outdoor activity resynchronize the internal body clock, which promotes sleep.

Q. How will a sleep disorder specialist help someone with sleep problems?
A. We ask patients to keep a sleep log for several weeks with information about when they go to bed and wake up, whether they nap, and how tired they are.

We advise patients to get out in the sunlight and exercise—walk or jog. It doesn't have to be particularly strenuous—a twenty- to thirty-minute walk offers cardiovascular as well as sleep benefits.

Q. Are sleeping pills safe and effective?
A. Many prescription medications are safe and effective. There should be no problem with a sleep medication if its use is supervised, the prescription is appropriate, it is not taken nightly (patients can then become tolerant and eventually it not will not elicit the desired effect), and the patient doesn't escalate the dosage.

Some patients unduly fear becoming addicted or dependent on sleep medications. This is a valid concern for a small part of the population, but an occasional (every third or fourth night) sleeping pill for most people will not be harmful.

We favor sleeping pills that are absorbed quickly. The effect usually lasts as long as the person wants to sleep and is no longer in the bloodstream the next morning. Medications that leave a hung-over, drugged feeling the next morning are not desirable.

Q. What about over-the-counter sleep medications?
A. We do not usually recommend over-the-counter sleep substances. Many of these medications have a long elimination half-life—patients often feel drugged the next day. Some studies suggest that they're not as effective as prescription medications.

Q. What is your take on melatonin as a sleeping pill?
A. Melatonin may not be as harmless as it is sometimes portrayed in the media. Some studies report that melatonin has a hypnotic (sleep-inducing and sleep-maintenance) effect, but no one knows how it's best used or whether it is safe.

There are melatonin receptors throughout the human body, not just in the brain. Melatonin has caused artery constriction in animal studies. I do not recommend melatonin for anyone who has a history of heart disease, stroke, or hypertension.

In dosages purchased off the shelf, melatonin is absorbed and eliminated quickly. Melatonin has a maximal physiologic effect of two or three hours—not the six to eight hours required of an acceptable sleep medication.

Q. What about using melatonin for jet lag?
A. The use of melatonin for jet lag is like shooting in the dark. Its effect depends on the person's internal body clock as well as the number of time zones that will be crossed.

Q. Are sleep disorders covered by health insurance?
A. The office visit and a polysomnogram (a diagnostic test used to diagnose sleep disorders) in a sleep disorders clinic usually are covered.

Q. What is in the future for the treatment of sleep problems?
A. A variety of sleep-inducing preparations are under investigation, including hormonal components derived from progesterone. New, short-acting hypnotic drugs soon will be marketed that are rapidly absorbed, safe, and don't interact with other medications.

Q. What is your advice to women in their fifties who want to sleep peacefully?
A.
- Take care of your body
- Keep your weight down.
- Exercise.
- Get outdoors in the sunlight.

- Make appropriate changes in your lifestyle—decrease the caffeine and alcohol, if they are contributing to the problem.
- Don't feel that you're chained to your bed. If you can't get to sleep, get out of bed, leave your bedroom, and distract yourself.
- Many factors contribute to poor sleep. Don't underestimate the value of a sleep disorders professional who can help solve your problem.

19

Stress, Anxiety, Panic Attacks, Depression

Helen Abramowicz, M.D.

Helen Abramowicz majored in math in college, graduating in 1964. She attended the Albert Einstein College of Medicine in New York. After graduation in 1968, she completed a pediatric residency at Bronx Municipal Hospital and did a two-year adult psychiatry residency at New York's Montefiore Hospital and a child psychiatry residency at the Westchester Division of The New York Hospital–Cornell Medical Center. She has taught on the volunteer faculty at The New York Hospital–Cornell Medical Center since 1979, where she now is a clinical assistant professor of psychiatry. Dr. Abramowicz has private psychiatry practices in Larchmont, New York, and New York City.

Q. Tell me about stress.
A. Stress is a range of symptoms experienced when someone perceives that she cannot master or control demands, conflicts, or problems.

Q. What are typical symptoms of stress?
A. Symptoms range from worry, muscle tension, and physical aches and pains to insomnia, diarrhea, distractibility, and irritability. In some cases stress can lead to anxiety and panic. The severity depends on the

degree of the stressors (causes of stress) and the person's ability to cope.

Q. Can stress be a good thing?
A. Yes. Learning to master stressful situations can be growth promoting. The ability to overcome stress allows us to handle future problems more easily.

Q. Does stress get worse as we age?
A. Not necessarily. Symptoms of stress don't usually get worse, but as people age, they are likely to have more stressors, such as difficulties with children, illness, or death of parents.

Q. Is there a link between menopause and stress?
A. The major link is that menopausal symptoms—hot flashes, changes in sexual functioning, mood changes, and the like—can be stressful for some women.

Q. How does stress lead to serious mental illness?
A. Overwhelming stress can lead to posttraumatic stress disorder (PTSD). Examples of massive stress might be living through catastrophes, such as an earthquake, a kidnapping, or a horrendous automobile accident. Severe anxiety and depressive symptoms also can result in posttraumatic stress disorder.

Q. Are some people prone to symptoms of stress?
A. Yes. Some people are genetically vulnerable to stress and become overwhelmed by even minor conflicts or problems. The manifestation of symptoms depends on a person's genetic predisposition and developmental experiences. A woman with high self-esteem whose life has run fairly smoothly usually will be able to deal with stress.

Q. When is it time to seek professional help?
A. People should seek professional help if symptoms persist and the discomfort is unbearable.

Q. How do therapists help people cope with stress?
A. Therapists teach patients to divide tasks into components and do things one day or even a few hours at a time.

Talk therapy helps people understand their own psychological makeup—their strengths, inner resources, and abilities. It also can help them resolve issues or conflicts from the past.

Cognitive therapy is a treatment that corrects distorted attitudes and beliefs and helps patients deal with problems in a more effective and realistic way.

Patients are encouraged to use relaxation techniques, such as yoga and meditation, which help them focus on inner peace and distance themselves from overwhelming I-can't-cope feelings.

Medications may be prescribed if symptoms are severe and disabling.

Q. What is anxiety?
A. Anxiety is a universal human experience characterized by fearful anticipation of an unpleasant event. Everyone suffers from anxiety at one time or another, but extreme anxiety is a psychiatric disorder.

Q. Tell me about the different forms of anxiety disorder.
A. One type is generalized anxiety disorder, characterized by restlessness, fatigue, difficulty concentrating, the "blahs," muscle tension, irritability, and sleep difficulties, either restless sleep, difficulty falling asleep, or trouble staying asleep.

There are also specific anxiety disorders, such as obsessive-compulsive disorder, in which anxiety takes the form of obsessions and compulsions. Obsessions are persistent, excessive, irrational thoughts, ideas, or images that are not based on actual problems or reality and cause extreme discomfort. Although the person tries to ignore or stop these impulses or thoughts and recognizes that they aren't realistic—"I know this is crazy but I keep thinking that I'm going to get AIDS just by being in this room"—her underlying anxiety has taken that form and she can't stop.

Compulsions are a manifestation of anxiety in which a person feels compelled to perform repetitive behaviors, such as hand washing, checking, and touching things according to a rigid set of rules. She may feel compelled to wash her hands repeatedly, pat twenty things before leaving a room, or dress in a certain order. Not doing those things causes her distress.

Another form of anxiety is phobia, in which someone is afraid of external things, such as bridges, elevators, or tunnels. The fear is out of proportion to the potential danger.

Panic attack is the most extreme form of anxiety. It is an overwhelming experience that causes intense fear or discomfort. Symptoms include palpitations, increased heart rate, sweating, shaking or trembling, shortness of breath, a feeling of choking, chest pain, nausea, abdominal distress, dizziness or light-headedness, numbness, hot flashes, chills, feelings of unreality or detachment (called derealization or depersonalization), and fears of going crazy, losing control, or dying. A patient diagnosed with panic attack abruptly develops four or more of these symptoms, which reach a peak within ten minutes.

Q. Are panic attacks the same as anxiety attacks?
A. Anxiety attack is a misnomer for a lesser form of panic. It is not a specific psychiatric disorder.

Q. Do people with anxiety suffer all the time?
A. No. Anxiety waxes and wanes. It usually comes on suddenly, but it isn't always a direct result of a stressful event.

Q. Does anxiety run in families?
A. Yes. Anxiety disorders run in families. Some people are biologically vulnerable.

Q. Does anxiety get worse with age?
A. Not necessarily. Most people with anxiety disorder are diagnosed before they reach age fifty. However, stress can increase anxiety in a vulnerable person. If stressful events increase with age, anxiety might worsen or recur.

Q. How common are anxiety disorders?
A. Five percent of the population suffers from anxiety disorders.

Q. Are women more prone to anxiety?

A. Yes. Anxiety disorders are more common in women—two-thirds female versus one-third male.

Q. Is there a correlation between hormones and anxiety?

A. Anxiety that is first experienced during menopause is usually mild and resolves quickly. Hormone replacement may help. However, menopause can be a stressor that brings on full-blown anxiety in women who have a history of clinical anxiety disorder.

Q. When is it time for people with anxiety to seek the help of a psychiatrist?

A. A psychiatric evaluation for anxiety disorder would be appropriate if a woman's discomfort intrudes on the quality of her life.

Q. Tell me about medications for anxiety disorders.

A. Tranquilizers such as benzodiazapines (Valium, Ativan, and Xanax) specifically treat anxiety. Antidepressants, especially selective serotonin reuptake inhibitors (SSRIs) (Prozac, Zoloft, and Paxil) are also useful in treatment of anxiety but take several weeks to have an effect.

Q. Let's talk about depression. How do "the blues" differ from clinical depression?

A. A person with the blues feels low, sad, disappointed, or discouraged. Blues are transient, everybody has them, and they don't impair functioning or interfere with the quality of one's life. Clinical depression is a full-blown psychiatric disorder.

Q. Tell me about the different forms of clinical depression.

A. There are two main forms of clinical depression—dysthymia and major depressive illness.

Q. What is dysthymia?

A. Dysthymia is a milder, chronic form of depression. People with dysthymia feel depressed most of the day, most of the time, for at least two years. An official diagnosis requires the patient to have at least two of the following: decreased appetite or overeating, insomnia or sleeping too much, fatigue or low energy, low self-esteem, poor concentration, difficulty making decisions, feelings of hopelessness.

Q. How does major depressive illness differ from dysthymia?
A. It is more acute and intense than dysthymia. People with major depressive illness feel hopeless. They don't believe that there is a way out of their depressed state. Their thinking is distorted and not based on reality. They have lost all perspective.

Patients diagnosed with this type of depression suffer severe symptoms for at least two weeks. Symptoms include depressed mood for most of the day, markedly decreased interest in previously pleasurable activities, major changes in eating behaviors, significant weight loss or weight gain, severe insomnia or excessive sleeping, intense agitation, a slowdown of movements (psychomotor retardation), extreme fatigue, loss of energy, low self-esteem, indecisiveness, and a preoccupation with death, which may include suicidal thoughts or even a planned suicide. If they don't get help, they could die.

Q. How common is depression?
A. Ten to 25 percent of women will suffer a major depression sometime in their life. That's a huge number. These figures are unrelated to ethnicity, education, income, or marital status. Some people are genetically predisposed to depression.

Q. Is depression most common for women at menopause?
A. No. That is a myth. Depression is most common in the twenty-five- to forty-four-year age group.

Q. What is bipolar disorder (manic depressive disorder)?
A. Bipolar disorder is a syndrome in which people have depressive and manic episodes. The manic phase is an unrealistic high that can get people in trouble—they may become delusional and grandiose, and their judgment often is impaired. It may be their way to escape from depressive feelings.

Bipolar disorder also has a genetic basis. Patients are unable to regulate their mood because of biological factors.

Q. Does talking it out help people resolve their depression?
A. Talking may help milder forms of depression but probably won't cure full-blown depression.

Q. What should someone do who is suffering from depression?
A. A person with a severe depression should be under the care of a psychiatrist.

Q. How do you deal with someone who comes in for the first time?
A. I take a history and we talk. Not just about her symptoms. I try to form a bond with her so that I will get to know her as a person.

People who are depressed feel hopeless. It's part of their condition to think that nothing will help. The psychiatrist or psychologist must give the patient a positive feeling that something can be done. There is a lot that we can do. We must give them hope that they will come out of this.

Q. Is depression curable?
A. Most depression is treatable. It certainly can go into remission. Depression seems to be cured for some people although others develop subsequent episodes.

Q. What if the depression is severe?
A. If symptoms are very severe at the first visit, I may recommend immediate medication. I also want the patient to have a medical workup to rule out physical conditions that might cause depression.

Q. What if the patient is suicidal?
A. If she is suicidal and in danger, we're talking about a different level of involvement. We need to have family members involved. We must monitor the patient very carefully. In some cases, hospitalization will be required.

Q. Tell me about medications used to treat depression.
A. There are several classes of antidepressants. The most widely used are the selective serotonin reuptake inhibitors, including drugs such as

Prozac, Zoloft, and Paxil. Although every drug has possible side effects, these tend to have fewer than most.

Q. What are the side effects of SSRIs?
A. SSRIs can cause restlessness, agitation, and insomnia. Some patients experience decreased sexual functioning—lower arousal or decreased orgasm. Weight gain is another possible side effect.

Q. How do antidepressants work?
A. Serotonin, a specific chemical in the brain, plays a role in regulating emotion. People with depression seem to have inadequate serotonin in certain brain pathways. SSRIs alter serotonin metabolism.

Q. What is the future for depressive illnesses?
A. Medications will become refined. There will be more specific drugs with fewer side effects.

New imaging techniques will better localize areas in the brain and brain pathways that are affected. That will help in drug development.

Creative, insightful people will think of new approaches and therapies. Cognitive therapy is an example of a successful method that was recently developed.

Q. What do you advise women in their fifties who want to maintain their mental health?
A.
- Try to turn negatives into positives. Don't dwell on perceived problems. View an empty nest as an opportunity, not a loss. Participate in pleasurable activities that you could never do before. Foster new interests and friendships.
- Don't have rigid expectations for yourself. Don't beat yourself up and feel guilty. Many women tend to take on too much. Don't make your entire day a series of obligations and negative experiences. Nobody can deal with difficulties unless she has something positive for herself.
- Exercise is good for emotional as well as physical well-being. It doesn't have to be a high-powered workout. A daily walk with a friend offers physical activity, interaction, and moral support.

- Use relaxation techniques such as yoga, exercise, meditation, and massage to counter stress or anxiety.
- If you experience a major crisis, find a support group. They exist for almost every condition and illness.

Each woman has to find what works for her.

20

Sexuality

Maj-Britt Rosenbaum, M.D.

Maj-Britt Rosenbaum was a premed major in college, graduating in 1959. She attended the Columbia University College of Physicians and Surgeons in New York and did her psychiatric residency at New York's Albert Einstein College of Medicine, where she has been on the faculty since 1967. She is the former director of the Human Sexuality Center at Long Island Jewish Hillside Medical Center. Dr. Rosenbaum is currently associate clinical professor of psychiatry at Albert Einstein College of Medicine and has a private psychiatric practice in Larchmont, New York.

Q. What is sexuality?
A. The purpose of our sexuality is to ensure the survival of our genes. In order to achieve this basic biological goal, our sexuality has evolved into a complex, ever-changing capacity, with a multitude of psychological, social, and physiological components. Today it is mainly these aspects we are interested in when we talk about sexuality.

Sexuality is a life force that permeates all aspects of our lives. Sexuality drives us to reach out for partners, for momentary sexual pleasure as well as for long-term commitments that help nurture our young. Sexuality encourages us to "advertise our wares," to display our reproductive value to its best advantage. Sexuality reinforces our sense of being female or male. Even if we never exercise our reproductive potential, the basic biology, the effect of the ebb and flow of our hormones have a powerful effect on our behavior and on our nervous system. This in turn affects how we behave in all our relationships, the intimate as well as more distant ones.

Q. How does sexuality change as we get older?
A. Sexuality becomes more complex. The clear-cut urgency for sexual expression of adolescent males and the more diffuse, often confusing bodily reactions of adolescent females become increasingly more integrated into the totality of our lives. As we get older, sexuality is a broader part of life. We can express our sexual energy in work, in art, in music, with friends and family, as well as in the erotic dimension.

Q. What about the sexuality of people in their fifties?
A. People in their fifties may not have as much sex-in-bed desire, but sexuality flourishes in a variety of ways. To feel attractive and close to others makes us feel sexually valuable.

Q. Tell me about the sexuality of women in their fifties.
A. Women who were sexual when they were younger tend to retain their sexuality. Their physiological response is maintained, and they have a full capacity for orgasm, but it might take a little longer because of decreased levels of estrogen and testosterone.

Q. What types of sexual problems do you see in women who are fifty to sixty years of age?
A. In addition to relationship difficulties, sexual problems in this age group of women are often hormonally related, illness related, medication related, or due to lack of partners or partners who are unable to have erections.

Q. How are hormones linked to a woman's sexual drive and response?
A. At menopause, estrogen and testosterone levels drop. In terms of sexuality, estrogens have more to do with receptivity—feeling ready to receive or engage in sex. Testosterone is responsible for the sense of wanting to have sex. Lower hormone levels can cause sexual problems in some women.

Q. How do drops in estrogen levels affect a woman's vagina?
A. Too little estrogen can cause atrophic vaginitis. The vaginal wall may become thin, sensitive, and less responsive to lubrication, causing painful intercourse. Also, women who don't have enough estrogen or who have not had intercourse for a period of time may find that their vagina has tightened.

Q. Will estrogen replacement help these sexual problems?
A. Yes. Estrogen keeps the mucous membranes soft and pliable and helps maintain the function of the genitalia. If there are no contraindications or other concerns, estrogen replacement can help.

Q. What other measures can ameliorate vaginal dryness or atrophy?
A. Water-soluble lubricants can help. Those that are specifically made for vaginal lubrication are best, even better than K-Y Jelly.

Q. What about a tightened vagina?
A. In addition to local or systemic estrogen, the vagina can be stretched with dilators. However, most women will respond just with estrogen replacement.

Q. Tell me about DHEA and testosterone, the new "love drug."
A. DHEA is an androgenic drug that is widely used in the holistic medical community. Many women find it to be quite energizing. The risk is of overdosage or overuse. DHEA is normally sold in 25 milligrams (mg), which is too much for women. The dose should be restricted to 5 or 10 mg. The side effect of DHEA and testosterone overdoses can be severe masculinization.

Women should have their testosterone levels checked; if needed, they can take androgen supplements under medical supervision.

Q. How are natural testosterone, androgens, and DHEA different?
A. Androgen is the broad category of masculinizing hormones. Testosterone is an androgen made in the ovaries and the adrenal gland. DHEA is another androgen made mostly in the adrenal gland.

Q. Should all women in their fifties have their testosterone levels checked?
A. No. Most women retain their sexual capacity and desire and don't need testosterone levels checked. They continue to produce fair amounts of androgens.

If they feel a marked lowering of sexuality or desire, they should have their hormone levels checked.

Q. How do men and women differ as they age in terms of sexuality?
A. Men are more fearful than are women of losing their sexual functioning. Many women, in an almost paradoxical way, feel more comfortable about their bodies as they get older. Although our society may consider them less attractive with the passing years, women tend to feel more at home with their bodies and more comfortable with their sexuality and its expression. Men, especially those who may have erectile faltering, can become very vulnerable. Women may be familiar with this feeling from their earlier days, when they were less secure about their bodies, even though they "objectively" looked better.

Q. How can women deal with husbands who are having sexual difficulties?
A. Keep up the verbal as well as the sexual communication. We need to share with our partners. Most therapy is not so much what you do but how you talk about it and express your wishes as well as your demands. Ask your husband, "What can I do for you?"

Q. At what point should a couple consider professional help?
A. When the problem becomes painful. When they cannot deal with it themselves. The earlier a couple talks to a therapist, the better. Problems are easier to resolve in the early stages.

Q. Do women have difficulty getting their husbands to seek help?
A. Many men welcome the help if it's not done in an atmosphere of blame. They're suffering. They want a solution to their problem. Urologists today have many diagnostic and therapeutic ways of handling erectile problems.

Q. Are men's sexual problems at this age physiological or psychological?

A. They're mainly physiological. Twenty years ago psychiatrists labeled most men's sexual problems as performance anxiety. The more we studied it, the more we saw a physiological slide as men got older. Sexual problems don't happen to every man. Many men function well into their eighties and nineties.

Q. What do you advise men who are having problems?

A. Try, but don't worry if it doesn't work each time.

Have a medical checkup to be sure that medical conditions or medications aren't causing your problem.

Q. Tell me about the effect of medications on sexuality.

A. Medications tend to affect men more than women. The worst culprits are antihypertensives. Antidepressants may cause sexual problems for both men and women. Prozac-type drugs can delay orgasm and sometimes make it impossible.

Q. Why aren't the antihypertensives a problem for women?

A. Women's sexual arousal is more diffuse than men's, and for some reason antihypertensives don't seem to interfere as much.

Q. How does illness affect sexuality?

A. Any chronic or debilitating illness will interfere with sex because of fatigue and general body problems.

Q. What if that illness involves surgical removal of a woman's reproductive or sexual organs, such as a hysterectomy?

A. The majority of women who have a simple hysterectomy without removal of the ovaries can maintain very good sexual functioning. Some women will miss the uterine component of their sexual response—that is, the contracting of the uterus with orgasm. This is referred to as "missing the echo chamber" or "the deeper response." Most of those women eventually will enjoy sexual response.

A small percentage of women who have a simple hysterectomy claim that their sexuality has changed completely. They feel nothing.

This lack of response could be due to neurological damage, or it may arise purely on an emotional basis. The lack of a uterus may cause them to feel that they are no longer fully women.

The uterus has been part of women's sexual response throughout their lives and certainly continues to be so in the fifties. Although it is no longer used for childbearing, the uterus is a sexual organ that takes part in sexual response.

I would not discourage a woman from having a medically indicated hysterectomy for sexual reasons. The chances are that she will continue to have a very good sexual response.

Q. What if the woman has her ovaries removed as well?
A. That can be a problem if she cannot have hormone replacement for the reasons that we previously discussed.

Q. What about breast surgery and sexuality?
A. Breast surgery tends to be a problem of body image. The breast is an erotogenic zone for most women. Many women will miss that aspect of sexuality. Some women will miss it intensely. Others will focus on the larger picture and be happy to be alive and free of cancer.

A mastectomy is a very real loss, especially a bilateral mastectomy. Breast replacement surgery can be helpful. I strongly recommend reconstructive breast surgery for women who want it, especially if it doesn't involve a second operation and there's little or no risk.

Q. What about the husband's response to mastectomy?
A. Some husbands may have negative responses. A difficult, conflicted relationship can have trouble. Divorces or losses of relationships sometimes result from a woman's mastectomy. In my experience, most men respond well. A good marriage or relationship will incorporate almost anything. Appreciation of the partner often deepens after such problems.

Sexual relationships can be healing. Women often feel sad and have a grief reaction. Cancer surgery and the loss of a breast can be very difficult if there's no support.

Q. How can women who have become single, through death of a spouse or divorce, cope with their sexual desires?
A. Some women experience feelings of sexual frustration and others don't at all.

Those who do can turn to masturbation, sexual fantasies, or erotica, which has become increasingly open and talked about. Although masturbation can be a release, it may not be enough. Many women complain because their main loss is of the partner, the reaching out to another person, and not just the sex.

Some women turn toward each other—for homosexual expression, either directly sexual or just for the cuddling, closeness, and physical touching.

Many women continue to search for relationships.

Much of the pleasure of sexuality is skin to skin touching. Direct contact is a sexual need that we can express in friendships or by taking care of family members and pets.

Q. What is a sexually healthy woman?
A. A woman who has incorporated sexuality with her whole self, who is comfortable with her body and who can express herself freely in a sexually satisfying way.

Q. What is your advice to women in their fifties who want to have active, enjoyable lives?
A.

- Don't be afraid to talk to others. It is helpful to share concerns, vulnerabilities, and losses and to get advice.
- Take care of your body—exercise and eat well, but also allow some indulgences.

The fifties is one of the best times in life. I hope that women will focus on themselves and say, "It is time for me."

Younger women may look with fear at becoming fifty. They don't know. The fifties can be a calmer, more accepting, a feeling good time of life. That includes owning one's own sexuality.

21

Alternative Medicine

James S. Gordon, M.D.

James Gordon was an English major in college. He attended Harvard University Medical School in 1962, where he also did a medical internship. After completing a psychiatric residency at the Albert Einstein School of Medicine in New York, he became a research psychiatrist at the National Institute of Mental Health in Bethesda, Maryland. For the past twenty-five years he has pioneered a new approach to medical care that combines conventional scientific methods with alternative techniques. He was the first chairman of the Advisory Council of the National Institutes of Health's Office of Alternative Medicine. Dr. Gordon is a clinical professor of psychiatry and community and family medicine at the Georgetown University School of Medicine, director of the Center for Mind-Body Medicine in Washington, and author of *Manifesto for a New Medicine: Your Guide to Healing Partnerships and the Wise Use of Alternative Therapies.*

Q. Tell me about the Center for Mind-Body Medicine.
A. The Center for Mind-Body Medicine is an educational program. We teach professionals (physicians, nurses, social workers, psychologists) and individual patients how to achieve optimal wellness through the use of alternative techniques such as acupuncture, biofeedback, manipulation, herbalism, massage, nutrition, exercise, dance, and med-

itation. Our emphasis is on the use of support groups as the best places for teaching and learning.

Q. Why are some people turning to alternative medical therapies?
A. In the past twenty-five years much of the promise of conventional medicine has been unfulfilled. Some people with serious illnesses do not get better. Patients who are unwell but have not been given a medical diagnosis feel ignored. Inadequacies such as these have led people to look for new approaches to medical care.

Q. What percentage of Americans use alternative medical therapies?
A. In 1990 approximately 34 percent of Americans were using some form of alternative medicine. That figure is now closer to 45 percent. Seventy to 80 percent of people with cancer or HIV have tried alternative therapies.

Q. Has there been resistance to alternative therapy from mainstream physicians and surgeons?
A. Initially, physicians and surgeons were resistant. They assumed that conventional medicine was at a pinnacle and provided most of the answers. They knew little of alternative therapies. Different concepts of health care were seen as peripheral or even superstitious. Their narrow vision was a result of their conventional training in biomedicine and an emotional, ideological, scientific, and economic investment in their work.

Q. Are physicians and surgeons beginning to accept holistic approaches to medicine?
A. Yes, there is much more openness. Many physicians are incorporating holistic medicine into their practices partly because patients have convinced them that alternative approaches offer health benefits.

Q. How can a doctor give patients the best of biomedicine and at the same time offer a holistic approach to medical care?
A. It's not a question of practicing one type of medicine or another but of being a good physician and using what works. I use approaches

205

and techniques that are most useful while abiding by the Hippocratic advice to first do no harm.

Q. Tell me about the different levels of health care that your holistic approach includes.
A. Self-care is the first level of health care, except in the case of an emergency. The next level includes techniques for self-healing, such as acupuncture, manipulation, and massage. Drugs and surgery are used only as a last resort.

Q. How can a woman find a physician who will offer her a holistic approach to care?
A. She should try to encourage her physician to move in this direction. The ideal primary care physician should be open to all approaches to medical care. He or she should try to help the patient find a holistic program that would work for her. If your doctor says "thanks, but no thanks," you may have to look elsewhere.

The American Holistic Medical Association, a group of several hundred physicians, can recommend someone in your locality.

Ask your friends for a recommendation. Many women in their fifties are under the care of a physician who incorporates holistic methods.

Q. In this day of managed care, will health insurance companies pay for alternative therapies, such as massage and biofeedback?
A. Some health insurance companies currently pay for alternative therapies. Many do not. They probably will change their policies if enough people demand it.

Q. Do osteopaths practice holistic medicine?
A. Osteopathy was originally a holistic approach to health care. Although the philosophy still exists—approximately 10 to 15 percent of osteopaths perform manipulation of the spine—most osteopaths practice conventional medicine.

Q. What about chiropractors?
A. Chiropractors are schooled in manipulation. They aren't allowed

to prescribe drugs or perform surgery, but they usually know when to refer a patient to a physician.

Q. What is homeopathy?
A. Homeopathy is the use of tiny doses of substances to relieve symptoms. Homeopathic medical schools no longer exist in the United States, and the practice of homeopathy is not licensed in most states. However, several controlled studies have shown that homeopathy has helped patients with arthritis, asthma, and hay fever.

Q. What's naturopathy?
A. Naturopathy is the use of natural, nonpharmaceutical remedies, such as herbs, supplements, diet, homeopathy, exercise, hydrotherapy (water therapy), and relaxation techniques, to treat illness and to maintain health.

Naturopaths are licensed in several states as primary health care providers. They are allowed to perform minor surgery and occasionally to deliver babies, but they cannot do major surgery or prescribe drugs.

Q. Tell me about acupuncture.
A. Acupuncture is a several-thousand-year-old technique of Chinese medicine in which needles are inserted in various points of the body to move what the Chinese call qi, or energy, a force that moves in the body and affects all aspects of physical and emotional functioning. The acupuncturist knows where the points are and can discover the imbalances by taking the pulse, looking at the tongue, and feeling the belly.

Q. What is acupressure?
A. Acupressure is using the fingers to stimulate the points that we discussed under acupuncture.

Q. What is reflexology?
A. Reflexology is a technique in which pressure is exerted on specific parts of the body—the sole of the foot or the palm of the hand, for example—to stimulate certain organs. It is based on the idea that

certain parts of the body are a hologram for other parts of the body—
that is, the entire body is represented on the sole of the foot and the
palm of the hand.

Q. Tell me about the safety of herbs and natural supplements.
A. Whether you're under the care of a professional or embarking on a
course of self-care, you should learn the proper use, appropriate dosages, and possible side effects of herbs and natural supplements. Substances that come from nature are not necessarily without harm.

There is nothing that can't be improperly used. You may be sensitive to a particular herb. Your gut may not tolerate certain supplements. What works for one person may not work for another.

Q. What do you think of DHEA?
A. DHEA is a very powerful hormone. I would not recommend that
anyone use DHEA indiscriminately or on a prolonged basis. It may
help people who are DHEA deficient or those who have low levels of
energy.

Q. What about melatonin?
A. Melatonin is another hormone that I would not use or prescribe
indiscriminately. It may be helpful for jet lag or sleeplessness. Studies
have shown melatonin is palliative in some cases of metastatic cancer.
I think that's worth exploring.

Q. What about St. John's wort as an antidote for depression?
A. St. John's wort is a potent herb that can have side effects and
should be used with caution. It seems to be effective for some people
as an antidepressant, but the real issue with depression is what's going
on in that person's life. Why is she depressed? She'd better do something about that. If she can't stand her job or her spouse, St. John's
wort may relieve symptoms, but she is still living an unfulfilled life.
The inappropriate use of antidepressants also concerns me. Many people take antidepressants but don't address their problems.

Q. How should medical education change to include alternative
medical therapies and mind-body medicine?

A. Alternative therapies and mind-body medicine should be part and parcel of every aspect of medical education. Only then will we see doctors with different perspectives and attitudes toward themselves, toward their patients, and toward medicine in general.

From the first year of medical school, physicians should be taught to respect, understand, and care for themselves. Self-awareness, relaxation, meditation, nutrition, exercise, and massage should be included in their basic training. If doctors learn to care for themselves, they will be better able to communicate that to their patients, resulting in a shift to patient self-care, away from the physician merely treating the symptoms of disease.

Q. What advice do you have for women in their fifties who are suffering from the symptoms of menopause?
A. Stop thinking of menopause as a disease. Menopause is part of an important life transition. The real problem with menopause is societal. Women in other cultures don't experience the kind or severity of menopausal symptoms that are suffered by women in the United States.

Many women find that natural herbs and hormones help to relieve or control the symptoms of menopause.

Q. What do you see as the future of health care in light of this new approach to medicine?
A. Health care will be transformed in the next twenty to thirty years. Virtually all primary care physicians will include a mind-body approach in their practices. Alternative medicine will become part of the treatment in every hospital in this country.

Q. What do you advise women in their fifties whose health problems are not being met through conventional medicine?
A.
- Try to find a physician, nurse practitioner, or physician's assistant who has the knowledge and expertise to help you develop a program of self-care.
- Designate a quiet time every day for relaxation or meditation.

This is a part of our heritage as human beings that has been squeezed out of the lives of many of us.

- Find time for regular exercise.
- A proper diet is essential. Each person must determine what makes sense for them to eat.
- Make use of mainstream medicine for its strengths, but don't be limited by it.
- Do not be mystified by medicine. You can learn about and understand your health problems. Knowledgeable people make informed choices and are not confined to conventional medicine.

SECTION IV
Disease Prevention

22

Preventing Heart Disease

Jerome L. Fleg, M.D.

After graduating from college in 1967 with a major in zoology, Jerome Fleg attended the University of Cincinnati College of Medicine. He then did his internship at the Baltimore City Hospitals, followed by two years of military service. In 1973 he moved to St. Louis to complete two years of internal medicine residency followed by a fellowship in cardiology, both at Washington University–Barnes Hospital. In 1977 he became a staff cardiologist at the Gerontology Research Center in Baltimore, a position that he still holds.

The Gerontology Research Center is part of the National Institute on Aging, one of the thirteen institutes of the National Institutes of Health.

Q. What is the function of the heart?
A. The heart's major function is to pump blood to all the other organs of the body so that every tissue and organ is viable and has enough oxygen and other required nutrients.

Q. What are common heart problems?
A. Coronary artery disease (CAD) is by far the most prevalent type of heart problem in the United States and most Western societies. The coronary arteries are the vessels that supply blood to the heart muscle. If the coronary arteries are blocked, the heart is deprived of oxygen and can't function properly. Coronary artery disease means blockages

of at least one of the three coronary arteries that supply the heart muscle with blood.

Q. What are the risk factors for coronary artery disease?
A. The major culprits are high levels of low-density cholesterol (LDL), smoking, and high blood pressure. These are modifiable risk factors. Age, gender, and a positive family history of CAD are unmodifiable risk factors. Being male and older are more potent risk factors than a positive family history of CAD as well as any of the modifiable risk factors.

Q. How common is heart disease in fifty- to sixty-year-old women?
A. Coronary artery disease is fairly uncommon in women ages fifty to sixty—it occurs in less than 5 percent of women in this age group. However, prevalence goes up dramatically above this age.

Q. Is the low incidence of heart disease in younger women due to estrogen? When does the risk go up?
A. Because of the estrogen effect, coronary disease is extremely low in women in their forties. Some women in their early fifties are not yet menopausal. At the end of this decade, essentially all have gone through menopause. It's in the decade of the fifties that we start to see a significant increase in the prevalence of coronary artery disease in women. Women don't suddenly develop an increased risk the minute they go through menopause. But after menopause, the risk gradually goes up. Up to that point, heart disease in women is quite uncommon.

Q. Do you believe that taking estrogen will prevent heart disease in women after menopause?
A. It's not an all-or-none phenomenon. You're not going to completely prevent heart disease by taking estrogen, but several large uncontrolled studies show that estrogen reduces the risk for a major coronary event by about half. However, carefully planned prospective studies are now in progress to determine more accurately the cardiovascular benefit of estrogen-replacement therapy (ERT).

Q. How does estrogen give protection against heart disease?
A. Estrogen seems to improve the lipid profile—it increases the good cholesterol (HDL) and lowers the bad cholesterol (LDL). Not surprisingly, the incidence of high cholesterol, particularly bad cholesterol, goes up significantly in postmenopausal women who are not on estrogen-replacement therapy.

Estrogen also improves endothelial function. Endothelial cells make up the inner lining of the blood vessels. It's thought that estrogen makes the endothelial cells dilate more readily, which increases the size of the arteries, thereby increasing blood flow to the body tissues.

Q. What is cholesterol?
A. Cholesterol is a lipid (a form of fat) that is manufactured by the body. Every cell membrane in the human body contains some cholesterol. It's is a necessary ingredient for life. But excess cholesterol that has dissolved in the blood tends to deposit in the walls of the coronary arteries, and this is a potent risk factor for coronary artery disease. The higher your total cholesterol—specifically the low-density cholesterol (LDL)—the higher your chances for coronary artery disease.

Q. What is the difference between LDL cholesterol and HDL cholesterol?
A. LDL and HDL are differentiated in a laboratory setting by the density of their particles. The HDL is a higher-density cholesterol and is actually protective against heart disease.

Q. How does the HDL cholesterol help?
A. Some people think that HDL cholesterol acts as a scavenger, getting cholesterol out of the blood vessel wall and then transporting it back to the liver. It takes the bad cholesterol (LDL) out of the areas where it could harm the blood vessel wall.

Q. When should women begin having their cholesterol levels measured?
A. That's an individual decision. Women whose close family members have had major coronary artery disease in their forties or fifties proba-

bly should get their cholesterol levels measured as teenagers or young adults. Women without a family history or other risk factors may wait until their forties to check their cholesterol.

Q. How often should cholesterol be measured after that? Are there guidelines?
A. An expert panel (National Cholesterol Education Program) suggests repeating every five years if total cholesterol is less than 200 or yearly if higher.

Q. Please explain cholesterol numbers. What about the HDL/LDL ratio?
A. A normal total cholesterol is less than 200. If you don't have other risk factors for coronary disease, an LDL of less than 160 is good. If you have other major risk factors, many cardiologists would like your LDL to be under 130. If you have overt coronary artery disease, you should try to get the LDL cholesterol under 100.

You can come up with all kinds of ratios—HDL to LDL or HDL to total cholesterol. For simplicity, most recommendations are based on the absolute LDL levels.

Q. What do you recommend if a patient's cholesterol is moderately high?
A. If they're smoking, we tell them to stop. Smoking lowers the HDL (protective cholesterol). We ask them to modify their diet—try to eliminate high-fat foods such as red meats, ice cream, and butter. If they're obese, losing weight can lower cholesterol to a certain extent.

Q. When do you decide to give cholesterol-lowering medications?
A. The first order of business is to put a patient on a low-cholesterol diet for about three months. In that time we can tell whether the target cholesterol can be attained. We treat each patient individually. If a patient has overt coronary artery disease and her LDL cholesterol is significantly above 100, most physicians would prescribe a cholesterol-lowering medication. If this woman did not have heart disease or other risk factors, the acceptable LDL level would be pumped up

accordingly—if the LDL was below 160, most physicians would treat with diet alone.

Q. Are there side effects to cholesterol-lowering drugs?
A. All medications have side effects. The side effects of cholesterol-lowering drugs are uncommon and quite mild. When they do occur, they're usually reversible.

Q. Will lowering cholesterol prevent heart disease or heart attacks in women?
A. In the past, most research studies have been done on middle-aged men who had high cholesterol or known coronary artery disease. There are really no data that tell us what to do with a healthy fifty- to sixty-year-old woman who has moderately elevated cholesterol.

Q. Are research studies now being done that will benefit women?
A. Yes. The National Institutes of Health is now attuned. In fact, a very large study called the Women's Health Initiative is specifically looking at the strategies to lower the risk of coronary artery disease in middle-aged women.

Heart disease research on women in their fifties is difficult because of the nature of the disease—women have a lower incidence. There won't be adequate numbers of female patients available at a single center for these studies. It's a lot easier to find fifty- to sixty-year-old men with the disease.

Q. How important are exercise and diet?
A. Exercise and diet influence the modifiable risk factors. Aerobic exercise and low-cholesterol diets can bring down high cholesterol and help to lower blood pressure as well. But it's naive to say that these lifestyle changes will ensure that you won't develop heart disease. You can't change your genetics.

Q. Do you prescribe aspirin for women to prevent heart attacks?
A. Aspirin is probably useful, but it is still controversial for women. There are no hard data about women in their fifties. Men who are fifty to eighty years old show benefit from taking aspirin regularly. How-

217

ever, if a woman in her fifties has known coronary artery disease or multiple risk factors, most cardiologists would prescribe aspirin.

Q. Does taking supplementary fiber, such as oat bran, help prevent heart disease?
A. Fiber does not provide a magic bullet that will automatically prevent you from developing heart disease. Some data show that high intake of fiber may reduce your cholesterol by 5 or 10 percent. But if your LDL cholesterol is 250, fiber alone is not going to bring it down to a normal range. You will still need drugs to achieve that goal. But you may need fewer drugs or lower doses. Fiber, like most nonpharmacological interventions, is useful but still relatively weak compared to drugs.

Q. What about antioxidants, such as vitamin E?
A. There's probably no compelling reason for a healthy woman in her fifties to take vitamin E to prevent heart disease. Some medical studies suggest that antioxidants are beneficial. They may be, as long as you don't go out on a limb. Too much vitamin E could cause toxic effects. Modest doses that are generally recommended probably will not harm you. It may be proven at some point that it does some good in preventing heart disease.

Q. And what about olive oil?
A. Greeks, who consume large amounts of olive oil, have one of the lowest incidences of heart disease. Is it their genetic makeup or is it the olive oil? It's a little difficult to tell. Most cardiologists don't think that olive oil markedly lowers your risk.

Q. Does alcohol consumption lower your risk of heart disease?
A. People who consume about two drinks a day have the best profile—that is, they have the lowest risk of coronary disease compared to people who drink more or who completely abstain.

Q. What mechanism causes alcohol to prevent heart disease?
A. It is thought that alcohol increases HDL, the good cholesterol.

That is probably the mechanism that gives a modest amount of alcohol its protective effect.

Q. What about the link among stress, the type A personality, and heart disease?
A. There are fewer data these days indicating that the type A personality is an important factor in heart disease. The typical traits of the overall type A, who is impatient, interrupts, and is hard-driving, may not be that bad. Psychologists now think that the hostility component to type A is the toxic component.

Q. How does high blood pressure increase the risk of heart disease?
A. High blood pressure increases the wear and tear on the whole arterial system. It accelerates the degeneration of the blood vessel wall that is caused by normal aging. Since systolic blood pressure rises with advancing age, aging is often considered a muted form of hypertension. Similarly, hypertension is an accelerated form of aging. The two have very similar effects on blood vessels. They both increase the rate of degeneration of elastin, the elastic tissue, and the deposition of calcium and collagen, which are very rigid substances. With aging and hypertension, the arteries become like rigid pipes instead of the nice, compliant vessels that they were in youth.

Q. Is there any reason for a woman in her fifties to have an annual electrocardiogram?
A. No, I don't think an annual electrocardiogram (EKG) would be useful. The resting EKG is not a sensitive indicator of coronary artery disease. If you have coronary narrowing and you haven't had a heart attack, the resting EKG probably would look normal. A stress EKG (one done while you exercise) might be of some benefit. Then again, because women in this age group generally have a low risk of coronary disease, there will be a lot of false positives—that is, abnormal stress EKGs in women without disease.

Q. What are the manifestations of coronary artery disease?
A. The manifestations are angina (chest pain), a heart attack, or sudden death.

Q. Although women in their fifties have a low incidence of heart disease, it can happen. What are the symptoms?
A. The symptoms of a heart attack are severe, unrelenting, pressure-like chest pain in the sternal area (the breast bone area). If she experiences any of these symptoms, she should go to an emergency room immediately to have a heart attack ruled out. Heart attacks in this age group are not nonexistent. Milder chest pressure that comes on with exertion and goes away promptly with rest usually indicates angina.

Q. Can someone have coronary heart disease or a heart attack without pain?
A. Yes. You can have a silent heart attack even without clinical history of heart disease. An EKG can pick that up. In addition, in many people, the only evidence of coronary artery disease is an abnormal stress test.

Q. What should healthy women in their fifties do to protect their hearts?
A. All of the common-sense things:

- Don't smoke.
- Be sure your blood pressure is okay—treat it if it's high.
- If your cholesterol is moderately high, you should be on nonpharmacological therapy (diet and exercise). If it's extremely high, you should be on drug therapy.
- Keep weight down to a reasonable level. Excess weight increases other risk factors, such as high blood pressure, high cholesterol, and diabetes, which is another independent risk factor for coronary heart disease.
- Exercise. It provides numerous benefits. Exercise may have some independent beneficial effects, such as improving endothelial function and improving anticoagulant activity in the blood, which makes it less likely to clot.
- Diet. The primary effect of a low-fat diet is to lower cholesterol and reduce weight.
- Estrogen seems to protect against coronary disease. Most cardiologists would recommend estrogen replacement unless a woman has contraindications, such as breast cancer or a family history of breast cancer.

23

Hypertension (High Blood Pressure) and Stroke

Jerome L. Fleg, M.D.

After graduating from college in 1967 with a major in zoology, Jerome Fleg attended the University of Cincinnati College of Medicine. He then did his internship at the Baltimore City Hospitals, followed by two years of military service. In 1973 he moved to St. Louis to complete two years of internal medicine residency followed by a fellowship in cardiology, both at Washington University–Barnes Hospital. In 1977 he became a staff cardiologist at the Gerontology Research Center in Baltimore, a position that he still holds.

The Gerontology Research Center is part of the National Institute on Aging, one of the thirteen institutes of the National Institutes of Health.

Q. **What is hypertension?**
A. Hypertension is the elevation of blood pressure above the normal range. It is the most common cardiovascular disorder.

Q. **What is normal blood pressure?**
A. The normal range of blood pressure is less than 140 systolic, the top number, and less than 90 diastolic, the bottom number.

Q. Would you briefly explain systolic and diastolic?
A. Systolic pressure occurs while the heart is pumping the blood through the vessels. Diastolic pressure occurs between heartbeats.

Q. When is someone considered hypertensive?
A. When the blood pressure is above 140 systolic and/or 90 diastolic.

Q. What happens to your blood pressure as you get older?
A. Your systolic blood pressure normally goes up with age, whereas the diastolic pressure remains fairly stable.

Q. What percentage of women in their fifties have high blood pressure?
A. Approximately one-third of women ages fifty to sixty have high blood pressure. According to American Heart Association data, the prevalence of hypertension in women forty-five to fifty-four is 23 percent and in women fifty-five to sixty-four is 47 percent. If you average these two numbers to approximate the prevalence in women fifty to sixty, the prevalence is 35 percent.

Q. What risk factors contribute to hypertension?
A. Controllable factors include obesity, consuming more than two alcoholic drinks per day, and taking in high amounts of salt.

Uncontrollable risks include genetic components—if your parents were hypertensive, you are more likely to become hypertensive. Other family patterns also may contribute to hypertension, such as a shared lifestyle and a tendency to be overweight. African Americans have more hypertension than whites. Some people are genetically more salt-sensitive and thus more prone to hypertension.

Q. Does stress contribute to high blood pressure?
A. Stress may elevate blood pressure. People used to think of hypertension as hyperstress. But the two are not synonymous. Not all people who are under stress have hypertension, and most people who have high blood pressure are not under a lot of stress.

Acute stress can make the blood pressure go up. You've probably heard about the white-coat effect. A small percentage of people will have dramatic increases in their blood pressure in the doctor's office. The physician may conclude that this person is hypertensive. However, as soon as the patient walks out of that office, the blood pressure goes back normal. In this case, the diagnosis can be difficult. We might outfit this person with a twenty-four-hour blood pressure monitor or ask her to have her pressure checked multiple times at home.

Q. What are the complications of untreated hypertension?

A. The major outcomes of untreated hypertension are coronary artery disease, strokes, and kidney disease. The negative effects of not treating high blood pressure are extremely well documented. It would be considered unethical not to treat someone who has hypertension.

Q. How do you treat high blood pressure?

A. The first line of treatment is the nonpharmacological: reducing weight, reducing salt in the diet, consuming only moderate amounts of alcohol, and a regular exercise program. Exercise can act to dilate the arteries, which lowers blood pressure.

Q. What if nonpharmacological treatment doesn't work?

A. We can get the blood pressure under control with medications that bring it into a normal range in the vast majority of individuals. Many classes of drugs reduce blood pressure. It's a matter of finding one that an individual tolerates well and that does the job. There's a certain amount of trial and error involved. It sometimes takes multiple drugs.

Q. Do you keep tabs on people with hypertension? Can blood pressure change when patients are on medications?

A. Any lifestyle change, such as diet or alcohol intake, can make the blood pressure change. Sometimes it changes spontaneously. Patients should be monitored frequently to be sure that their high blood pressure is controlled adequately.

Q. Isn't high blood pressure often called the silent killer?

A. Yes. That's because hypertension doesn't cause any symptoms. People used to talk about headaches or nose bleeds as symptoms of high blood pressure, but the vast majority of hypertension patients don't have any symptoms that are related to their blood pressure.

Q. Is there good news about high blood pressure?
A. Yes. The good news is that we have medications that control blood pressure very well. Treating high blood pressure brings the risks of kidney dysfunction, heart disease, and stroke down significantly. If treated adequately, having high blood pressure merely makes you cognizant of your health.

Q. What do you advise women in their fifties with regard to hypertension?
A. Women in their fifties have about a 35 percent prevalence of hypertension, which is substantial. They should have their blood pressured measured every year. If their blood pressure is high, it should be treated. Anyone walking around with hypertension should get treated.

Q. How common is stroke in women in their fifties?
A. In the Framingham Study, the annual incidence is 1 in 1,400 women ages forty-five to fifty-four and 1 in 800 women ages fifty-five to sixty-four.

The Framingham Study is a longitudinal observational study of cardiovascular disease in over 5,200 residents of Framingham, Massachusetts. The study began in 1948 and is still ongoing. Subjects are examined at two-year intervals.

Q. What are causes of stroke other than hypertension?
A. Other major causes of stroke include brain aneurysms (congenitally weakened blood vessels that can rupture), valvular heart disease, drug abuse (especially cocaine and intravenous drug use), atrial fibrillation and other cardiac rhythm disturbances, congestive heart failure, heart attack, and congenital heart disease.

Q. What is ischemic stroke?
A. Ischemic stroke is a stroke caused by occlusion of a brain blood vessel that was narrowed already by atherosclerotic plaque.

Q. Is there a link between diet and stroke?

A. There is no firm link, although some studies have shown that elevated blood cholesterol and heavy alcohol use may increase stroke risk. A high-potassium diet was associated with lower stroke risk in at least one study.

Q. What do you recommend as treatment for people with hypertension?

A. Treatment choices should be guided by the individual's physician.

For mild blood pressure elevation, nondrug approaches such as weight loss, salt restriction, moderate intake of alcohol, or aerobic exercise training can be used.

For more serious hypertension, drug therapy is necessary as soon as the diagnosis is made.

Q. What are the common treatments?

A. Major drug classes for hypertension treatment include diuretics, beta blockers, alpha blockers, calcium antagonists, angiotensin-converting enzyme inhibitors, and angiotensin receptor blockers.

Q. Are there choices?

A. The choice of both nondrug and drug treatment depends on multiple factors, particularly physician's experience, patient preference, associated medical conditions, and side effects.

Q. What is your advice to women in their fifties with high blood pressure?

A. Get it treated. High blood pressure is not a benign condition over the long term, despite a complete lack of symptoms in most patients.

24

Preventing Diabetes— Living with Diabetes

Richard Jackson, M.D.

Richard Jackson majored in math and biology in college, graduating in 1972. He attended medical school at Ohio State University School of Medicine. After graduation in 1976, he did an internal medicine internship and residency at Memorial Hospital in Worcester, Massachusetts. He completed his fellowship in endocrine metabolism at Duke University in 1982 and then went to the Joslin Clinic in Boston, where he has remained. Dr. Jackson is senior physician, medical director of the Diabetes Outpatient Intensive Treatment Program, and head of the Immunology Research Section at the Joslin Clinic. He also holds an appointment as assistant professor of medicine at the Harvard Medical School.

The Joslin Clinic, the world's largest diabetes center, was founded in 1898. Outpatients are seen and treated at the seven-story clinic, but inpatients are admitted to nearby hospitals. Members of the Joslin staff have appointments at various Boston hospitals.

Q. What is diabetes?
A. Diabetes is a disease in which the glucose (sugar) levels in a person's blood are too high.

Q. What are the symptoms of diabetes?
A. Symptoms include excessive thirst, frequent urination, and weight loss.

Q. What causes these symptoms?
A. Excess blood sugar spilled into the urine draws water to it, producing a large urine volume, which causes the person to urinate often. People drink a lot in response to the large amount of excreted urine. They experience weight loss because sugar calories go down the toilet.

Q. What are other symptoms of diabetes?
A. Other symptoms can be blurred vision and infections, particularly recurrent vaginal or urinary tract infections.

Q. What if someone ignores the symptoms of diabetes?
A. Symptoms can progress and become deadly. A person with uncontrolled diabetes may quickly develop medical complications.

Q. Tell me about the complications of uncontrolled diabetes.
A. Complications range from death due to heart attack, stroke, or kidney disease; to eye disease and blindness; amputations because of poor circulation to the limbs; and neuropathy (nerve damage that is painful and difficult to take care of).

Q. What happened to people with diabetes before insulin was discovered?
A. They died. In 1910 diabetes patients lived only two or three years. The discovery of insulin was a medical miracle.

Q. Tell me about the different types of diabetes.
A. There are two types of diabetes—type 1 and type 2. The causes are different but the result of both is high blood sugar. Once high blood sugars develop, the symptoms and the complications are the same.

Q. What causes type 1 diabetes?
A. In type 1 diabetes, the immune system, which usually protects us

227

from the outside world of viruses, bacteria, and the like, turns against a part of our own body—the insulin-producing cells in the pancreas. (Insulin is the major hormone in the body that controls blood sugar.)

Diabetes occurs slowly. When it gets to the point at which there are very few insulin-producing cells and sufficient insulin is no longer made, blood sugar levels begin to increase. Once glucose levels are high, symptoms develop and diabetes is clinically identifiable.

Q. Why is type 1 diabetes called an autoimmune disease?
A. It's called an autoimmune disease because the body's own immune system turns against itself. However, diabetes is a very specific aberration. The immune system works properly in other areas.

Q. Is type 1 diabetes the same as juvenile diabetes?
A. Type 1 diabetes is sometimes called juvenile diabetes, but the name is incorrect because most people develop type 1 diabetes as adults. The median age for developing type 1 diabetes is the early thirties.

Q. What is type 2 diabetes?
A. Type 2 diabetes, the more common form, has nothing to do with the immune system. It is caused by a combination of insulin resistance and the improper secretion of insulin.

Normally, insulin floats in the bloodstream and eventually hooks up to a receptor on a cell surface, which fits like a key in a lock. In type 2 diabetes, the insulin and receptors are normal, but something inside the cell resists the effects of the insulin. In addition to this insulin resistance, people who develop type 2 diabetes don't secrete insulin properly.

Q. Are women in their fifties more likely to develop type 2 than type 1 diabetes?
A. Yes. If a woman in her fifties develops diabetes, the chances are that it is type 2. It is sometimes called adult-onset diabetes because almost all people who develop type 2 diabetes are over forty.

Q. Does the risk of type 2 diabetes increase with age?
A. Yes.

Q. Does diabetes run in families?
A. Type 1 and type 2 diabetes both run in families.

Q. How common is diabetes?
A. By age seventy, 4 percent of the population will have diabetes. Type 1 accounts for about 15 percent of that total. Over 3 percent of fifty- to sixty-year-old women have diabetes.

Q. Do bad habits, such as overeating and poor diet, lead to diabetes?
A. No. You can't *cause* diabetes. You can't eat so badly, weigh so much, or be so inactive that you get diabetes. Many people are wrongly blamed for their diabetes. They did nothing to bring on this disease.

Q. What if I had the gene for type 2 diabetes? How could I help myself?
A. If you have genetic background for type 2 diabetes, your good physical fitness, optimal weight, and proper diet could delay or even prevent its onset.

Q. Tell me about treatments for type 2 diabetes.
A. The approaches in treating type 1 and type 2 diabetes are similar in terms of diet and exercise. Exercise is useful for type 1 but essential for type 2 diabetes.

In type 2 diabetes, exercise has an immediate effect of lowering the blood sugar because your muscles use the glucose as a fuel. Regular aerobic exercise also allows your body to become more fit, resulting in less insulin resistance and lower blood sugars. That's a very powerful effect because insulin resistance is one of the causes of the disease.

What you eat is very important. You need to eat slow-release foods, such as complex carbohydrates, that your sluggish, resistant, inefficient insulin system can take care of.

With type 2 diabetes, your body has insulin but it's not working well. Your system can't eliminate a lot of simple sugars that raise your blood sugar quickly. It can deal with combinations of foods that allow a slower increase of blood sugar.

Q. **Tell me about medications used to treat type 2 diabetes.**
A. Four different classes of medicines are available. None of the pills works so well that you can ignore exercise or proper nutrition.

Q. **Who takes insulin injections?**
A. People with type 1 diabetes take insulin. People with type 2 diabetes can be treated initially without insulin.

Q. **How does someone with diabetes know her blood sugar level?**
A. She must check her blood sugars using a little gadget that pinches her finger and reads the sugar level from a drop of blood.

An even better test, called an AIC, reflects average blood sugars over a period of several months. That test must be done in a laboratory. If the number on this test is lowered, her chance of future problems is greatly reduced.

Q. **Is diabetes increasing in the United States?**
A. Yes. We don't know why.

Q. **How does longevity of the population correlate with diabetes?**
A. Some scientists think that if people live longer, there will be more type 2 diabetes.

Q. **What are the criteria for diagnosis of diabetes?**
A. A diagnosis can be made if you have symptoms accompanied by high blood sugar. Your fasting blood sugar would be above 126.

Q. **What are normal glucose values?**
A. A normal glucose value is below 110. It should optimally be below 90 and in women may be 80 or lower.

Q. **Should everyone get regular diabetes screening test?**
A. It is reasonable to screen for diabetes because it is such a common problem.

Q. **How does diabetes affect a person's life?**
A. That depends on the person. I saw a patient this morning who has

had diabetes for twenty years and is doing very well. I saw someone else who checks his blood sugars too often, worries about what he eats, how much he eats, when he eats, when he should run, how long, and which adjustments he must make.

A third patient had been in good health until she was diagnosed with breast cancer. She had a lumpectomy followed by radiation. Several years after that she developed type 2 diabetes. She considers her diabetes a worse problem than the breast cancer.

Q. How can breast cancer be less of a problem than diabetes?
A. People would rather have something bad happen and have it taken care of once and for all. My patient's breast cancer was a problem and something was done. She may do well and she may not, but she doesn't have to do anything but live with the concern. She has to deal with her diabetes every day.

Q. How is diabetes different from other diseases?
A. Diabetes is the most onerous disease. No other condition requires such a high degree of coping by the patient. It affects people on a daily basis. They always have to think about what they eat, how much, when, their exercise, and balancing that with other treatments and checking blood sugars. Diabetes can be managed, but if a patient doesn't take care of herself, she risks terrible complications.

Q. Is the life expectancy of people with diabetes shortened?
A. Yes, if they don't control their diabetes well.

Q. What is the future for people with diabetes?
A. There will be new medicines for type 2 diabetes.

Studies are under way on transplants of islet cells (the cells that make insulin) in the pancreas.

Q. What do you advise women with diabetes who want to live long, healthy lives?
A.
- Take care of your diabetes. If you're not doing well, seek the help of a specialist. You may need to consult a dietitian.

- Have regular eye exams by an ophthalmologist trained in diabetes. This is crucial. Diabetes is the leading cause of blindness in this country. Under the care of a good ophthalmologist, the chance of developing severe visual problems is less than 2 percent. Treatments are available that can prevent or slow the progress of eye disease.
- Blood pressure, cholesterol, and triglycerides (the fats in the blood) must be well controlled because they increase the risk of heart attack and stroke, as does diabetes.
- Don't smoke. Smoking multiplies the risk of complications.
- The microalbumin test, a test for early signs of kidney problems, should be performed annually. Medications can reverse kidney disorders in diabetes if started very early.
- Diabetes is reflected not by how you feel but by your blood sugar numbers. Although you feel good, your diabetes can be out of control.
- The more you learn about diabetes, the more comfortable you will be, and the less you will worry.
- It is bad luck to have diabetes. You didn't cause it, but you have to deal with it and go on with your life. A doctor cannot take care of your diabetes without your cooperation. This disease changes every day. If you don't learn to cope with it efficiently, you will have problems. If you ignore diabetes, it can get you. You can do well with diabetes and live a long life if you have a good understanding of how your body responds to foods, medications, and exercise and if you have the knowledge to control the disease. Your diabetes will never disappear, but you can get the upper hand and live with it successfully.

25

Arthritis and Autoimmune Diseases

Patricia L. Maclay, M.D.

Patricia L. Maclay majored in biology in college. She attended the Medical College of Pennsylvania for two years and completed medical school at Mount Sinai in New York, graduating in 1974. She did an internal medicine internship and residency at Mount Sinai, where she also completed a two-year fellowship in rheumatology. She then went into practice in Pittsburgh, Pennsylvania, and was an associate clinical professor of medicine at the University of Pittsburgh Health Center. In 1992 she moved to Orlando, Florida, where she has implemented the use of the new medical specialty psychoimmunology as an educational model to help people understand stress and its link to disease. Dr. Maclay is currently in private practice in Orlando.

Q. What is the meaning of the word "arthritis"?
A. Arthritis is a Greek word. *Arth* means joint; *itis* denotes inflammation. The literal definition of "arthritis" is joint inflammation. The word "arthritis" is used by the general population for anything that hurts in their musculoskeletal system.

Q. What is the medical definition of arthritis?
A. Arthritis is a change, inflammatory or degenerative ("wear and

tear"), that occurs at the joints and creates swelling, pain, and discomfort. Medically, the term "rheumatology" has a greater spectrum. It covers not only classical osteoarthritis and rheumatoid arthritis but anything that affects the joints, such as ligament problems, bursitis, and tendonitis. It also covers other rheumatologic diseases, such as systemic lupus erythematosus, psoriatic arthritis, and ankylosing spondylitis.

Q. What are rheumatologic diseases?
A. Approximately one hundred diseases fall under the category of rheumatologic diseases. They include any illness that involves the connective tissue of the skeletal system, ranging from autoimmune diseases such as rheumatoid arthritis and systemic lupus erythematosus; degenerative conditions such as osteoarthritis; and metabolic disorders such as gout.

Rheumatologists are specialists who treat all of these diseases. We cover musculoskeletal problems, generalized aches and pains of bursitis and sciatica, and back and neck problems. We also see patients with fibromyalgia.

Q. What is the role of the rheumatologist in treating arthritis and autoimmune diseases?
A. The rheumatologist is the medical counterpart of the orthopedic surgeon, as the cardiologist is the medical counterpart of the cardiac surgeon.

Rheumatologists diagnose and educate patients to better understand and deal with their disease.

Q. What causes rheumatic diseases?
A. The cause of each is different. Arthritis has no specific single etiology. We think there are strong genetic links. Your lifestyle also may affect the development of arthritis.

Q. In what medical category is rheumatoid arthritis?
A. Rheumatoid arthritis is an autoimmune disease.

Q. What is an autoimmune disease?
A. *Auto* means "oneself." *Immune* refers to your immune system. "Autoimmune" means that your body reacts against something that is a part of yourself.

Your immune system is always on guard against substances that are foreign, called antigens. If an antigen enters its surveillance that is partly, but not completely, identical to the body, the immune system will react against it and try to fight it off. If the immune system does not function properly and loses the ability to distinguish between its own cells and the foreign antigen, a cross-fire occurs that includes your body's own cells.

Hypothetically, rheumatoid arthritis may be triggered by a foreign antigen that enters the body—such as part of a bacterium from the intestine that goes into the bloodstream—and leads to the development of "cross-fire" antibodies against itself. This is an example of an autoimmune disease.

Q. How common is rheumatoid arthritis?
A. In the United States about 2.5 million people, or 1 percent of the population, have rheumatoid arthritis. Its onset is predominantly in young or middle-aged people, although children can develop it (juvenile rheumatoid arthritis). The peak incidence is between ages fifteen and forty, but there is another peak in the elderly.

Q. Tell me about rheumatoid arthritis in women, especially those in their fifties.
A. The presence of estrogen may be protective. Postmenopausal women on hormone replacement have a lower incidence of rheumatoid arthritis. It also may protect them against subsequent exacerbation of rheumatoid arthritis.

Q. What are treatments for rheumatoid arthritis?
A. The most important place to start is with education about the disease, diet, and the role stress plays in the cause and continued activity of disease.

We may prescribe medications, such as aspirin and nonsteroidal anti-inflammatory drugs and occasionally prednisone, a corticosteroid.

Drugs that allow patients to go into remission may be given, which include methotrexate, gold, Plaquenil, and the relatively new approach of using antibiotics such as minocycline and tetracycline.

Q. Can rheumatoid arthritis be cured?
A. As of yet, there's no real cure. Remission is a key word in arthritis. Since we don't know the cause of rheumatoid arthritis, a cure probably will be based on a better understanding of the gene, and the role that lifestyle and stress play in allowing diseases to happen.

Q. Tell me about osteoarthritis.
A. *Osteo* means "bones." Osteoarthritis is the most common form of arthritis. Long thought to be due to "wear and tear," we now are understanding the dominant role both the gene and lack of exercise have in allowing what is sometimes referred to as degenerative arthritis to occur. Many people have a genetic predisposition to osteoarthritis, and when coupled with obesity and a sedentary lifestyle, arthritis occurs.

Q. How does osteoarthritis differ from rheumatoid arthritis?
A. Osteoarthritis probably is caused by a genetic predisposition coupled with a lack of exercise and, in some cases, aggravated by obesity. Rheumatoid arthritis probably is the result of genetics and the autoimmune process. Osteoarthritis is a result of cartilage deterioration while rheumatoid arthritis involves an attack on the cartilage by the immune system.

Q. How common is osteoarthritis in women in their fifties?
A. It is very rare for anyone in that age group *not* to have some area of cartilage degeneration—the fingers, thumbs, knees, or hips. Osteoarthritis is also commonly found in the cervical or lumbar spine.

Q. Tell me about the different types of osteoarthritis.
A. There are three types of osteoarthritis: hand and feet, large weight-bearing joints, and the cervical (neck) and lumbar (low back) spine. You can have one, two, or all three types. A person should see a physician regardless of the level of symptoms.

Hand involvement was the first type of osteoarthritis to be documented as genetically associated. It occurs in people as young as twenty to thirty years old.

Q. What type of osteoarthritis is common in women in their fifties?
A. In women at age fifty, we see osteoarthritis at the base of the thumb, the knees if associated with obesity, the cervical and/or lumbar spine, or the feet. Hand involvement is common in this generation of women because of past domestic activities, such as cleaning, wringing wet clothing, and changing diapers.

Osteoarthritis can be caused by injury or repetitive overuse. In the future, it will be interesting to observe which joints will be affected by osteoarthritis as today's young women turn fifty. We will probably see the base of the thumb due to the use of the computer and knee and ankle arthritis as a result of years of running, jogging, and aerobics if done on poor surfaces with inadequate shoes and minimal warmup.

Q. How can osteoarthritis be prevented or the onset delayed?
A. Osteoarthritis can be prevented or delayed with weight control and exercise. It has its greatest predisposition in the knees of overweight women. Exercise strengthens the muscles that control the joints, thereby allowing cartilage repair and preservation.

Q. Is it okay to ignore the symptoms of osteoarthritis if you can bear the pain?
A. No. The body is a wonderfully fine-tuned instrument. Any signal from the body, especially pain, is critically important and should not be ignored.

Pain is a warning sign, a red light. Your body is telling you to stop and pay attention. An aching back, knees, or hand is abnormal. Ask your physician to evaluate it. Once you have a diagnosis, you can get information from books or the Internet that will help you understand the disease and find ways to reverse it or at least prevent its progression.

Q. How can the pain of osteoarthritis be controlled?
A. We first teach people about diet, weight control, and an exercise

program. The more protected the joint is by a strong muscle, the better patients feel. The association between reducing stress and the reduction in the perception of pain is critically important also.

Topical analgesics may reduce pain. Oral analgesics also might be prescribed. Patients must be careful because aspirin and nonsteroidal-based medications can irritate the stomach. We may give narcotic analgesics for severe pain, when the patient isn't ready for surgery. Steroids are sometimes given by injection to allow a more immediate relief, although this is not a permanent effect.

Q. What is systemic lupus erythematosus (lupus)?
A. Lupus is an autoimmune disease in which antibodies attack a part of the cell, especially the cell nuclei throughout the body. Lupus patients often present with a myriad of signs and symptoms. Three of the most common symptoms are fever, rash, and arthritis. Often associated with sun exposure, the rash commonly occurs in areas of the skin most often exposed to sunlight. The classic area involved is the face, where the rash takes on the appearance of a butterfly across the upper cheek, below the eyes, and across the bridge of the nose (malar rash). There also may be a diffuse red rash, hair loss, and oral ulcers. Other symptoms can include stiffness, joint swelling, and fatigue, at times severe. Inflammation of the lining of the heart (pericarditis) and lungs (pleuritis) can cause tremendous pain. The most serious areas of lupus involvement are renal (kidney), which can lead to renal failure, and central nervous system.

Q. Who gets systemic lupus erythematosus?
A. Lupus is usually diagnosed in young and middle-aged women— five females to every one male. Lupus is unusual in menopausal women, although they may present with this disease as a side effect of certain medications used to treat hypertension, unusual heart rhythms, or tuberculosis. Some lipid-lowering drugs cause symptoms that mimic or actually cause SLE. When the drug is removed, most patients get better.

Q. What is the treatment for lupus?
A. The treatment regimen for lupus is similar to that for rheumatoid

arthritis, but we depend more on corticosteroids and immunosuppressant drugs.

Q. Tell me about gout.
A. Gout is a metabolic form of arthritis. (Metabolic refers to the physical and chemical processes by which the human body produces substances and energy.) In gout, the body is unable to remove uric acid. When uric acid reaches a certain concentration, it begins to precipitate or form needlelike crystals in the tissue. The crystals are very irritating to the body. The arthritis is usually in the lower extremities—the toes and the ankles—because those are the areas in the body that are most acidic. When the crystals form, the immune system recognizes them as abnormal and starts the attack. When the immune cells begin to eat up (phagocytize) these needles of uric acid, the cells break apart, causing local inflammation. Gout usually affects the great toe and is called podagra. Ben Franklin had gout.

Gout is predominately a male disease but occurs in equal numbers in genetically predisposed postmenopausal women.

The symptoms of gout are swelling, redness, and pain so intense that many people can't wear a sock or have bed clothing touch their swollen toe.

Q. How do you treat gout?
A. Diet is very important because gout is caused by a buildup of uric acid. Uric acid is a breakdown product of purine, an amino acid found in certain foods. Both red and white meats (especially organ meats), beer, wine, and certain types of fish with high levels of purine should be avoided.

Certain anti-inflammatory drugs may be prescribed, especially indomethacin. Other medications can put the disease into remission. Different drugs stop the production of uric acid (allopurinol), accelerate the excretion of uric acid (Benemid) from the urine, or curtail the activity of the disease (colchicine). These medications may be given in combination with one another.

Q. Tell me about fibromyalgia.
A. Fibromyalgia is an illness that presents with multiple areas of body

aches and pains in all four quadrants of the body. It is predominantly a disease of women.

Patients experience many of the following symptoms: fatigue, disturbed sleep patterns, stiffness, mitral valve prolapse, TMJ (temporomandibular joint dysfunction), migraine and muscle tension headaches, irritable bowel and irritable bladder syndrome, sensitivity to the environment, difficulty with cognitive function, and reduced memory. Research involving this disease has shown low blood serotonin levels, high P substance (the substance that has been associated with the occurrence of pain), and difficulty with basic parasympathetic nervous system function (balance and dizziness). These symptoms seem to reflect abnormalities in the autonomic nervous system thought to be one reason, hypothetically, for disease occurrence.

Q. How common is fibromyalgia?
A. Fibromyalgia has been found to occur in as high as 15 percent of the population in a rheumatology practice and 5.7 percent in the general medical practice, but it is probably *under*diagnosed.

Q. How common is fibromyalgia in women in their fifties?
A. It is very common at menopause, probably because of the significant stress that can occur during this transitional phase of life.

Q. How do you treat a patient who presents with symptoms indicating fibromyalgia?
A. First, I make sure she has no other disease. The multiple symptoms of fibromyalgia can be misdiagnosed as an endocrine abnormality or an autoimmune disease. Patients with fibromyalgia may go from one doctor to another. They are often mislabeled as neurotic, psychotic, or depressed.

When a diagnosis of fibromyalgia is verified, although medications can be prescribed, the most important step is education about the disease and the critical role the individual has in dealing with the disease.

The field of medicine has no specific answer for patients with fibromyalgia, although research is beginning to strongly implicate prolonged stress and the negative effect it has on the autonomic nervous system leading to disease development.

Q. What is your hope for the future of arthritis and autoimmune diseases?
A. Arthritis research will alter disease occurrence and outcome in the future. The results of gene research will play vital roles in these changes, especially those of genetic manipulation and vaccine production.

Data supporting the role of weight control and exercise in preventing arthritis continue to be published. That walking significantly improves osteoarthritis of the knee is now accepted.

Research in surgical replacement is exciting. Joint, hip, and shoulder replacements will continue to improve. Artificial joints in which the bone grows into the joint prosthesis will create a stronger bond that will last a lifetime, we hope.

Q. What is your advice to women in their fifties who have arthritis or autoimmune diseases who want to live long, healthy, pain-free lives?
A.
- Get a diagnosis.
- Ask questions and understand everything you can about your disease.
- Exercise. It helps with weight loss, strengthens muscle around the joints, and enhances overall wellness.
- If you're overweight, plan and carry out a gradual weight reduction program.
- Eat a proper diet, regardless of your weight. Understand the negative effects that fat, sugars, and refined carbohydrates have on your health.
- Seek sources of support. Don't be afraid to allow someone to help you.
- Investigate the opposite roles that stress (negative) and spirituality (positive) play on your health.
- Don't let arthritis stop you. Do everything you can to get back into total wellness.

Q. What is your philosophy about women in their fifties?
A. These are the richest years of our lives. Women in their fifties often have a wealth of knowledge and ability. In maturity, we have a greater understanding of life. Although we may experience problems, maturity in spirit, mind, and body allows us to overcome stress, to deal with problems, and to achieve the lifelong goal of wellness.

SECTION V

Preventive Health Strategies

26

Preventive Health Strategies

Deborah Rhodes, M.D.

Deborah Rhodes's college major was history/literature. After graduation from Cornell University Medical College in 1992, she did an internal medicine internship and residency at the Johns Hopkins Hospital in Baltimore, where she also worked for two years as a Robert Wood Johnson Clinical Scholars fellow. In 1997 Dr. Rhodes joined the staff of the Mayo Clinic in Rochester, Minnesota, where she is a senior associate consultant, dividing her time between general internal medicine and the Breast Clinic.

Q. How often should a healthy woman in her fifties get a medical checkup?
A. Every healthy woman in her fifties should get a medical checkup once a year, but she doesn't necessarily need a complete physical.

Q. Which screening tests should she undergo that could save or prolong her life?
A. There are a handful of diseases for which regular screening is effective and actually reduces the incidence of illness and death. Those include tests for cervical cancer, breast cancer, colon cancer, hypertension, and high cholesterol.

Q. What about diseases that don't have screening methods?
A. Unfortunately, for most diseases, screening tests either are not available or are not effective. Diseases for which no effective screening

method exists usually are diagnosed only after the patient develops symptoms, prompting the doctor to perform specialized tests that will lead to diagnosis.

There are some special-case scenarios in which screening for certain diseases is helpful in select women, but not in all women. For example, women with obesity, a history of gestational diabetes, a family history of diabetes, or who are in a high-risk ethnic group (such as Native Americans, Hispanics, and African Americans) would probably benefit from annual screening for diabetes (with a blood test for fasting glucose). As another example, women with a strong family history of ovarian cancer should be screened with ultrasonography every year beginning at age twenty-five or five years earlier than the earliest onset in a relative. Note, however, that familial ovarian cancer accounts for only 5 to 10 percent of all cases.

Recommended Screening Tests and Procedures for Women in Their Fifties

Annual Exams and Screening Tests
- *Blood pressure, weight, height, and breast exam*
- *Pelvic exam* (including rectal exam)
- *Pap smears* should be done annually if the woman has had more than two sex partners in her lifetime; if her age at first intercourse was less than eighteen; if she has a history of a sexually transmitted disease; if she has had abnormal Pap smears in the past; or if she smokes. If she has none of these risk factors and she has had at least two normal Pap smears in the past, she can have Pap smears every two to three years. Patients who have had hysterectomies with removal of the cervix still need annual pelvic examinations but do not need to have Pap smears.
- *Mammogram*
- *Skin cancer check*—a thorough skin exam for suspicious moles.
- *Counseling* on diet and exercise, substance abuse, safe sex practices, injury prevention, and smoking cessation (if relevant).

Every Three to Five Years Beginning at Age Fifty
- *Colon cancer screening* with either flexible sigmoidoscopy plus barium enema *or* colonoscopy. Note that flexible sigmoidoscopy should

be combined with a barium enema in order to achieve thorough screening for colon cancer.

Every Five Years
- *Cholesterol level* (including total cholesterol, LDL, HDL, and triglycerides)

Baseline Value at Age Fifty; Repeat at Age Sixty
- *TSH* (a test of thyroid function)
- *Hearing and vision screen* (including glaucoma check). Note: This recommendation is for women who have no known hearing or vision problems; any woman with known problems should have a hearing and vision test every year; it is essential for diabetics or patients with known glaucoma to have yearly eye exams.
- *Urinalysis:* This is a matter of controversy; many physicians do not believe that routine urinalyses are very useful. Urinalyses can be used to test for protein in the urine (an early sign of kidney dysfunction), blood in the urine (a sign of kidney dysfunction or of kidney/bladder cancer), and bacteria in the urine (a sign of urinary tract infection, which may not be causing any symptoms).
- *Hematocrit* (a test for anemia): This is my personal bias; many physicians do not obtain routine hematocrits, but I feel that as a women enters menopause, it is reasonable to test for iron deficiency anemia, to make sure that the years of menstrual blood loss have not caused depletion of her iron stores.

Once at Age Fifty
- *Tetanus-diphtheria booster* (or immediately after a skin-puncturing wound if the woman cannot recall whether she had a tetanus-diphtheria booster at age fifty)

Once at Age Sixty-five and Then Every Year Thereafter
- *Influenza vaccine:* A new vaccine is designed each year to protect against those strains of influenza virus that are likely to be prevalent during the coming flu season. All women age sixty-five and older should receive this vaccine on an annual basis, as should all younger women with chronic lung disease, such as asthma and emphysema, heart disease, diabetes, renal disease, liver disease, or

immunosuppression, such as from cancer, steroids, or another cause. Anyone who works or lives in a health care or chronic care facility should have the influenza vaccine every year.

Once at Age Sixty-five

- *Pneumococcal vaccine:* This vaccine protects against a common type of pneumonia. For healthy women, this vaccine should be given once at age sixty-five. Women with certain chronic conditions should receive the vaccine at age fifty and then every six years thereafter. This includes women with chronic lung disease, such as asthma and emphysema, heart disease, diabetes, renal disease, liver disease, alcoholism, sickle cell disease, absence of a spleen, or immunosuppression, such as from cancer, steroids, or another cause.

Q. Who officially makes recommendations for preventive health care?
A. There are many sources for recommendations on the type and frequency of tests for preventive care and health maintenance. Furthermore, different sources often disagree as to the most appropriate frequency and type of preventive care. I tried to include the recommendations for which there is a broad consensus. The main sources of my recommendations were the American Cancer Society; the American Heart Association Postmenopausal Health Curriculum; R. L. Byyny and L. Speroff, *A Clinical Guide for the Care of Older Women: Primary and Preventive Care* (2nd ed) (Baltimore, MD: Williams and Wilkins, 1996); the Canadian Task Force on the Periodic Health Examination, *Clinical Preventive Health Care* (Ottawa: Canada Communications Group, 1994); and the Report of the U.S. Preventive Services Task Force, *Guide to Clinical Preventive Services,* U.S. Department of Health and Human Services, 1996.

Q. Tell me about heart disease in women over fifty.
A. Heart disease is the most common cause of death in women over fifty. It is essential that they reduce their heart disease risk factors.

Q. What are some heart disease risk factors?
A. Heart disease risk factors include increased age, premature meno-

pause without hormone replacement, high blood pressure, high cholesterol, smoking, obesity, diabetes, a family history of heart disease, and race—the incidence of cardiovascular disease is higher in African American women than in white women.

Q. Tell me about cancer in women.
A. It has been estimated that over half of cancers in women are related to lifestyle factors such as smoking, obesity, diet, infectious diseases, reproduction, and sexual behavior. Although many women fear breast cancer, lung cancer is more common. In 1995 over 24 percent of cancer deaths in women were from lung cancer compared to 18 percent from breast cancer, 11 percent from colon cancer, 5.6 percent from ovarian cancer, and 4.1 percent from uterine/cervical cancer.

Q. How can women prevent cancer?
A. They can prevent cancer by having an annual pelvic exam and Pap smear, breast exam, and mammogram; doing a monthly breast self-examination; getting a regular colon screening; avoiding the sun; or applying sunscreen when outdoors; eating a low-fat diet with limited red meat and lots of high-fiber foods; drinking moderate amounts of alcohol; and controlling their weight.

Q. Tell me more about vaccines.
A. If a woman has never had chicken pox, she should receive the varicella virus. This is a relatively new vaccine that is given in two injections administered one to two months apart. This vaccine protects against chicken pox, which can be a far more serious disease in adults than it typically is in children.

Hepatitis A vaccine is needed only if she travels to developing countries.

Hepatitis B is recommended if a woman is exposed to blood products or participates in high-risk personal behaviors such as multiple sexual partners.

Q. Are women in their fifties at risk for sexually transmitted diseases (STDs)?
A. Yes. Many women in this age group are divorced, separated, or

widowed and may have new sexual relationships. Older women are at risk for STDs just as is any woman with a new sexual partner. These women must use condoms and should be wise about their choices of sexual partners. However, we do not normally screen for sexually transmitted diseases in this age group.

Q. What are the most common sexually transmitted diseases?
A. Sexually transmitted diseases include gonorrhea, chlamydia, syphilis, genital herpes, genital warts, and HIV (human immunodeficiency virus), the AIDS (acquired immunodeficiency syndrome) virus.

Q. Tell me about gonorrhea, chlamydia, syphilis, genital herpes, and genital warts.
A. Gonorrhea is caused by a bacterium. Gonorrhea may cause a thick, puslike discharge from the vagina and urethra and/or painful urination, but it also may be totally asymptomatic. Gonorrhea causes an acute infection of the pelvic organs that may become chronic if not treated. It can spread through the bloodstream, resulting in fever, rash, and joint pain. Women in their fifties would most likely be tested only if they have symptoms or if they have had multiple sexual partners. Gonorrhea is diagnosed by taking a culture of the cervix. It can be treated with antibiotics. There are usually no long-term consequences if it is promptly and adequately treated.

Chlamydia, also caused by a bacterium, may have no associated symptoms, or it may cause painful urination and/or vaginal discharge. Chlamydia causes inflammation and infection of the pelvic organs. It can be treated with antibiotics. Women in their fifties would most likely be tested only if they have symptoms or if they have had multiple sexual partners.

Syphilis is caused by a spirochete. In the first stage, symptoms include painless sores on the genitals. In the second stage, a rash may develop anywhere on the body, but especially on the palms of the hands and soles of the feet. Headache, fever, and joint pain are also common in this stage. The last stage results in widespread infection, often including the brain. Syphilis can be completely cured if diagnosis is made early and treatment is adequate. Any postmenopausal woman with unexplained gait disorder or other neurologic symptoms (such as early dementia) should be tested for syphilis.

Genital herpes is caused by the herpesvirus (usually type 2). Symptoms include pain, itching, and blisters or open sores in the genital area. Blisters form, rupture, and then begin to heal after three to four days. The virus then lies dormant in the infected areas. In most cases, the virus periodically reactivates, especially in times of stress, causing a new outbreak of blisters. The virus is extremely contagious whenever blisters are present. Herpes generally does not cause any long-term complications in postmenopausal women. The frequency and severity of outbreaks can be lessened with medications such as acyclovir.

Genital warts are caused by human papillomavirus (HPV). Symptoms include venereal warts that often resemble warts elsewhere on the skin. These warts are not always apparent. Both men and women may be infected with HPV and have no symptoms or visible warts, and so may unwittingly transmit the infection to their partners. HPV can be deadly to women. While most strains of the virus cause warts that are no more harmful than warts on the skin, some strains of the virus actually can lead to cervical cancer. In fact, most cases of cervical cancer are believed to be related to HPV infection. Treatment includes removing the warts with cryotherapy or laser therapy. For women with high-risk strains of HPV, frequent pelvic exams and Pap smears are essential.

AIDS is a disease of the immune system caused by HIV (human immunodeficiency virus). HIV can be transmitted through four main body fluids: blood, semen, vaginal fluids, and breast milk. Transmission can take place through sexual contact (oral, anal, or vaginal), direct blood contact (for example, through the sharing of needles contaminated with infected blood), mother to child (during pregnancy, delivery, or breast feeding), or blood transfusions. The virus causes progressive impairment of the body's defenses against infections. Symptoms of infection may include persistent fever, night sweats, weight loss, enlargement of lymph nodes, and chronic cough and shortness of breath. Although new medications offer hope for improved quality and duration of life for people infected with HIV, AIDS is generally a fatal disease.

251

Q. Tell me about osteoporosis prevention.

A. Certain risk factors increase a woman's risk of osteoporosis. They include declining estrogen levels, race (white women are at higher risk than Asians or African Americans), family history (a mother or grandmother with the disease), diet (if you rarely included milk products or calcium supplements when you were younger), heavy alcohol consumption, smoking, a sedentary lifestyle, body composition (very thin women or those who have had eating disorders), medications such as heparin (a blood thinner), anticonvulsants, steroids, some thyroid medications, and chemotherapy.

Postmenopausal women who have significant risk factors for or symptoms of osteoporosis should have a bone density scan.

Many insurance companies will not pay for routine baseline bone density scans unless there is a specific indication (such as a fracture or many risk factors for osteoporosis). I think women should have a baseline bone density scan at around age fifty to help them in their decision as to whether to take estrogen and to enable them to get appropriate treatment if their bone density is low. However, if their insurance company will not cover it, this may not be possible. If they're going to take estrogen regardless of the results of the bone density scan, many physicians would argue that the scan is not necessary.

Q. Tell me about asthma. Does it develop as late as the fifties?

A. Asthma is a lung disease in which inflammation and hyperreactivity of the trachea and bronchioles cause the airway to narrow. Asthma can develop for the first time in adulthood. While it typically presents as wheezing and shortness of breath, it also may present as a cough that won't go away. Anti-inflammatory medicines, such as steroid inhalers, usually relieve the symptoms.

Q. What is emphysema?

A. Emphysema is a chronic, obstructive lung disease, usually caused by smoking, which results in destruction of the terminal portions of the lung.

Q. Tell me about vaginal problems.
A. Aging and the loss of estrogen can cause atrophy of the vaginal tissues, which may result in itching, inflammation, and painful intercourse. Sex does not make this problem worse. In fact, sexual activity can increase the circulation of the vaginal tissues. Sexually active women in their fifties often experience less atrophy of the vagina.

Q. How does loss of estrogen affect the urinary tract?
A. Loss of estrogen and age can cause the urethra and bladder walls to thin, which can result in inflammation, painful urination, incontinence, and urinary tract infections.

Q. Tell me about incontinence.
A. The most common type of incontinence is called stress incontinence, in which pressure on the bladder from coughing, sneezing, laughing, or jumping up suddenly causes loss of urine. A second type, urge incontinence, is an immediate, sudden need to urinate—the woman feels as if she can't hold her urine long enough to get to the bathroom. The third type, overflow incontinence, is a constant dribbling of urine due to an inability to completely empty her bladder. Some women suffer with a combination of the three types of incontinence.

Q. What are common causes of incontinence?
A. Excess weight, frequent constipation, or childbirth can weaken pelvic floor muscles, leading to incontinence. Decreased estrogen levels can cause weakening of the urinary sphincter muscle and thinning of the urethral lining (reducing bladder support). In addition, some diseases, such as diabetes, Parkinson's, stroke, and multiple sclerosis (MS), can damage nerves that control the bladder, leading to incontinence. Some medications (diuretics, anticholinergic medicines) also can cause incontinence.

Q. How can a woman prevent or cure incontinence?
A. She can lose weight, prevent constipation with a high-fiber diet, and strengthen her pelvic floor muscles with Kegel exercises.

Q. What are Kegel exercises?
A. A Kegel exercise is accomplished by squeezing the pelvic floor muscles, the same muscles used to stop passing gas. In a Kegel, the woman tightens those muscles for a count of three, relaxes for a count of three, and repeats for five minutes, ideally three times a day. These exercises, done regularly, can strengthen a woman's pelvic floor muscles and help to prevent or relieve incontinence.

Q. Tell me about other measures to cure incontinence if these don't work.
A. Certain medications can reduce or eliminate incontinence. Bulking agents can be injected into the urethra to increase resistance to urine flow. If nothing else works, surgery can eliminate the problem.

Q. Let's talk about the physician. What should a woman in her fifties look for in a physician?
A. Women in this age group should have an internist or a family practitioner instead of or in addition to her gynecologist, who is board certified and experienced in the care of menopausal and postmenopausal women. This physician should have a good bedside manner and be comfortable discussing a range of possibly difficult issues.

Q. Is the physician's affiliation with a women's center an advantage?
A. Affiliation with a women's center may be a logistical advantage—may allow a woman to get her exam, lab tests, and mammogram done at the same visit—but the physician's competence and sense of caring for patients is of primary importance.

Q. When is it appropriate for a woman to get a second opinion after consulting her physician?
A. A woman should get a second opinion if a screening test is abnormal, yet her physician has a wait-and-see attitude.

She should get a second opinion if surgery is recommended.

Any unexplained symptom that her doctor cannot diagnose deserves a second opinion.

A diagnosis of cancer may require a second opinion, particularly with regard to treatment options.

A woman should get a second opinion if she is diagnosed with advanced cancer and her physician says there's nothing more he or she can do or if she recommends an experimental treatment.

Finally, a second opinion is appropriate if she doesn't feel comfortable with that of her physician.

Q. What do you advise women in their fifties who want to keep healthy?
A. I will answer by quoting from the *Mayo Clinic Women's Healthsource* (August 1997, vol. 1, no. 7). The newsletter asked Mayo Clinic physicians to give their opinions on growing older healthfully and to reveal what they did personally to improve the length and quality of their lives. The top five recommendations were:

1. Exercise, exercise, exercise.
2. Don't smoke. If you do, quit.
3. Take hormone-replacement therapy (HRT) after menopause (unless you have a medical condition for which HRT is not recommended).
4. Exercise your mind.
5. Enjoy life. Have fun. Love someone.

27

Dietary Behaviors That May Protect Your Health

Katherine Tucker, Ph.D.

Katherine Tucker's college major was nutrition. After graduation in 1978, she joined the Peace Corps, where she worked with undernourished mothers and children in the Philippines. In 1981 she returned to the United States to earn her Ph.D. in international nutrition, which she completed in 1986. She then joined the faculty at McGill University in Montreal, where she taught nutrition for three years. In 1989 Dr. Tucker moved to the School of Nutrition at Tufts University in Boston, where she is currently an associate professor of nutritional epidemiology.

Q. What is good nutrition?
A. A formal definition of good nutrition would be a state of optimal balance in the consumption and utilization of nutrients. But it's more than that. We now include body conditioning and exercise in our definition. So it's really having your body performing optimally by consuming the right foods and maintaining a balance in your energy metabolism through physical activity.

Q. How can someone put together a healthful diet?
A. They can follow the United States Department of Agriculture (USDA) Food Guide Pyramid and Dietary Guidelines.

Q. Tell me about the Food Guide Pyramid.
A. Twenty years ago the food intake recommendations were based on four major food groups—meat, dairy, fruits and vegetables, and grains. There was lot more emphasis on meat and milk.

The Food Guide Pyramid is now focused more on fruits and vegetables, fiber, and grains, and it also suggests quantities. The USDA recommends three to five daily servings of vegetables and two to four servings of fruits. Six to eleven servings of breads, cereals, rice, and pasta per day are the base of the pyramid. Meat and dairy products are included but in limited amounts.

Q. Why is the emphasis away from meats and dairy products?
A. The primary reason is because these foods are high in saturated fat.

Q. What is bad about high intakes of saturated fat?
A. Many studies have shown that high intakes of saturated fat are related to risks of heart disease and possibly colon cancer.

Q. How can women, especially women in their fifties, get enough calcium in their diet and keep saturated fats to a minimum?
A. Women should have three to five servings of dairy products a day. They can limit the high-fat dairy by drinking skim milk, a really good source of calcium, and eating low-fat yogurt. Part of the solution is acquiring a taste for skim milk and low-fat or nonfat yogurt. There are also low-fat cheeses in the grocery stores, although they are less popular. Nondairy sources of calcium include tofu, sardines, and some green leafy vegetables.

Q. How does saturated fat increase the risk of heart disease?
A. A diet high in saturated fat can lead to an accumulation of plaque in the arteries. Plaque is a lipid (fat) material that collects on a lesion in the artery. It narrows the arteries and increases the formation of blood clots, which causes heart disease.

Q. What about the link between saturated fat and colon cancer?
A. The colon cancer data are less clear. The link seems to be between high fat intakes and slow transit time. The hypothesis is that if you've

got a high fat intake, the food sits in your intestine longer and inter-acts to form compounds that can negatively affect your colon.

Q. Are you implying that chronic constipation is harmful to colonic health?
A. Yes. That's another reason to eat a high-fiber diet—fruits and vege-tables and grains with fiber. You want to keep things regular. Regular-ity can become a problem as we get older.

Q. Tell me about fiber.
A. There are two main types of fiber—soluble and insoluble fiber. Soluble fiber, found in oats, apples, and other fruits, gets into the blood and can protect against heart disease. Insoluble fiber, found in wheat bran, tends to protect against colon cancer. It is better to ingest fiber from food than from supplements.

Q. What are trans fats?
A. Trans fats in our diets come largely from hydrogenated fats, which are oils that have been chemically altered to be more solid at room temperature. The chemical structure of hydrogenated fat is different from that of most naturally occurring fats. Margarine and shortening are examples of trans fats.

Q. What about margarine?
A. With the movement away from saturated fats, nutritionists told people to use margarine. Margarine is made by hydrogenating polyun-saturated oils. Hydrogen is added to make them more saturated. Trans fats act like saturated fats, so new evidence suggests that you're not doing much better by eating hard margarine. If you choose margarine, use the soft tub, which has less of the trans fats. The liquid margarines are even better. Current recommendations are to try to avoid both saturated fat and trans fat as much as possible.

Q. Are there hidden trans fats that people might not realize?
A. Yes. French fries are an example of a hidden source of trans fats. Many if not most fast-food restaurants cook French fries in hydroge-nated oil. Other hidden trans fats are in crackers and snack foods.

Those could be problems when people are trying to cut their saturated fats.

Q. What is the goal of fat in the diet?
A. The guideline is to stay below 30 percent of calories from total fat, to keep the saturated fats below 10 percent, and to balance polyunsaturated, monounsaturated, and saturated fats. We don't usually have to worry about a minimum level of fat in the diet—in the United States we're far above the minimum levels.

Q. Many studies have shown that high homocysteine levels are strongly related to heart disease. What is homocysteine?
A. Homocysteine is an amino acid that is an intermediate product of normal metabolic processes. Homocysteine occurs as a result of the metabolism of methionine (another amino acid) from protein in our diets. Normally homocysteine is transformed into harmless substances. But if there is a deficiency of folic acid (folate), vitamin B-12, or vitamin B-6, the pathways that metabolize homocysteine are interrupted, causing an accumulation of homocysteine.

Q. How do high levels of homocysteine cause heart disease?
A. The mechanisms aren't completely defined but the associations are very clear. High levels of homocysteine in the blood appear to promote the accumulation of plaque in the arteries and cause damage to the artery wall.

Q. Which foods in our diet contain folate, vitamin B-6, and vitamin B-12?
A. Cereal, particularly breakfast cereals, fruits, and vegetables are the best sources of folate and vitamin B-6. Vitamin B-12 is in all animal products. However, many older people have difficulty absorbing the vitamin B-12 found in foods. Taking a B-complex supplement is therefore a good idea for people over fifty.

Q. What is the recommended daily allowance (RDA) for folate, vitamin B-6, and vitamin B-12?
A. Current RDAs for women ages fifty-one and over are 180 micro-

grams folate, 1.6 milligrams B-6, and 2.0 micrograms B-12. However, based on recent research the new RDAs will be higher. At least 400 micrograms folate will be recommended.

Q. If you follow a diet with high meat and fat intake and low fruit-vegetable-grain intake, it seems that you're at risk for heart disease for two reasons simultaneously.
A. Yes. According to the Food Guide Pyramid, you don't want to have really high meat or saturated fat intake. And you should have very high fruit and vegetable consumption. The increased risk of heart disease is multicausal.

Q. Some studies claim that monounsaturated fats such as olive oil are good for one's health. How did that come about?
A. Years ago it was recommended that people avoid saturated fat by switching to highly polyunsaturated fats, such as safflower oil. However, research showed that while such fats lowered total cholesterol, they also lowered the HDL (the good cholesterol). It was observed that people in sections of Europe where the rates of heart disease were much lower than in the United States, consumed much more olive oil than we do here. That's when the Mediterranean diet came into vogue. Studies then done in the United States and elsewhere revealed that higher proportions of olive oil reduce total cholesterol without such a reduction of HDL; therefore, olive oil is more protective of the heart.

Q. If olive oil is good for your heart, should people add it to their diet?
A. Yes, it's better to use olive oil in cooking, on vegetables, and in salad dressing. All of that is good in moderation, but you shouldn't feel free to increase your total fat by adding olive oil. You still have to work on reducing your fat intake.

Q. What are some other differences in the Mediterranean diet that are protective against the risk of heart disease?
A. The Mediterranean diet includes less meat, more fruits, vegetables, and grains, and more wine.

Q. What about alcohol to prevent heart disease?
A. Moderate drinking seems to protect against heart disease. People who imbibe tend to have slightly better lipid profiles, particularly higher HDL. The current recommendation is no more than one daily glass of wine for women and two glasses for men. Red wine seems to be especially protective because it contains a phytochemical called res-versital, found in the skin of the grape. It is not found in white wine. (*Phyto* means plant. Phytochemicals appear to protect our health in a variety of ways which we are just beginning to learn about.) Of course, too much alcohol is harmful and therefore the recommendation is that if you do drink, do so in moderation.

Q. What is your take on substitute fats such as Otrim and Z-Trim?
A. Research suggests that substitute fats like Otrim, which contains soluble fiber, can help to lower blood lipids under controlled conditions. However, we don't know how it will work in general use or about other potential effects. Z-Trim, which is made with insoluble fiber, is newer and is currently being tested. We still need more research.

Q. What about fake fats such as Olestra?
A. Olestra is very controversial. We don't know enough about it yet. There are side effects, such as bloating and abdominal pain. More serious, fat substitutes absorb and bind the fat-soluble nutrients in the diet, including the carotenoids and some other phytochemicals. Those are the very factors that may be protective against heart disease and cancer. Their loss is of great concern.

More than that, fat substitutes in the diet have not been shown to help with weight loss. Some people believe that since they are nonfat, they can eat more of them. Replacing high-fat junk food with nonfat junk food doesn't solve the problem. These are not nutrient-rich foods. They usually contain high amounts of sugar. They may be fat-free, but they may still have a lot of calories.

Q. What do you think about sugar in the diet?
A. There's nothing wrong with sugar in itself. It's a natural food. It's fine in moderation. Sugar provides pure energy, but it doesn't contrib-

ute other nutrients. If you eat lots of pastries, you're getting fat and sugar, high calories and low nutrients. If you're eating candy, you're getting lots of sugar but essentially no other nutrients.

Q. Tell me about the salt in the diet.
A. Studies on salt have been inconsistent, but it seems that salt intake contributes to high blood pressure in some, but not all, persons. If you have high blood pressure, I would recommend limiting your salt. There is plenty of sodium already in our food supply and no need to add salt from the salt shaker. Salty snacks and processed foods are other major sources to watch. Fortunately, sodium content is listed on food labels.

Q. Are there bad foods?
A. There are no bad foods. I would not recommend excluding any foods from your diet. The key is to practice portion control and to limit the frequency of use of high-fat, low-nutrient foods.

Q. Isn't fish a better choice than red meat?
A. Yes, fish is generally a better choice than red meat. Fish contains omega-3 fatty acids, which have been shown to reduce the clotting that leads to arterial plaque formation. But it's fine to eat a little red meat, in small portions and limited frequency. Red meat provides iron, which you don't get from fish.

Q. If fish oils are protective, should people take supplementary fish oil pills?
A. That is an individual decision. We don't yet have enough evidence to be sure that the benefits of supplementation outweigh any unidentified risks. It is possible to take too much from pills, while this is unlikely from diet.

Q. Why is variety so important in the diet?
A. Because there are different beneficial nutrients and different potential toxins in different foods. It's not good to go on any diet where you eat all the same things. For example, toxic minerals such as mercury can concentrate in certain types of fish. Aflatoxin contamination can

be present in peanut butter. In small amounts these aren't dangerous. If you eat a variety of foods you get a variety of nutrients and you'll avoid the intensity of any toxin, including those we don't yet understand.

Q. How can vegetarians get a well-rounded diet?
A. It depends on the kind of vegetarian. Ovolacto vegetarians get complete protein from eggs, milk, and other dairy products. Iron is a nutrient to be concerned about, however.

Strict vegetarians, who do not consume any animal products, should be careful. The old recommendation for balancing the amino acids can help. Soy products, such as tofu, dried beans and peas, peanuts, and peanut butter, eaten with whole grains can cover most protein requirements. Supplementation with iron, vitamin B-12, calcium, and vitamin D is important.

Q. What about older vegetarians?
A. It's important for older vegetarians to get adequate protein and vitamin B-12. With aging, protein requirements seem to go up. Both exercise and adequate protein are important to protect against loss of lean body mass.

Q. What is the worst thing that people do in terms of their diet?
A. The worst thing they do is to go on extreme diets, where they're eating only a few foods or eliminating entire categories of food. They can create dietary imbalances or even serious health problems.

Q. What is your recommendation for dietary behaviors that may protect a woman's health?
A.
- Eat a balanced diet.
- Eat a variety of foods.
- Limit intake of meat, high-fat desserts, high-fat dairy products, soft drinks, and candy, but don't try to be extreme. Splurge occasionally with small portions of the foods you really love.
- The more fruits and vegetables and whole grains, the better for protection from heart disease and cancer.

- Use skim milk and low-fat dairy products. Supplements to consider include calcium and vitamin D to protect against bone loss and osteoporosis, vitamin B-12 to protect against neurologic deterioration, and possibly vitamin E. For those without specific medical conditions, a good multivitamin for seniors may offer protection but should never be considered a substitute for a good diet.

28

Nutrition and Changing RDAs: Vitamins, Minerals, Supplements, Antioxidants

Jeffrey Blumberg, Ph.D., F.A.C.N.

Jeffrey Blumberg received his undergraduate degrees in pharmacy and psychology. He completed his Ph.D. in pharmacology in 1974 at the Vanderbilt University School of Medicine and did postdoctoral training in biochemistry at the University of Calgary in Alberta, Canada. He began his academic career at Northeastern University in Boston, where he worked in pharmacology and toxicology. Dr. Blumberg moved to Tufts University in 1981, where he is now professor of nutrition, chief of the Antioxidants Research Laboratory, and associate director at the Jean Mayer USDA Human Nutrition Research Center on Aging.

Q. What is the mission of the Jean Mayer USDA Human Nutrition Research Center on Aging?
A. The mission of the Jean Mayer USDA Human Nutrition Research Center on Aging, a federally funded agency jointly contracted by the United States Department of Agriculture and Tufts University, is to study the role of nutrition in the aging process. This effort is already providing important new information useful for defining specific dietary allowances for older adults and revealing the ways in which our

265

diet can promote health and longevity. This is the only such center in the world.

Q. Tell me about Recommended Daily Allowances (RDAs).
A. The Food and Nutrition Board of the Institute of Medicine develops the RDAs. They were created to recommend minimal amounts of essential nutrients needed to prevent deficiency diseases. But deficiencies such as scurvy, beri-beri, and pellagra are no longer public health problems in this country, nor in most of the developed world. The greatest health challenge we face is the growing prevalence of chronic diseases common to older adults—for example, heart disease, cancer, osteoporosis, age-related dementias, and visual impairment due to cataract and macular degeneration. These are diseases that people worry about, and with good reason. Even when these conditions don't kill (and heart disease and cancer are the leading causes of death among Americans), they significantly diminish the quality of life. What we really need to do—and scientists are doing this now—is to reconceptualize what we mean by nutrient requirements and identify intakes associated with achieving optimal health. The RDAs are important because these numbers are eventually translated to the Daily Values used on all food labels—and manufacturers formulate their products with these nutrient requirements in mind.

Q. How are the RDAs changing?
A. The Food and Nutrition Board is meeting now to develop new RDAs. As they exist now, there are RDAs for different age groups with the oldest as fifty-one plus. But a fifty-one-year-old and a ninety-one-year-old don't have the same nutrient requirements.

Q. Why were people as young as fifty-one grouped with ninety-one-year-olds?
A. Until the last decade, there was not enough information to make more precise recommendations. Unfortunately, there was an inappropriate stereotyping of what aging and the elderly are really like. The thinking was that as people age, they become more sedentary and they get smaller and, therefore, they don't require as much nutrition. However, we have learned that the requirement for many nutrients

increases, not decreases, with age—the exact opposite of the old paradigm. This is especially true when we consider the goals of maximizing physiologic functions, promoting optimal health, and preventing chronic diseases. But this means the gap between what older people actually eat and what they require for optimal health is quite wide.

Q. What's wrong with cutting back on fat?
A. The typical American is consuming too much fat, especially saturated fat, a dietary risk factor for heart disease. However, the nutrition message that many people have fixated on is reducing fat. They think if they achieve it—for example, by consuming reduced/low-fat food products—they are eating healthfully. But what consumers also must understand is the need to reduce total calorie (energy) intake, not just fat. They also must recognize the health benefits associated with increasing the consumption of fruits and vegetables, not just because they are low in fat and contain lots of vitamins and minerals but because they are rich in phytochemicals.

Q. What are phytochemicals?
A. *Phyto* is Latin for "plant." There are thousands of natural chemicals in plant foods. We are now beginning to appreciate that they may possess important health-promoting properties independent of the essential nutrients found in the same foods. Interestingly, as we have come to recognize the benefits of increasing our intake of vitamins and minerals through supplementation, some companies are beginning to market phytochemical supplements.

Q. What about the importance of calcium and vitamin D for women as they age?
A. As women age, their ability to absorb calcium decreases. The rate and efficiency with which they can synthesize vitamin D in their skin from the sun also slows. These age-related changes are an important part of why vitamin D requirements increase with age. This is an example of how we can compensate for age-related physiologic changes by increasing our intake of specific nutrients through changes in our diet and the use of supplements. Several studies have now demonstrated that women who supplement their diet with calcium and

vitamin D can significantly reduce their loss of bone density and rate of hip and vertebral fractures by 30 to 40 percent.

Q. Tell me about the recent concern about folic acid.
A. Folic acid is a B-vitamin, an essential nutrient, and one that we know is very low in the diets of most women. Typical intakes of folic acid are about 150 micrograms (mcg), yet studies show that pregnant women must consume at least 400 mcg daily to prevent neural tube birth defects and that older women need at least the same amount to reduce the risk of cervical cancer and colorectal cancer and to reduce their level of homocysteine.

Q. Why is homocysteine one of the hottest new stories in nutrition in the last few years?
A. Homocysteine is now recognized as an independent risk factor for heart disease and stroke. Homocysteine is an amino acid found in every cell of our body. It is a normal part of amino acid metabolism. Amino acids are the building blocks of proteins. Folic acid is very important in many cellular functions, including DNA synthesis, and it has now been recognized that folic acid also works to maintain low levels of homocysteine. Scientists have wondered why some people who don't smoke and who have low cholesterol and a healthy weight have heart attacks and strokes. We are now finding that many of these people have high homocysteine levels. But now we know a simple nutritional intervention—increasing our intake of folic acid (and often vitamins B-6 and B-12 as well)—can convert homocysteine into a useful amino acid (methionine) or nontoxic metabolites. Clinical trials are now being undertaken to determine whether lowering homocysteine with B vitamins is an effective way to reduce the risk of heart disease and stroke.

Q. Are folic acid and homocysteine levels associated with other diseases?
A. Homocysteine appears to be associated with cognitive impairment similar to age-related dementias like Alzheimer's disease. While this does not mean that folic acid can cure Alzheimer's, people with high homocysteine levels do more poorly on tests used to diagnose

Alzheimer's disease than do those with low homocysteine levels. This is an exciting new area: nutritional neuroscience. The decline in cognitive function with age is more feared than any other chronic disease. And it is exciting to think that simple changes in our diet or the use of vitamin supplements may be found to help reduce the risk of certain dementias.

Q. Which foods contain folic acid?
A. Green leafy vegetables are a rich source of folic acid. Orange juice is easy to drink and a good source of folic acid as well. However, most people, and especially women, are not getting enough folic acid—that is, at least 400 mcg daily—from their diet. Most multivitamins contain 400 mcg folic acid and thus represent a good "insurance policy" to guarantee this level of intake. Although very high intakes of folic acid can mask the signs of vitamin B-12 deficiency and allow damage to nerves to develop, the same multivitamins with folic acid almost always contain vitamin B-12.

Q. Do you believe that antioxidants, such as vitamin E, can reduce the risk of heart disease?
A. An extensive body of scientific evidence suggests that vitamin E can reduce the risk of heart disease. People who take vitamin E supplements have been shown to have a 40 percent reduction in their risk of heart disease. And people who already have had a heart attack and then were treated with vitamin E supplements have been shown to have a 77 percent reduction in the risk of having a second one. But vitamin E is not the only important antioxidant nutrient.

Q. Tell me about antioxidants.
A. Antioxidants include vitamin E, vitamin C, carotenoids such as beta carotene and lycopene, and plant polyphenols like the flavonoids. Generous intakes of carotenoids have been associated with many health benefits, including a reduced risk of cancer. Flavonoids from fruits and vegetables as well as from tea and red wine also have been linked to a reduced risk of cancer and heart disease.

Q. What are oxygen-free radicals?

A. We live in an environment of oxygen. We need oxygen to breathe. But oxygen can be a dangerous friend. When oxygen is metabolized in the body, a small amount (usually 1 to 5 percent) is converted to free radicals, which are highly reactive and very toxic molecules. These molecules immediately attack adjacent molecules in the cell, the lipids in cell membranes, the amino acids in proteins, and even the DNA in the nucleus. Free radical damage to the cell constituents can lead to the development of chronic diseases. For example, damage to DNA may lead to cancer and perhaps even the aging process itself.

Q. What is the free radical hypothesis of aging?

A. The free radical hypothesis of aging proposes that the aging process results from the accumulation of injury caused by free radicals. There is some experimental evidence to support this theory but also some evidence that is not consistent or supportive. However, it continues to be one of the most provocative and testable theories of aging that scientists are pursuing today.

Q. Are oxygen-free radicals always bad?

A. No. For example, certain immune cells kill bacteria and viruses by releasing free radicals. However, Mother Nature, in her wisdom, said, "If I'm going to put you in an environment of oxygen, I'll give you antioxidant defenses." And, indeed, our food contains literally hundreds of antioxidant compounds, such as vitamins C and E, carotenoids, and polyphenols. We also make some antioxidants in our own cells, compounds such as glutathione and coenzyme Q10 and enzymes such as superoxide dismutase and catalase. This broad array of antioxidant defenses protects us from our own metabolism as well as from the free radicals created by certain environmental pollutants, such as cigarette smoke and smog. The size of this antioxidant army also suggests just how dangerous the free radical enemy is.

Q. What can happen to our body if we're not adequately protected from oxygen-free radicals?

A. We may see excess oxidation of LDL (the "bad" cholesterol) leading to heart disease, oxidation of DNA resulting in cancer, oxidation of the clear proteins in the eye lens precipitating cataracts, and many other chronic diseases, such as emphysema and lung cancer caused by smoking—the best instrument ever designed to deliver free radicals into your body is the cigarette.

Q. Do you advise people to take supplementary antioxidant vitamins?
A. We know that most people do not consume optimal amounts of antioxidants in their diet. It would be helpful if they followed the Dietary Guidelines for Americans and ate at least five, and preferably more, servings of fruits and vegetables each day. Dietary supplements containing antioxidants are a practical way to increase antioxidant intake, especially of vitamin E, the richest sources of which are vegetable oils and nuts, which are also high-fat foods. Fortunately, even very high supplemental doses of antioxidants are quite safe.

Q. What do you recommend to women in their fifties who want to eat right and take supplemental vitamins to ensure proper nutrition?
A. Cut back on total fat, particularly saturated fat, increase dietary fiber, and eat at least two servings of fruit and three servings of vegetables a day. Of course, this advice represents a radical change for many people. It is hard to change a dietary pattern that you have been following for more than fifty years. But you can change your food habits a little at a time, and then eventually you will be following the Food Guide Pyramid. For dietary supplements, I recommend a multivitamin/multimineral formula that includes one to two times the RDA, 500 to 800 mg calcium, and 100 to 400 IU vitamin E. Other supplements also might be advisable, depending on the individual. However, it is essential to recognize that dietary supplements are not dietary substitutes; it remains critical to follow a healthful eating pattern as well. Dietary supplements are not magic pills but rather are analogous to seat belts—they can help protect you from injury but do not provide a license to drive recklessly.

Q. What would you advise women in their fifties who want to live long, healthy lives?

A.
- Don't smoke.
- Eat a healthful low-fat, high-fiber diet.
- Keep active, both mentally and physically—with the physical exercise, include both aerobic and strength training regimens.
- Educate yourself about nutrition and how to select dietary supplement(s) appropriate to your individual needs.

29

Weight Control

Aviva Must, Ph.D.

Aviva Must graduated from college in 1976 with a major in biology and a minor in psychology. She entered graduate school at Tufts University in Massachusetts to study nutrition. She completed her graduate work in 1992. In 1994 she joined the Department of Family Medicine and Community Health at the Tufts University School of Medicine as an assistant professor. Her primary research interest is the epidemiology of obesity, especially in the pediatric population. She teaches epidemiology and biostatistics and serves as director of the dual Master's in Nutrition and Master's in Public Health program.

Q. How do our bodies normally change as we age?
A. What normally happens is that we gain weight. The word "normally" in this context is unfortunate because it implies that gaining weight is ideal or optimal. Most studies suggest that weight gain is not optimal for health.

Q. Gaining weight isn't unique to women. Why do women perceive weight gain as a major problem?
A. Probably for two reasons. The first reason is that there are significant health effects associated with weight gain. Risk of non–insulin-dependent diabetes, heart disease, and stroke is linked to weight gain during adulthood for women. Second, and perhaps more often, the

reason that women perceive weight gain as a major problem is esthetic. Women tend to associate weight gain with loss of their youthful appearance.

Q. As a woman gets older, she is likely to get heavier. But even if she doesn't gain weight, her body changes. What's happening?
A. The woman is likely to be losing lean body mass—muscle. Among the many changes experienced by the woman as she ages are changes in body composition. As she ages, even if she maintains the same weight, the amount of fat she carries increases. For example, if she keeps her weight at 145 pounds from her twenties through her thirties, forties, and fifties, at fifty she will have a higher percent body fat than she did in her twenties. Her body may not look different. But if you squeeze her upper arm, for example, it may feel softer because it has more fat and less muscle.

Q. Why do women gain weight as they age?
A. Lean body mass, the major determinant of caloric need, is metabolically active tissue. The amount of calories your body requires is directly proportional to your lean body mass. As people age and lose muscle, their caloric needs decrease, but often their caloric intake does not. If they continue to consume the same number of calories, they gain weight. In addition, physical activity usually decreases with age, and sedentary habits increase. If your activity level goes down, the energy balance equation is in positive balance, and you gain weight.

Q. What is the energy balance equation?
A. Your body is in energy balance when the amount of energy your body uses is equal to the amount of energy you get from diet. If your body uses less energy than you take in, you will gain weight, and you are said to be in positive energy balance. If your body uses more energy than you take in, you will lose weight, and you are said to be in negative energy balance. As you get older, calories necessary for metabolism decrease because your lean body mass and energy spent in activity are both going down. Unless your energy intake decreases, you will be in a positive balance and, over time, you will gain weight.

Q. How much of a positive energy balance causes weight gain?
A. Small imbalances will cause weight gain. If you're out of balance by only 100 calories a day, over the course of a year you would gain approximately ten pounds. That's just from 100 calories, which is equivalent to one piece of bread, an apple, or a small banana. If you're in a very small positive energy balance every day, over time you would amass a large quantity of adipose (fat) tissue.

Q. What is obesity?
A. I use the terms "obesity" and "overweight" interchangeably. The definition of obesity is variable because fatness is measured on a continuous scale. Defining weight is similar to describing height. What makes somebody tall? I could define a tall woman as one who is over five feet ten. You might say she is tall at five feet nine. We could argue all day about cut-off points for tallness. Similarly, cut-off points for overweight and obesity are somewhat arbitrary.

Q. How can someone judge that she is overweight?
A. There is no absolute standard for defining obesity. However, the World Health Organization has recommended cut-off points based on body mass index.

Q. Tell me about the body mass index.
A. The body mass index (BMI) is calculated by dividing one's weight measured in kilograms squared by one's height in meters. The cut-off points suggested for body mass index are: Grade 1 overweight if your body mass index is over 25; grade 2 overweight if it is over 30; and grade 3 overweight for BMIs over 40. People with body mass indices over 30 are severely overweight. People with BMIs over 40 are morbidly overweight.

It is important to remember that the body mass index is based on weight, not on fat. But if you're very overweight, it's an almost forgone conclusion that you are also fat.

Q. When do health risks kick in?
A. Most health risks start with body indices over 25. More than half

of all women over fifty have a body mass index above 25. That is alarming.

Q. Which medical problems are associated with being overweight?
A. Heart disease, diabetes, hypertension, gallbladder disease, arthritis, and certain cancers. Non–insulin-dependent diabetes mellitus is a common condition that is very sensitive to weight.

Q. Do you think that thinner is better for women in their fifties?
A. The question is, thinner than what? There are significant health risks associated with extreme thinness in this age group, such as osteoporosis and fracture. The social environment of American culture has set up a standard whereby we joke that a woman cannot be "too rich or too thin." Sadly, this joke translates into pressure on many women and teenage girls to perceive body weight and weight gain as a major problem. And while many adults need to monitor their weight to prevent weight gain, many women who are intensely preoccupied with weight are of normal weight. On a population basis, it appears that substantial weight gain (more than 5 BMI units, or eleven pounds) is twice as common in women as in men, although rates of new cases of obesity are similar.

Q. Should a woman in her fifties who is thirty pounds overweight go on a strenuous diet?
A. Probably not. Losing thirty pounds on a strict diet could be dangerous. This woman might starve herself or take pills—behaviors that in themselves carry health risks. Actually, she could improve her long-term health risks markedly by gradually losing ten or fifteen pounds, which represents a far more feasible task.

Q. Are some people more prone to weight problems because of genetic factors?
A. Yes. Studies of twins reared apart indicate that there is a strong genetic component to overweight. But to blame the problem of obesity and adult weight gain on genetics misses the point. We have

substantial scientific evidence to suggest that the environment plays an extremely important role in obesity and weight gain as well.

Q. Tell me about obesity in the United States.
A. We are presently experiencing an epidemic of obesity in the United States. Although there has been no major change in the genetic composition of the population over the last fifty years, the number of people who are overweight has doubled.

Q. What is an epidemic?
A. An epidemic is an observed incidence greatly in excess of scientists' expectations. If it stays that way and we come to expect it, we call it "endemic."

Q. Why is there an epidemic of obesity in the United States?
A. We are not sure. The epidemic of obesity appears to be related to decreased activity and a generally more sedentary lifestyle. There is little evidence that it is linked directly to changes in diet.

Q. Tell me about research that shows that obesity in our country is not due to diet.
A. The National Health and Nutrition Examination Survey has tried to figure out what people have been eating for the past thirty five years. The data from those surveys suggest that caloric intake has *decreased*. If eating were to blame for overweight in this country, the caloric intake would have gone up.

Data from a number of studies suggest that physical activity has declined and sedentary behavior is on the upswing. Sedentary activity is not just the opposite of physical activity. It is an entity in itself.

Q. What is sedentary activity?
A. Sedentary activity sounds like an oxymoron. A better term might be sedentary habit or sedentary behavior. I'll use myself as an example of someone who is both sedentary and active. I participate in several exercise classes each week. During those three one-hour aerobics classes I probably burn off a total of 750 calories. At work, I mostly sit

in front of a computer terminal. I might circle the parking lot three times to get a parking space that is close to the grocery store. I spend my evenings reading or in front of the television set with the remote control. Despite my exercise classes, I am very sedentary.

Q. Tell me about the concept of apple shapes versus pear shapes.
A. Women with slender legs who are thick through the middle but don't have much fat in the hip and thigh area have android (male) body shapes. They are the apples. In contrast, most women with voluptuous rear ends and broad hips and upper thighs are pear shapes; this shape is called gynoid. A large body of research suggests that people with android body shapes have a higher risk for heart disease and for non–insulin-dependent diabetes.

Q. Why are apple-shape women at higher risk for heart disease and diabetes?
A. Apple-shape women are at higher risk because central fat distribution is an independent risk factor for heart disease, hypertension, and diabetes. *Where* you carry your fat is important in addition to the amount of fat you store. Visceral fat is fat stored around the internal organs in the abdominal cavity. Regardless of weight, apple shapes have a more central fat distribution pattern in which there is excess fat around the body organs, which can cause greater health risks.

Q. Is this fat distribution pattern genetically determined?
A. Yes. Fat distribution appears to be more tightly genetically linked than fatness itself.

Q. Can a woman change her body shape?
A. No. Body shape is largely genetically determined. You cannot change from apple to pear, although some evidence suggests that certain lifestyle factors, such as smoking and alcohol intake, increase central fatness; and physical activity decreases it.

Q. What if you lose total body fat?
A. That will result in less fat around your organs and will improve

your risk profile. But losing fat can't change your overall shape. If you regain fat, it will return to the places it left. That is because you cannot lose fat cells, you can only shrink their size.

Q. How does menopause affect a woman's fat distribution?
A. When women lose estrogen, they generally begin to store fat centrally. The body shape of a postmenopausal woman becomes more like that of a man.

Q. Does this postmenopausal fat distribution pattern change women's health risks?
A. Yes, it does. By ten years after menopause, a woman's heart disease rate is the same as a man's.

Q. Is the apple-pear concept the reason that premenopausal women have lower heart disease rates than men?
A. We think so. It appears to be dictated by hormones. Estrogen protects against heart disease in the premenopausal woman.

Q. What is the biggest problem for women who are overweight?
A. The biggest challenge is weight maintenance. This may be surprising. Although it is difficult to lose weight, it's much more difficult to maintain weight loss.

Q. Why is weight maintenance so difficult?
A. We are not sure. One commonly mentioned explanation is the set-point theory.

Q. Tell me about the set-point theory.
A. Fat storage in nonobese adults appears to be regulated in a manner that preserves a specific body weight. In animals and in humans, deliberate efforts to starve or overfeed are inevitably followed by a return to the original weight. It is as if there is a set point for weight that your body wants to go back to. Proving this theory has been a very active area in obesity research. Some studies seem to suggest that the so-called set point can be reset if weight change is maintained over time. This theory, if correct, has important lessons for weight control.

First, it is far easier to prevent weight gain than it is to try to treat it. Second, individuals should be patient with plateaus during weight reduction; if negative energy balance is maintained, additional weight loss should follow any plateau.

Q. Why do so many people gradually gain weight as they get older?
A. Probably due to the behavioral changes and body composition changes I've already mentioned. But the medical community may bear some responsibility as well. Nobody bothers you when you put on a couple of pounds. It's only when your weight is out of control that your health care provider says, "Gee, you've gained thirty pounds. You'd better take it off." Where was that provider back when you gained the first five pounds, which you could have more easily lost?

Q. What should women with a weight problem do?
A. A severely overweight individual should be referred to a physician who specializes in the treatment of obesity. Moderately overweight women should try weight maintenance as a first goal. Find a physical activity that you enjoy. An activity that suits you is key because you're signing on "for life." The same goes for dietary changes. If you hate eating breakfast, don't go on a diet that insists on a big breakfast. It will be doomed to failure. The notion of a diet, in general, probably should be avoided. Going *on* a diet implies that at some future point in time you will go *off* it. That is why it is preferable to adopt an eating style, one that suits you and can become second nature.

Q. Is it a good idea to weigh yourself daily?
A. Some people like to get on the scale each morning as a check-in and a reminder. If the scale is a low-key reinforcement, okay. If it's going to make you crazy, don't do it.

Q. Do women in their fifties have eating disorders?
A. Yes, sadly, some do. There is tremendous pressure in our society to be thin. Binge eating disorder—bingeing but not purging—is a problem for middle-aged women. Bulimia (binge eating followed by purging) is also seen in this age group.

Q. Are diet pills helpful in weight reduction and control?
A. They may be useful for people who have severe weight problems. But I have very serious concerns. I am concerned about diet pills in today's environment where women have surgery just to remove small amounts of fat. I worry about the abuse of these medications. And as we saw in 1997, some may carry substantial health risks. Two drugs were recently taken off the market at the request of the United States Food and Drug Administration.

Q. What are the worst things women do to lose weight?
A. They go to extremes. They take laxatives and over-the-counter diet medications or drugs sold through the mail, which may or may not hurt you but probably won't help. They exercise excessively. They starve themselves. A frightening number of women undergo surgery to remove fat. Or they try other dangerous procedures that don't work. None of the incredible and terrible extremes that women go to achieves weight maintenance. At best, these extremes buy weight loss.

Q. What discourages you about obesity?
A. What discourages me most is that people want a quick fix. The prescription that I have described is nothing new. It's not sexy, there's no market—nobody's going to make money off my advice.

Huge numbers of people are obese. Prevention before age fifty is the answer. But don't give up if you're overweight at fifty. Even moderate weight loss has salutary effects. Losing weight and keeping it off can lower your blood pressure, improve your glucose and lipid profile, and improve health and longevity.

Q. What is your feeling regarding pressures on women to look good?
A. It's unfortunate that society puts pressure on women so they feel that they have to go to extremes to meet some ideal of beauty. Sadly, some women respond to this pressure with surgery to reduce body weight or to reshape their nose or to eliminate puffiness under their eyes. We carry a lot of baggage as aging women, trying to live up to that unrealistic ideal of youthful beauty. And, of course, it is doomed for failure. You can't turn back the clock. It's just going to get worse.

Q. What is your prescription to women who want to lose weight, with a goal of optimal health and longevity?

A.

- Eat a variety of foods, especially fruits and vegetables, with most calories coming from carbohydrates, grains, and cereals. Use fats, oils, nuts, and meats sparingly.
- Participate in physical activity that suits you and make it part of your daily lifestyle. Avoid sedentary behavior.
- Start small and be happy with little victories.

30

Exercise and Fitness for Health and Longevity

Michael O'Shea, Ph.D.

Michael O'Shea was a premed major in college. After graduation in 1973, he opted for a career in athletic training and rehabilitation and opened a sports medicine gym. He now holds a master's degree and a Ph.D. in sports medicine. He earned his Ph.D. at Union Graduate School in Cincinnati. He has served as personal trainer to numerous professional athletes and celebrities. He is a fellow of the American College of Sports Medicine and a former team doctor for both the National Basketball Association and the National Hockey League. He is a Healthy American Fitness leader selected by the President's Council on Physical Fitness and Sports. Dr. O'Shea continues to run a gym in New York City.

Q. How has the scientific community changed its view of exercise in the last ten years?
A. Ten years ago exercise wasn't considered beneficial unless it was done vigorously enough to get a person's heart rate up into the training range.

Q. What are the present thoughts about exercise?
A. New studies have shown that even moderate exercise lowers blood pressure and decreases risk factors for heart disease and other medical

conditions. People who exercise live longer. The point is, in the old days, it was believed that if you weren't getting your heart rate over 150, you wouldn't make gains. That has changed because of research. Just walking, gardening, and working around the house will burn calories and lessen many health risks.

Q. What is a person's training range?
A. The training range is a guideline for aerobic conditioning. The goal is to elevate your heart rate high enough for aerobic conditioning without being dangerously high—that is, you shouldn't go above the top number in your training range. On the other hand, you won't get the optimal benefit if your heart rate is below the lower number.

Everyone's training range decreases with age. You don't have to undertake vigorous exercise. Even walking can get you into your training range.

Q. How do you calculate your training range?
A. To calculate your training range, subtract your age from 220. Seventy percent of the result is the low end of your training range and 85 percent is the high end. For example, if you are fifty years old, subtract 50 from 220, and the result is 170. Seventy percent of 170 equals 119, the low end of your training range. Eighty-five percent of 170 equals 145, the high end of your training range.

Q. What differentiates moderate from vigorous exercise?
A. That depends on the person. A woman who walks a couple of blocks for ten minutes is doing minimal to moderate exercise. Someone who runs a six-minute pace for ten miles is participating in vigorous activity. Nonetheless, those two people have worked fairly hard and may have stressed themselves similarly. In the exercise business we call this perceived exertion.

Q. Tell me about perceived exertion.
A. When you exercise, you should feel that you've exerted yourself. Perceived exertion is essentially how hard someone is working.

Q. If we feel we're working hard just walking a couple of blocks, how can we increase our level of exertion?
A. Each time you exercise, your body adapts so that you can do more and more. The next time you exercise, you should do at least as much as you did the last time and perhaps a little bit more.

Q. Should you feel pain or soreness?
A. You don't want to feel pain or soreness but you want to feel as if you're working.

Q. How would you start someone, say, a woman in her fifties, on an exercise program?
A. After I get medical clearance from her doctor, I explore her goals and assess her level of fitness. Then I set up a gradual exercise program. I'd probably start her walking or swimming. What she accomplishes on day 1 will be a building block for the next session.

Q. You seem to promote moderate rather than strenuous exercise.
A. Yes. Especially for people over fifty.

Q. Why?
A. Because consistency is the key to longevity. Typically when people start a rigorous program, such as running three or four times a week, at some point they stop and they never begin again. I'd rather see that person walk for an hour five times a week and keep it up for the rest of her life.

Q. Walking for an hour five times a week sounds boring. How do you create motivation to keep it up?
A. Exercise with friends. That's one of the key motivators. If you and I and a couple of friends begin a walking program and you all show up at my house, bang on the door, and pull me out, it's a lot harder for me to sit and watch TV.

Q. Let's say I'm walking forty-five minutes four or five days a week and it's easy. I'm not working that hard. What's the next step?
A. Eventually you'll want to walk faster to get your heart rate up to a

training range. Ideally, when you start to walk, you can bring a stopwatch to monitor your heart rate. The harder you work, the higher your heart rate. The higher your heart rate, the stronger it becomes. You are conditioning your cardiovascular system. You might consider jogging, swimming, or biking as the next step.

Q. Are stretches important when you get to this level?
A. Yes. Stretching exercises before and after your workouts loosen your hamstrings, your calves, and your lower back. Stretching ultimately helps prevent injuries.

Q. Walking and jogging stress the bones in the lower body, which can prevent osteoporosis. What can women do to help their upper body?
A. This is where strength work comes in, which can be as minimal as doing push-ups against a wall or lifting soup cans. Strength training and weight-lifting allow you to tone your muscles while you stress your bones. You've got to stress the bones to make them absorb the minerals that help prevent osteoporosis.

Q. Will exercise help with weight reduction and overall health?
A. Weight reduction is a tremendous plus. People who exercise burn extra calories, and they can lose weight. If they weigh less, their blood pressure probably will go down, and their cholesterol levels may improve.

Q. Do time and intensity of exercise correlate with increased health benefits?
A. Yes. Benefits increase with the added time and the level of intensity. But too much vigorous exercise, too soon, can be detrimental. If you don't increase your exercise level slowly, you can hurt yourself.

Q. Tell me about fitness machines.
A. There are probably thirty different pieces of aerobic equipment for home or health club including exercise bikes, treadmills, stair-stepping machines, Versa climbers (a machine that works legs and arms with a climbing type of motion), cross-country-ski machines, and so on.

The advantage of walking or jogging is that all you have to invest in is a pair of sneakers. You can do it anywhere, at any time of the year.

Q. What are the benefits of a professional trainer?
A. A trainer can test you and set up a program. He or she will show you your limits and prescribe appropriate workouts. Probably 3 or 4 percent of people who exercise hire a trainer.

Q. What about health clubs?
A. Health clubs are another way to increase motivation. You're not nearly as bored at a health club with forty other people and a good instructor as you would be sitting home alone on your exercise bike.

Most health clubs have aerobic and strength equipment as well as exercise and yoga classes. They usually are staffed with talented people who may have degrees in exercise physiology. These instructors will test you, demonstrate the equipment, and set you up in an exercise program.

Q. What if lack of time is an excuse for not exercising?
A. We're all busy. You've got to find time to exercise. If you're that busy, you really need to exercise. George Bush exercised at least five days a week when he was the President of the United States. If he could find the time, anyone can. There's no time better spent than in exercising. An added benefit is that exercise releases endorphins, nature's own mood enhancers, which can make you feel really good.

Q. What is your philosophy of exercise?
A. Exercise is the ultimate medicine and even stronger preventive medicine. It can reduce stress, promote sleep, and help with weight reduction. Exercise improves the symptoms of diabetes and high blood pressure. It may prevent certain cancers and other diseases.

There is no better investment than exercise. That investment gets more important every day we get older.

It's hard getting started, but you don't have to become a zealot. Walking for thirty minutes a day, five days a week, is great for your heart, good for your bones, and it's fun. Just three ten-minute walks a week can decrease risk factors for many diseases and increase longevity. Why wait until the doctor tells you you're overweight, your blood pressure is too high, your lipids are up, your sugars are bad, and you've got to change your lifestyle?

Exercise is like brushing your teeth. If you don't brush them, they'll fall out. If you don't use your body, you're not going to live as long and the quality of your life isn't going to be as good as that of people who are fit.

31

Strength Training for Strong Bones

Miriam E. Nelson, Ph.D.

Miriam Nelson graduated from college in 1983 with a degree in human nutrition and foods. She completed her Ph.D. at Tufts University in 1987. Dr. Nelson spent a year in Washington, D.C., working as a legislative assistant with Senator Patrick Leahy, but she missed the research and returned to Tufts in 1989, where she remains as Associate Chief of the Human Physiology Laboratory at the Jean Mayer Human Nutrition Research Center on Aging.

The Jean Mayer Human Nutrition Research Center on Aging is a federally funded agency, jointly contracted by the United States Department of Agriculture and Tufts University, that is dedicated to conducting research on the effects of nutrition on the aging process. It is the only such center in the world. "Nutrition at our center is defined quite broadly," says Nelson. "I work on physical activity and body composition, which we consider part of nutrition."

Miriam Nelson's book, *Strong Women Stay Young*, coauthored by Sarah Wernick, Ph.D., was published by Bantam in 1997. It is now in paperback. Her new book, *Strong Women Stay Slim*, was published by Bantam in April 1998.

Q. Your book Strong Women Stay Young came about as a result of 1994 research in which you studied the effects of strength training on various physiological processes of older women. What were some of the results of that study?

A. Women who strength-trained twice a week for a year became approximately 75 percent stronger, gained about three pounds of muscle, and lost three pounds of fat. Their balance improved. Their bone density at the hip and spine increased about 1 percent. (Bone density of women in the control group declined 2 to 2.5 percent.) Without any prompting from us, these women took up a more physically active lifestyle.

Q. Tell me about strength training, weight-lifting, and progressive resistance training.

A. Strength training, weight-lifting, and progressive resistance training are different terms for the same thing. They mean lifting a weight or pushing against a resistance so that your muscles contract against the heavy load. You can do only a few repetitions—up to ten—and then the weight or resistance becomes so difficult that you can no longer lift or push it in proper form and you need to rest.

Q. What happens to your body with this type of training?

A. Your muscles become much stronger. As those muscles strengthen, you need to increase the amount of weight that you're lifting. Every week, every other week, or every third week, as you become stronger, you lift heavier and heavier weights to continue gaining benefit.

Q. What is the goal in increasing muscle mass?

A. The goal is to strengthen your entire body. But our body is made up of pieces. Just one exercise won't improve your entire body. Strengthening exercises are specific to certain muscles in your arms, your back, your thighs, and your lower legs.

Q. Does strength training help with weight reduction?

A. Yes. Muscle is the true energy source for our body. The amount of energy we burn throughout the day is due to our muscle mass and the amount of physical activity we participate in. If we have more muscle, we burn more calories, which in turn helps with weight control. As we get older we lose about a third of a pound of muscle every year and gain that much fat. Therefore, we don't have as much muscle to burn the energy. If we don't eat less, we gain weight.

Many overweight people find aerobic activities such as running and walking unpleasant. They sweat. They huff and puff. Yet their doctors tell them to "go out and walk." But overweight people often excel in strength training because they have a lot of muscle. Suddenly they excel at something physical. This is great positive feedback. Once they're stronger, it's easier for them to walk, bike, swim, or do other athletic activities.

Q. What are other benefits of strength training?
A. Major benefits include a shift in body composition with increases in muscle and decreases in body fat, increases in bone density, better dynamic balance, less frailty, higher energy levels, and improved quality of sleep. We see improvement in mood, especially in people who have been clinically depressed. Strength training may be beneficial for reducing risk for diabetes. The muscle is the largest reservoir for glucose. If the muscle is in better shape, it probably can better dispose of glucose. Weight training also may decrease the risk of heart disease. The more muscle and less fat, the better your cholesterol levels.

Q. Why isn't walking good enough as a weight-bearing exercise?
A. You do place a load on the bones when you walk. You take many, many steps when you walk. But you're not applying a great load to the bones.

Q. How does weight training increase bone density?
A. Bones, like muscles, adapt to the forces applied to them. If you lift a heavy weight—let's say you're doing a biceps curl with a dumbbell in your hand, you lift the weight eight to ten times and it is so heavy that you need to rest—you're applying a very high load to the bone.

There also may be a systemic effect to strengthening exercises. Some of the hormones, such as osteocalcin, a bone-building hormone, also are increased.

Q. Does strength training decrease the risk of fractures for reasons other than increasing bone density?
A. Strength training does increase bone density, but it also gives better balance, increases muscle mass, improves strength, and motivates an active lifestyle. Suddenly weight training affects many risk factors for osteoporosis—not just bone density. If a woman is strong and has very good balance, she will be much more resistant to falling. If she doesn't fall, she won't break her hip.

Q. Will strength training result in aesthetic changes as well as better health?
A. Yes. Strength training will make you look better. As I've said before, we naturally lose muscle and gain body fat with aging. Body fat over a little bit of muscle can be jiggly and unfirm. The backs of our upper arms (known as wattles or bat wings) are a notoriously weak and flabby area for women. If those triceps muscles can be strengthened while the body fat decreases, that arm will be much firmer. Another problem area for women is the shoulders, which help her stand tall and look graceful. Strengthening exercises that target the shoulders, upper arms, and the upper back will help women have toned muscles and more definition.

Q. Do strength-training exercises pose risks?
A. Strength training done properly is safe for almost everybody, even women with chronic but stable medical conditions. We won't work with anyone who has had major surgery in the last six months or has an unstable medical condition. If in doubt, check it out with your physician.

Q. How should a weight training program be started?
A. We usually begin by asking participants to answer a questionnaire called the PAR-Q, which stands for Physical Activity Readiness Questionnaire. The seven simple self-assessment questions will help determine whether strength training is safe for you.

When starting a weight training program, it's a good idea to use some professional guidance, such as my *Strong Women Stay Young* program. The exercises are simple. There's no need to get down on the

292

floor (and struggle up again), because everything is done standing or seated on a chair. But many women prefer to get a trainer or go to a fitness facility where they can get more personal instruction.

Q. How can progress be assessed?
A. The best way is to see if you can lift heavier weights. If you started with three pounds and in three months you lifted ten pounds and several months later you're lifting fifteen pounds, you are obviously becoming very strong. You may suddenly realize that carrying two bags of heavy groceries is easy. There's a lot more spring in your step. You could also get a bone density test to follow your progress.

Q. What is the optimal number and length of strength-training sessions?
A. Two to three times a week for thirty to forty minutes a session.

Q. Do you believe in no pain, no gain?
A. No. It doesn't need to be painful. But it should be fatiguing. That is not a familiar sensation for many women until they begin their sessions.

Q. What advice do you have for women in their fifties who want to lift weights?
A. Stick with it. Have it become part of your life.

32

Curbing Addictive Behaviors

Robert L. DuPont, M.D.

Robert DuPont was a humanities major in college. After graduation in 1958, he attended the Harvard Medical School, where he also did a psychiatric residency after graduating in 1963. He completed his training at the National Institutes of Health in Bethesda, Maryland. In 1968 he became the director of Community Services (Parole and Halfway Houses) for the District of Columbia Department of Corrections. He started its addiction treatment program, which was expanded to become the citywide Narcotics Treatment Administration in 1971. In 1973 he was appointed by President Richard M. Nixon as the second White House "Drug Czar," while also serving as the first director of the National Institute on Drug Abuse. In 1978 he left government work to become Clinical Professor of Psychiatry at Georgetown University School of Medicine in Washington, D.C. He has concentrated his professional activities on addiction and anxiety disorders. He was the founding president of the Anxiety Disorders Association of America and is founder and president of the Institute of Behavior and Health in Rockville, Maryland. Dr. DuPont is author of *The Selfish Brain: Learning from Addiction*, and with his two daughters (Elizabeth Spencer, a social worker and Caroline DuPont, a psychiatrist) of *The Anxiety Cure—Eight Steps to Getting Well*.

Q. Tell me about the word "addiction."
A. "Addiction" is similar to words such as "anxiety," "paranoia," or "depression." They have relatively precise medical and scientific meanings but they are also words used casually to describe a variety of common behaviors and disorders.

"Addiction" applies to almost any repetitive, pleasure-driven behavior. There are so-called addictions to running, television, chocolate, sex, gambling, or even work. There are also addictions to cigarettes, alcohol, marijuana, prescription drugs, cocaine, and heroin.

Q. What is the core experience in addictive behavior?
A. Everything that is addictive is related to the brain's pleasure center. The same brain mechanisms are involved in all types of addictive behaviors.

Drugs hit the pleasure centers, the dopamine neurotransmitter in the nucleus accumbens, directly pirating the brain's own communication system for biologically vital behaviors such as eating and sex. Other addictive pleasures act more indirectly and generally are less compelling. They are also not impairing of brain function—they do not produce intoxication and impairment—the way alcohol and other drugs do.

Like all addictive behaviors, addiction to alcohol and other drugs is both cruel and unfair. Some people, for genetic and other reasons, are far more susceptible than are others. For example, some people gamble or have poor eating habits but never develop gambling addictions or eating disorders, while other people who engage in similar high-risk behaviors do not simply walk away from these behaviors but suffer from lifelong addictions. Think of high-risk behaviors as similar to riding in a car without seat belts or speeding—many people get away with these behaviors but others (a large minority of people engaging in high-risk behaviors) suffer terrible problems as a result.

Q. How is addiction to drugs and alcohol different from addiction to television, running, cigarettes, sex, or gambling?
A. Drugs and alcohol are much more effective stimuli to the brain's pleasure center. The intensity of these addictions is greater, as are the consequences.

True addiction to alcohol and drugs produces intoxication and mental impairment. The life of an alcoholic or drug addict is in disarray. In contrast, the everyday life of a cigarette smoker or even a compulsive gambler is not necessarily in shambles, although the ultimate consequences can be equally disastrous.

Q. Why is it inappropriate to compare addictive behaviors with addiction to drugs and alcohol?
A. Addictions can be compared and useful lessons can be learned from these comparisons. However, to equate addiction to chocolate to addiction to cocaine, or to compare alcohol addiction to caffeine addiction is terribly misleading because it trivializes the tragic consequences of addiction to alcohol or other drugs. When someone says "I have an addiction to cocaine and you have an addiction to chocolate so we're really just the same," they are wrong.

Q. Is there an addictive personality—that is, a person who is prone to becoming addicted?
A. There has been a lot of interest in the concept of the addictive personality. The most sophisticated, scientific answer to your question is that there is no such thing as an addictive personality. However, the popular culture says yes, there are addictive personalities, because most of us feel vulnerable to addiction and to one extent or another we are all "addictive personalities." It is also true that a person with one addiction—say, alcoholism—is more likely to have other addictions—such as gambling or sexual addiction.

Q. Many people self-identify as addictive personalities. Are they different from other people?
A. No. Their self-description doesn't distinguish them from most other people. An addictive personality is a human or even a mammalian characteristic. This phenomenon, if not universal, is certainly very widespread.

Q. What is the difference between the person who becomes an addict, such as the alcoholic, and the person who does not?
A. No one knows. Everyone is vulnerable, some more than others.

One way people differ is in their willingness to engage in high-risk, addiction-generating behaviors. Some people have values and behavior patterns that are relatively protective against addiction; others are reckless in their indulgences and this puts them at added risk of addiction. The more rebellious, willful, and private the person, the higher the risk of addictive behaviors. The more conventional, religious, and open a person is, the lower the risk of addiction.

Q. Is there a genetic link to this vulnerability in humans?
A. Genetics plays a role but it is not the whole story. Addiction has both environmental and biological roots. Some students drink a lot of alcohol in their college years and become alcoholics after they graduate. Most others do not; they simply drink less as they assume adult roles. Again, we don't know why, but how long people engage in potentially addictive behavior and how much they like it are important factors.

Q. Is there a psychological link to drug and alcohol abuse?
A. Drug and alcohol abuse is not the result of a psychological defect. It is mostly triggered by the desire for the drug experience, the drug "high."

Q. What constitutes a true addiction?
A. A true addiction includes two prerequisites. One is the loss of control. The other is dishonesty.

Q. Do you see addiction problems in women in their fifties?
A. Drug problems, such as addiction to cocaine or heroin, are unlikely to begin in this age group, but addiction can persist from youth into the fifties and beyond.

But alcoholism is of special concern. Alcohol addiction occurs most often in chronic, heavy drinkers. The onset of alcoholism is common in this age group, usually in the context of an upset in the person's life, such as loss of a job, divorce, or some other family disruption.

The excessive use of sleeping pills or antianxiety medicines, such as Valium or Xanax, can also be a problem of women in their fifties.

Even more common than addiction to antianxiety medicines and sleeping pills is inappropriate worry about addiction to these generally useful medicines. A woman can tell if she is addicted to these potentially addicting medicines by assessing her use: Is it a greater dose and greater frequency than her doctor has approved? Does she get medicines from many doctors without each knowing about all the medicines (and illicit drugs and alcohol) she uses? Does she lie to her doctors and others about her use of antianxiety medicines or sleeping pills? Do these prescription medicines cause her problems, such as intoxication to alcohol (slurred speech, memory loss, confusion, falls, automobile accidents)? If the answer to any of these questions is yes, she may well have a problem, and it could be addiction. If she answers no to all these questions, as do most women in their fifties who use these medicines, then she is not addicted at all. She is simply taking a useful medicine for a serious but treatable problem.

Q. Is a woman considered a drug addict if she takes modest doses of Valium or sleeping pills?
A. She probably is not addicted, although she may be physically dependent—that is, if she stops taking Valium or Xanax, she may experience withdrawal symptoms such as increased anxiety, insomnia, and symptoms like the flu. Symptoms last a week or two after stopping the medicine. She is not addicted if her problem of physical dependence can be solved by a very gradual reduction of the medication over several weeks or several months.

Q. What if she takes more than modest doses of these medications? Is she a true addict?
A. Again, the key to self-diagnosis is whether she is out of control or dishonest about her drug use. There is no such thing as an honest addict. If her doctors and family members know what she is doing, and she has no problem as a result of her use of the medicine, she should not label herself an addict. She may, however, want to try a period of three months or more off the medicine to see if she still needs it.

Q. What if a woman determines that she is an addict? Her life is in disarray and she has been dishonest with doctors and/or her spouse about her use of Valium or other medications? What should she do?
A. The best way to get well from addiction is to use the fellowship of Alcoholics Anonymous (AA). The simple standard for participation in twelve-step programs is to go to ninety meetings in ninety days. That is how to get the best out of AA and other twelve-step programs. Get a sponsor, work the twelve steps, do what the people in the meetings suggest. These programs are free and available to anyone, from the richest to the poorest person with addiction to alcohol and other drugs. Participants in twelve-step programs learn a new way of thinking about addictive behavior and staying well.

Q. Why Alcoholics Anonymous if she is hooked on medications?
A. People who are addicted to drugs or medications often have an alcohol problem at the same time, and in that case they fit very well into Alcoholics Anonymous.

Q. What if she doesn't have an alcohol problem?
A. If she's just taking pills and not alcohol, she should contact Narcotics Anonymous (NA), a companion program to AA that deals with all addictive substances except alcohol.

Q. Where are drug treatment programs found?
A. AA and NA phone numbers are listed in the yellow pages of any phone book under alcohol and drug abuse treatment. Or call the American Society of Addiction Medicine at 301-656-3920.

Q. Can addictions be treated successfully?
A. Yes. People who were addicted to drugs—including prescription drugs—and alcohol can get better and live perfectly good lives, but it takes hard work.

Addiction treatment is not the same as AA or NA. It is medical treatment that can help with detoxification and stabilization as a person becomes free of alcohol and other drugs. Addiction treatment can smooth the way to lifelong participation in the fellowships of AA and NA.

Q. Do addictions recur?

A. Addictions can recur; it's called a relapse. If the first treatment doesn't work, the second one often will. Addiction is not like an infectious disease, in which we kill the bug and it's gone. Addiction exists for a person's lifetime.

Q. Does medical insurance cover addiction treatment?

A. Yes, it usually does, although seldom as completely as it covers other medical disorders.

Q. What is your advice to women in their fifties who want to be addiction-free?

A. The one-word antidote to addiction is honesty. If you can tell your doctors and the people who love you the truth, the whole truth, and nothing but the truth about any behavior—including prescription drug and alcohol use—you do not have an addiction. This very simple standard will work across the board to prevent addiction because dishonesty is a central feature of addiction.

33

What Medical Studies
Mean to You

Mark Abramowicz, M.D.

Mark Abramowicz majored in government in college,
graduating in 1956. He attended Washington University
Medical School in St. Louis and did his internship, residency,
and fellowship training in pediatrics at Boston City Hospital
and Massachusetts General Hospital. From 1962 to 1964 he
served in the United States Army in Germany, where he prac-
ticed pediatrics in the largest American community outside of
the United States. In 1966 he became an assistant professor of
pediatrics at New York's Albert Einstein College of Medicine.
Succumbing to a long-standing interest in journalism, he began to work part time at the newsletter *The Medical Letter*. In
1973 Dr. Abramowicz accepted the position of full-time editor, a position he has held since that time.

The Medical Letter was first published in 1959. Its major
agenda is to review drugs that have been recently approved by
the Food and Drug Administration. The semimonthly newsletter takes no advertising and is totally independent of the phar-
maceutical industry. Its audience is mostly physicians, including approximately 125,000 in North America and 25,000
overseas.

Q. Tell me about medical studies.

A. There are two major types of medical studies—randomized double-blind, controlled studies, known as prospective studies, and epidemiologic (observational) studies, which are referred to as retrospective studies.

Q. How does a randomized double-blind study compare to an epidemiologic study?

A. A randomized double-blind study usually tests the effectiveness of a drug or treatment of a disease. It is prospective because researchers follow people for years to come.

An epidemiologic study observes the frequency, distribution, and causes of disease. It is retrospective because researchers look back in time to see what groups of people have done that might account for the differences in disease or disease patterns.

Q. Tell me about the design of a randomized double-blind study.

A. In a randomized study, an investigator gathers a group of people who agree to be included. Half of the subjects receive the real treatment, and the other half (the control group) are given a placebo (a sugar pill or something that looks like the true medication). The actual treatment and the placebo must be randomly assigned and should look and taste exactly alike. Neither the investigators nor the people in the study know who receives the treatment or who gets the placebo—thus the term "double-blind." Results of the study are evaluated before the code is broken.

Q. Give me a hypothetical example of an epidemiologic (observational) or retrospective study.

A. A researcher could design a retrospective study to determine whether estrogen causes breast cancer in women. He would include two groups of women—one hundred who had breast cancer and one hundred who did not—and look back in time to see differences that might account for the incidence of breast cancer. He might observe their diet, their pregnancies, when they went into puberty, when (and if) they became menopausal, whether they took estrogens, and many other variables.

Q. Tell me about actual observational studies that have tried or are trying to determine whether estrogen causes an increased risk of breast cancer in women.

A. Researchers have done many observational studies on the effects of estrogen on breast cancer. The best known one is the Nurses' Health Study, which looks at a variety of behaviors in more than 30,000 women for many years to account for differences in diseases.

Q. What is the problem with this type of study?

A. The problem with this type of study is that the investigator can't be sure that the two groups of women are alike in every way. Women who took estrogen may have been different from those who did not. They may have been from a higher social class, had different genetic backgrounds, had earlier puberty, later pregnancy, or consumed alcohol, which could account for differences in the outcome of the study. If they took estrogen, the cancer might have been caused by the hormone, but it also could have been a result of other factors. The confusion with the results of this type of study is in interpretation— whether these are associations or actual causes of the disease.

Q. Are randomized studies better?

A. Yes. There is no substitute for a randomized, controlled prospective study.

Q. What if your hypothetical study could be randomized?

A. If my hypothetical study could be prospective, as randomized studies are, the researcher would gather a group of women, randomly assign them estrogen and placebo, and follow them for many years to see whether they get breast cancer.

Q. If randomized studies are better, why aren't they done more often?

A. Scientists are reluctant to undertake randomized studies because they're time-consuming and much more expensive, and many people don't want to take a placebo. Essentially, it's easier for researchers to look backward than to control what people do in the future.

Q. How can women in their fifties interpret the information from studies about the relationship between estrogen and breast cancer?
A. The results of these studies are confusing. As I said before, it's very difficult to sort out the difference between associations and causes. Unfortunately, right now there isn't any magic answer that can help women make sense out of most studies. I think it's fairly clear, though, that the beneficial effect on cardiovascular mortality would outweigh the negative effect on breast cancer, if both effects turn out to be causal.

Q. Why is the public frustrated with medical studies?
A. One reason is that people want to draw conclusions about what they can do for themselves based on the results of studies. It's tempting to assume that two things that have changed together are causally related—that women who took estrogen in a study had a higher incidence of breast cancer for that reason. But it's unjustifiable to draw that conclusion unless a controlled experiment establishes cause and effect.

Q. How does the public know that the results of a study are worth listening to?
A. A study's validity can judged to some extent by the journal it was published in.

Q. Tell me about the hierarchy of medical journals.
A. With regard to medical studies, the main dividing point is between journals that are peer reviewed—that is, where several experts in the field decide whether a study is worth publishing—and those that are not, in which the editor of the publication decides, and he or she could have an interest other than the quality of the study.

Q. Do some journals publish only peer-reviewed studies?
A. Yes.

Q. If a study was in a journal that publishes only peer-reviewed articles, are we assured that the results are worth looking into?
A. Yes.

Q. Which journal is at the top of the hierarchy?
A. The best drug trials are published in the *New England Journal of Medicine*. If an important study in the treatment of diseases is not published in that journal, you almost have to ask yourself "Why not?"

Q. Why do the results of studies sometimes conflict and cause confusion to the public?
A. Sometimes studies conflict because they're done on relatively small numbers of people and the results occur by chance. Differing results also may be due to different populations. For example, one study might be done with people who have an early, milder form of a disease, while another might use those who have more advanced disease, allowing a drug to be more effective in one group than the other. The summary reported in newspapers may not take that into account, which can be confusing to the public.

Q. Give me an example of the results of an observational study that appeared innocuous but yielded a surprise when a prospective controlled study was done.
A. Several years ago observational studies showed that people who took supplemental beta carotene, an antioxidant found naturally in many foods, had a reduced risk of coronary heart disease. But in two later prospective studies, beta carotene supplements appeared to slightly increase the incidence of lung cancer. I don't think anybody expected that.

Q. What is your advice to women in their fifties with regard to decisions based on medical studies?
A. My advice would be to rely on the judgment of their primary care physician, assuming they have one whom they trust. Media reports on new treatments tend to be overoptimistic about effectiveness and not cautious enough about adverse effects. The actual medical reports can be difficult for nonexperts to interpret and may lead them to the wrong conclusion, even when they have M.D. degrees. That may sound patronizing, but I truly believe it's good advice. Even though I know a lot about medical treatment, I follow that policy with my own family.

305

SECTION VI

Maintenance, Rejuvenation, and Reconstruction

34

Skin: Maintenance and Rejuvenation

Michael H. Gold, M.D.

Michael H. Gold graduated from college in 1981 with a degree in biology. He attended the Chicago Medical School and did his internal medicine internship at Emory University School of Medicine in Atlanta. In 1989 he completed his dermatology residency at Northwestern University School of Medicine in Chicago. He then moved to Nashville, where he joined an established dermatology practice. After eight months Dr. Gold founded the Gold Skin Care Center in Nashville.

Q. What do you recommend as a daily skin care program for the face of a woman in her fifties?
A. The basic skin care program for a woman who wants her skin to look good should be as follows.

In the morning:
- Apply a glycolic acid cleanser and lotion. Glycolic acids are naturally occurring fruit acids that have shown promise in helping rejuvenate photodamaged skin if used regularly in concentrations readily available.
- If you have pigment abnormalities, use a glycolic bleaching medicine.

- Put on sunscreen—this is essential.
- Apply oil-free makeup.

In the evening:
- Wash your face with a glycolic acid cleanser.
- Apply a tretinoin product—Renova or Retin-A. If you don't wish to use tretinoin, apply glycolic acid cream or lotion.

Q. What is Retin-A?

A. Retin-A (the generic name is tretinoin) has been a tried-and-true treatment for acne. In 1988 the results of a study the University of Michigan published in the *New England Journal of Medicine* showed that tretinoin reduced fine lines and wrinkles. Tretinoin is also used as a wound-healing agent. When applied to actinically damaged skin, the photodamage improves. The epidermis (the top layer of the skin) normalizes, thickens, and actually grows new cells. Some of the damaged cells disappear. In that process, fine lines and wrinkles are also eliminated.

Retin-A is marketed in six types of creams and gels as well as in solution form. It must be prescribed by a physician. It is the number-one-selling dermatology medicine in the world.

Q. What is Renova?

A. Renova is an emollient form of the middle-strength Retin-A. Renova also can be obtained only on a prescription basis, and it is the only medicine FDA approved to treat photodamage.

Q. Is there a proper way to use these products?

A. Yes. Patients should wash their face, dry it but not totally, and apply a pea-size portion of the Renova or Retin-A to their slightly damp skin.

The proper strength depends on the patient's tolerance. If the lines aren't reduced after several months, the dermatologist can increase the dose.

Q. Tell me about alpha hydroxy acids for the skin.

A. Alpha hydroxy acids are fruit acids that have been manufactured for skin care. They include glycolic acid and lactic acid.

Alpha hydroxy acids are essentially moisturizers that can revitalize aging skin. At high concentrations (up to 90 percent and applied only in the physician's office), glycolic acid has been found to alter the collagen under the skin, allowing it to return to some of its original tone. Over-the-counter products contain between 5 and 10 percent alpha hydroxy acid. Daily use of these products has been shown to be useful in normalizing the skin tone and reducing pigments and skin irregularities.

Brand names include Neostrata, MD Formulations/MD Forte, Alpha Hydrox, and Murad. There are many found on cosmetic counters—too many to list.

Q. Tell me about beta hydroxy acids.
A. Beta hydroxy acids are really the old salicylic acid repackaged in a cosmetically elegant way. Salicylic acid was a classic treatment for acne many years ago.

Q. Does hormone therapy, such as estrogen, help the skin?
A. No. We don't use estrogen to treat aging skin.

Q. Are facial exercises good for toning skin?
A. The jury is out on that one.

Q. Are facials helpful to aging skin?
A. Facials are wonderful for cleaning the skin and getting the impurities out. They're not harmful and should be done on a regular basis.

Q. Should soap be used to wash the face?
A. I recommend only nonsoap cleansers. There are many soapless cleansers on the market that clean the skin very well, such as Cetaphil or Aquanil.

Q. What is your take on drinking eight glasses of water a day?
A. We know that hydration is important and therefore recommend that everyone drink a couple glasses of water a day. But it's not the end-all that will keep your skin healthy.

311

Q. Tell me about chemical peels.

A. There are four types of chemical peels. From weakest to strongest, they are the alpha hydroxys, the beta hydroxys, trichlorocetic acid (TCA), and phenol. Each of these provides a different response. The weakest results in a refreshing treatment that may reduce fine lines and wrinkles. The most potent peels are big time—we chemically peel the patient's entire face with hopes that she will have a "baby" skin face when we're done.

The success rates of most chemical peels are high. Light chemical peels utilizing alpha hydroxy, beta hydroxy, and low-potency TCA will require several peels over a period of time to see a desired effect. Deep TCA or phenol peels work fairly quickly but have more of a "down-time" period for healing. The lighter peels have no real down time.

Q. Tell me about fillers and implants for deep lines and wrinkles.

A. Fillers are injections of substances that temporarily fill in lines and wrinkles. Collagen, an insoluble protein that comes from cows, is the most common filler. Two types of collagen are Zyderm and Zyplast. Fibrel, which comes from pigs, is used on patients who are allergic to cow collagen.

Fat transplants also are used as fillers. Fat is excised from the patient's abdomen or buttocks and injected into her facial wrinkles. People are never allergic to their own fat, but with skin testing, most patients are almost guaranteed not to be allergic to other fillers.

Several drug companies are experimenting with human collagen. They use skin from cadavers or take it from patients to manufacture their own collagen. If the companies can prove longevity, these may replace collagen at some point.

Implants, such as Gortex, can be placed into large furrows or lines. Gortex probably will be replaced by a newer material called Soft Form, which has yielded promising results in early studies.

Botox, or botulinum toxin, is a good treatment for frown lines on the forehead and crow's feet around the eyes. Botox temporarily paralyzes the muscles that form these lines. The dosages used are very small. Botox has been shown to be safe when injected properly.

Q. Tell me about dermabrasion.

A. Dermabrasion is a process in which the skin is "sanded" using a special machine. It works well for patients with actinically damaged skin or scars on the face. Dermabrasion is messy and bloody, but there is still a place for it.

Q. Why is there still a place for dermabrasion if it is messy and bloody?

A. Many cosmetic dermatologic surgeons feel there is more control with their dermabrader and that the healing postsurgery is more regular.

Q. What about dermabrasion for a woman in her fifties?

A. A woman in her fifties would benefit because aging skin does respond to dermabrasion.

Q. Tell me about lasers for skin treatment.

A. There are many types of lasers for a variety of skin problems. Various new lasers can eradicate blood vessels on the face and legs, brown spots, and unwanted hair. Resurfacing lasers with the carbon dioxide (CO_2) or erbium-YAG lasers are popular ways to smooth the skin or repair scars. The new erbium-YAG laser doesn't penetrate as deeply as the CO_2 laser, allowing faster healing and recovery. There is no bleeding with laser surgery.

Q. What do you advise women in their fifties who want to maintain youthful skin?

A. Ask your dermatologist for a good skin care routine and stick with it.

35

Lasers for Cosmetic and Other Skin Surgeries

Roy Geronemus, M.D.

Roy Geronemus graduated from college in 1975 with a degree in biology. He attended the University of Miami School of Medicine and did an internship in internal medicine at the Beth Israel Medical Center in New York. He then completed a residency in dermatology and a fellowship in Moh's micrographic surgery and dermatologic surgery at the New York University (NYU) Medical Center. After completing his training, he joined the full-time faculty at the NYU Medical Center, a position he held for ten years. During that time he established NYU's Dermatologic Laser Center and ran the dermatologic surgery program. Dr. Geronemus opened the Laser and Skin Surgery Center in New York in 1993. According to Dr. Geronemus, that center is one of the world's most comprehensive laser facilities in terms of the numbers of lasers used and scope of cutaneous laser surgeries performed.

Q. What are lasers as they're used in skin surgery and dermatology?
A. The word "laser" is an acronym for light amplification by the stimulated emission of radiation. The laser delivers different types of light (wavelengths) to accomplish surgery of the skin or blood vessels. The laser beam cuts, seals, or vaporizes skin tissue and blood vessels. There are many different types of lasers, each used for a different purpose.

Q. Why do you use different lasers?
A. There has been a proliferation in the development of laser systems for various purposes. Many factors impact on the choice of a particular laser. It will depend on the problem—whether we're treating a large blood vessel or a small blood vessel, a brown spot or a tattoo, a wrinkle or hair removal, or a person with light skin or dark skin.

Q. Tell me about some of the lasers and their common uses.
A. A carbon dioxide (CO_2) laser, which emits a colorless infrared light, is used to remove fine lines, wrinkles, and acne scars.

A yellow-light laser uses a cameralike flash with an organic dye to produce short pulses of yellow light. It is used to treat enlarged blood vessels.

The argon laser gives out a blue-green light. It also can be used in the treatment of enlarged blood vessels as well as port wine stains and birthmarks.

Red-light lasers send short high-energy pulses that remove tattoos and brown spots.

Q. What are the advantages of laser skin surgery over conventional surgery?
A. Laser surgery can give immediate results, it is bloodless, it can cause less scarring, and there is less risk of infection.

Laser surgery can redefine (smooth) lines, tighten skin, and increase skin tone. Lasers can ablate and soften lines from the outside and stimulate new collagen formation within the dermis, or under layers of skin. A biopsy of the skin after a laser procedure will show a newly formed band of collagen.

Q. Is laser surgery performed in the physician's office?
A. Yes, but the office must be properly set up so that the procedures are performed safely and effectively.

Q. There has been a big push recently for the use of lasers in wrinkle removal. How has this affected the quality of laser skin surgery?
A. Many inexperienced physicians have begun to do this procedure

without appropriate training or expertise, resulting in unsatisfactory results in many patients.

Q. So it's best to go to someone who does these procedures often and regularly?
A. Yes. Experience is critical. There is a learning curve for each laser system. The learning curve with a new laser is very fast if a physician has been working regularly with lasers for years. But a physician who has been doing just standard scalpel surgery should not suddenly use a laser—he or she won't know its proper use, indications, or parameters.

Experience varies from person to person. Physicians who want to perform laser surgery should have didactic training, hands-on experience, and perhaps a preceptorship, where they follow someone around who does this type of work on a regular basis. If you're patient number 1, number 10, or even number 20, your physician won't have the experience needed to deal with your problem.

Q. How can a woman find a physician who is well qualified to perform laser surgery?
A. It's best to get a referral from another physician. In all likelihood, the laser surgeon's work will have been critically scrutinized by his or her peers.

Q. Who should give this referral?
A. Someone who works in a comparable field—the woman's dermatologist, plastic surgeon, or internist.

Q. Are anesthetics required for laser surgery of wrinkles?
A. That depends on whether we're treating an isolated area or doing a full-facial procedure. For limited areas, such as the upper lip or eyes, a local anesthetic can be used. Sometimes we use only a topical anesthesia or no anesthetic. When treating a broad area, I prefer to use intravenous sedation, which effectively removes all pain and any memory of the procedure.

Q. Tell me about laser treatments for large areas of the face.
A. We've been doing more full-facial procedures in recent years be-

cause lasers improve skin tone and texture. We have seen more tightening of the skin than we originally thought possible. Unless they had excessive redundancy of skin or deep jowls, people get the kind of tightening that they expected from a face lift.

Q. What is the most commonly requested procedure of women in their fifties?
A. The most commonly requested procedure is the removal of fine lines. Lasers will reduce or remove facial wrinkles and skin that's starting to sag. Lasers can't improve deep lines or extensive sagging of the skin, but you wouldn't expect that in a woman in her fifties.

Q. Why don't deep lines and sags respond to laser treatment?
A. They're probably just too deep.

Q. Tell me about the recovery period after laser surgery for wrinkle removal.
A. The recovery depends on the type of laser used and the depth of the procedure. The healing process is difficult for the first five days. Pain is not the issue. It's just oozing and swelling. This has been the problem with laser surgery—no doubt about it.

Laser surgery can result in a prolonged recovery process—the skin is raw, taking five to ten days to heal. There is significant redness that can last from weeks to many months and, in rare cases, up to a year. The redness begins as bright red. After the healing begins, it gets to a pink color. Women can cover it with makeup.

Some of the newer lasers, such as the erbium-YAG, are indicated for more superficial lines. This system results in much faster healing.

Q. What are the risks and complications of laser surgery for wrinkle removal?
A. In good hands, the risks are minimal. We don't see many long-term complications. There are risks of scarring and of changing pigmentation. One can get increased pigmentation over the short term and lightening of the skin or loss of pigmentation over the long term. There is also the risk of infection.

Q. How can these risks be minimized?
A. The risks can be minimized with the use of the proper technique on the right patient.

Q. How long do the results of laser skin surgery last?
A. The response to laser treatment for superficial lines and mild sagging of the skin can last for years. Some lines may recur, particularly those that move, such as lines around the corners of the mouth, nose, and between the eyes.

Q. When would laser skin surgery be contraindicated?
A. A woman with excessive sagging or prominent jowls would not be the right person for a laser procedure. Women with dark skin do not do as well. They are more prone to changes of pigmentation.

Q. Tell me about broken capillaries, another problem commonly seen in fifty- to sixty-year-old women.
A. Dilated blood vessels and broken capillaries of the face, legs, and other parts of the body are an unbelievably common problem. We do much more of this type of laser surgery than wrinkle removal.

Q. What about age spots?
A. Age spots (also known as liver spots) on the face and top of the hands and arms can be treated very nicely with lasers. It's a great treatment. They usually disappear.

Q. What are cherry angiomas?
A. Cherry angiomas or senile angiomas are little red bumps found on the trunk or legs. These mounds can be pinpoints up to the size of a pencil eraser. They're common in women in their fifties and very easily removed by laser.

Q. Do you remove varicose veins with lasers?
A. Yes. Superficial veins can be treated by laser. Some physicians use the standard techniques of sclerotherapy (injection of a sclerosing agent into the vein, which actually shrinks it) in conjunction with laser treatment.

Q. What about the standard treatment of stripping varicose veins?
A. Physicians still strip varicose veins in certain circumstances.

Q. Are lasers used to remove tattoos?
A. Yes. Whether they are cosmetic tattoos—eyeliner or eyebrows—or decorative tattoos on the body, they are removed nicely with lasers.

Q. What about scar removal?
A. It's not uncommon for women in their fifties to have had breast surgery for mammoplasty or lump removal. Scarring is not an uncommon result of these procedures. The pulsed-dye laser that we use for blood vessels is very effective in treating scars.

People who had acne earlier in life can have their scars improved with lasers.

Q. Do you completely remove scars with lasers?
A. No. But lasers soften them and make them much less noticeable.

Q. Do you remove moles with lasers?
A. Yes. Certain types of moles can be removed effectively with lasers. We would get a biopsy before taking off a mole that looks suspicious.

Q. What about hair removal?
A. We remove hair with lasers, sometimes in conjunction with topical creams. That includes facial hair, underarms, bikini lines, and full legs. The results are longer lasting than with other techniques.

Q. What is the cost differential between laser hair removal and a can of Nair?
A. Laser hair removal is much more expensive than Nair over the short term but over the long term it can be considered a cost-effective alternative.

Q. What is the future for laser skin surgery?
A. We're presently investigating laser techniques that will remove lines without injuring the skin. It may be possible to correct aging or sagging skin without any postoperative wounding. There has been

recent interest in the erbium-YAG laser, which does much of what the carbon dioxide laser does, but more superficially. As a result, the healing is much quicker and redness doesn't last as long. It is not as effective as the carbon dioxide laser for deeper lines but is effective for superficial lines and scarring.

Q. What do you advise women in their fifties who want to improve their looks with laser skin surgery?
A. Women seeking laser skin surgery should have realistic expectations of what lasers can and can't do.

Laser treatment is better than other techniques for many problems. But the correct laser must be used by a qualified physician for an appropriate procedure on the right patient.

My final piece of advice? Buyer beware.

36

About Cosmetic Surgery

Gerald Imber, M.D.

Gerald Imber graduated from college with a bachelor of arts degree in biology, art history, and the classics. He earned his medical degree in 1966 from Downstate Medical School in Brooklyn, New York, followed by a year of internship and a year of surgical residency at Long Island Jewish Hospital. After two years in the United States Air Force, he went to the Kaiser Foundation Hospital in Panorama City, California, in 1970 to finish his surgery residency. He then moved to The New York Hospital–Cornell University Medical Center in New York City for his plastic surgery residency, which he completed in 1974. Dr. Imber has been a clinical assistant professor of surgery (plastic) at Cornell University Medical Center and attending surgeon at The New York Hospital since that time. He has a private cosmetic surgery practice on Fifth Avenue in New York and is author of *The Youth Corridor*, published by William Morrow & Co. in 1997.

Q. Tell me about skin.
A. Human skin is an approximately eight-pound organ that covers the body and separates the external from the internal environment. Skin keeps toxins out and moisture, fluids, and important body components in.

Sweat glands in the skin regulate body temperature by stimulating evaporation when we're hot and shutting down blood vessels (to prevent heat loss) when we're cold.

Skin mirrors the body's internal environment. Certain skin changes reflect particular medical conditions.

Q. What causes the skin to age?
A. Skin ages when collagen and elastin (elastic fiber) in the dermis (the deep layer of the skin) break down. Collagen and elastin give substance and resilience to the skin. In youth, collagen fibers are organized in a smooth, parallel fashion. When collagen fibers break down and become disorganized in the course of normal aging, the skin thins and wrinkles.

Q. Why do collagen fibers break down with age?
A. Collagen breakdown can be due to ordinary wear and tear, such as constant motion of the skin in the course of daily life, or from chemical oxidation of the collagen fibers that occurs when circulating free radicals (negatively charged oxygen atoms that have a free electron) attach to the collagen. Ultraviolet rays from sunlight speed up this process, resulting in loose skin and wrinkles.

Q. Tell me about the skin of a fifty-year-old woman.
A. There is no typical fifty-year-old skin. A fifty-year-old woman who has good genes, stays out of the sun, is of normal weight, doesn't gain or lose large amounts of weight, takes vitamins E and C, and has no aggravating factors will have better skin than her peers who drink too much alcohol, gain and lose weight, don't have the proper nutritional and supplemental intake, and get too much sun.

Q. What makes some women age better than others?
A. Aside from genetics, skin care, and lifestyle, a woman's facial bone structure may help her age better. Skin that is draped over strong cheekbones and a strong jaw line looks better.

Q. When does the skin begin its aging process?
A. Chemical changes and breakdown of the skin begin early in adult

322

life. They are noticeable in the thirties and forties and continue to worsen over the course of the years.

Q. At what point is it appropriate for a woman to consider cosmetic surgery?
A. There is no absolute answer to that question. Cosmetic surgery should be based on the mirror and not on the calendar. My philosophy is, when something new and unflattering shows up in the mirror that is a sign of aging and it bothers you, that's the time to get rid of it. A woman can and should expect to look virtually the same throughout her adult life if proper care is taken, and that may include cosmetic surgery.

Q. Tell me about cosmetic surgery procedures that are commonly performed on women in their fifties.
A. The eyelids, which have the thinnest skin and take the worst beating from life's ups and downs, are vulnerable by age fifty. Most women in this age group have excess eyelid skin. Removal of the extra skin from the upper lid and tightening the skin of the lower lid are commonly performed on women in their fifties.

At this age, the nasal-labial folds between the corners of the nose and mouth tend to deepen. Fat pockets around the corners of the mouth become noticeable. When the nasal-labial fold and the little pouch of fat drop toward the jaw line and condense with some of the cheek fat, a jowl is formed. Everyone in their fifties has some of this going on. Based on one's genetic makeup, bone structure, and lifestyle, it may or may not warrant taking care of.

Many women have alpha hydroxy acid face peels to remove fine wrinkles and blemishes or laser resurfacing to remove wrinkles and smile lines.

Some women in this age group complain of a thinning of their lips—the upper lip particularly gets longer and thinner. The best way to deal with that is fat transplants—the injection of her own fat into the lips. This procedure usually needs to be done twice and the result can be permanent.

At this age, the tip of the nose drops with gravity and the nasal configuration also changes. A woman who had a slight hump in the nose and a normal angle of the tip at youth may notice at age fifty that the hump has become more noticeable and the tip of the nose is starting to look down at her chin. The tissues have stretched with gravity. The simplest way to deal with this, which we often do during a face lift, is to lift the tip of the nose and put it back where it used to be. Suddenly the hump looks less dramatic, the nose looks straighter, and the angle between the nasal tip and the lip is in its original place. Her nose looks more youthful, but it still looks like her.

Another procedure done in this world of fiftyish antiaging surgery is the use of chin implants. These are made from silastic, a hardened silicone, the same material used to make artificial joints. They are quite safe. A formed implant is placed on the chin through the inside of the lower lip and slipped under the two vertical muscles. A couple of stitches are sewn in so it can't move. The chin implant helps the profile, takes up slack, makes the jaw longer and stronger, and makes jowls less noticeable, giving an attractive angularity to the jaw.

At this age, many women notice an accumulation of fat just outside of the bra strap in the underarm area. That, too, can be removed completely by liposuction.

Q. How should a woman go about finding the best surgeon to correct a perceived flaw?
A. Cosmetic surgery is not a blind item. Nor is it an emergency. A woman should search for a surgeon in her community who is associated with the best hospital or medical center, who has the best reputation, who her friends have used, or her primary care doctor recommends.

It's important that the surgeon is experienced in the procedure she is contemplating. The most talented, ingenious physician who has done three eyelid operations is not nearly as good as a talented, ingenious surgeon who has done 3,000 eyelid operations. Every doctor has to start someplace, but not on you!

It's important to do the best shopping you can in this arena where nothing is certain. It's a good idea to consult more than one surgeon, unless you happen to click with the first one you meet and feel that he or she is the right person for you.

Q. Tell me about the following cosmetic surgery procedures.

A.
Collagen Injections

Collagen injections fill in skin defects caused by collagen break-down. The most common are the vertical frown lines between the eyebrows, some of the fine smile lines on the outside of the eyes, and the deep nasal-labial lines from the corners of the nose to the corners of the mouth and vertical lip lines. Collagen injections work well on early changes. The more collagen necessary to fill in the defects, the poorer job it will do.

Collagen is made from the collagen protein in the skin of cows. There is a great similarity between the protein in cow collagen and that of human collagen. For that reason, collagen is fairly well toler-ated in humans.

Cow collagen is purified and injected in a gel form. A skin test is given first to detect whether the patient is allergic to this product. Most people are not. However, some people develop an allergy over the course of the treatments.

The little pinprick from the injection is not terribly uncomfort-able, but there is a little swelling. Patients often go to lunch after the procedure and no one knows the difference. The result, at least for the time being, is quite good.

The down side to this procedure is that collagen is broken down by the body, metabolized, and disappears over the course of four to six months. Most people need to be reinjected.

A number of products are being tested in which the patient's own collagen from a piece of skin that has been removed at surgery or specifically for this purpose is processed. The advantage is that the patient is never allergic to his or her own collagen, and it seems to last slightly longer that the cow collagen. The down side is that you have to lose a piece of skin, which is also an additional step to the proce-dure, and the result is not permanent.

Fat Transplants

Fat transplants have become the backbone of most fill-in and presurgery strategies. This has been an excellent procedure for filling in the vertical frown lines between the eyebrows and the nasal-labial lines, the same areas where collagen would have been used, with the exception of the very fine smile lines. Fine lines are not filled using this process because a larger needle has to be used with fat transplant to preserve the living cells.

We remove the fat cells using liposuction technique, but with a 10 cubic centimeter (cc) syringe, which is very small, and a needle that is a little larger than the average needle. We apply a couple of drops of local xylocaine (painkiller). We take small amounts of the patient's own fat in the syringe (the equivalent to two thimblesful of fat), condense it in a centrifuge for a few minutes, and then reinject it sterilely. We want to inject live fat cells without destroying them so they can find a blood supply in the tissue that will give a permanent correction. There's very little discomfort. I have not seen damage to the area from which the fat is removed. The entire process takes fifteen minutes.

This is a transplant, not an injection. The fat survives because the fat cells are alive. They've just come out of your buttock or abdomen or wherever you can spare a few ccs of fat. About 25 percent of the fat cells find a permanent home and live forever. The patient gets that 25 percent correction with one injection. If she has this done two or three times, she will come close to a permanent correction of the defect.

Fat injections are better than injecting the patient's own collagen because none of the collagen will last permanently.

Chemical Peel, Dermabrasion, and Laser Resurfacing

Chemical peel, dermabrasion, and laser resurfacing are used when trying to correct the irregular surface of the skin, whether it's wrinkles, superficial residuals from acne, or just an irregular surface. These techniques do the same thing. They remove the epidermis of the skin down to the dermis, and new skin grows in.

The difference between a laser resurfacing and chemical peel and dermabrasion is that laser is a computerized dermabrasion. The laser resurfacing results in skin destruction by a light beam that is of a computerized strength and depth, so that the physician knows exactly how much he or she is burning away. The depth is exactly the same throughout the skin. For the first time, we can calibrate what we're doing against what we want to do.

Dermabrasion is a spinning wheel that tears off a certain amount of skin until bleeding gets to a level that we associate with a smoothing effect. Dermabrasion is not a very precise procedure.

Chemical peels are similar in concept. A deep peel destroys skin down to the superficial epidermis by creating a chemical reaction that destroys the skin. Deep peels combine a variety of phenyl products (phenyl is the active ingredient). The physician is unable to control or even visualize the exact depth of the destruction.

You run more risk of complication with the dermabrasion and the deep peel than you would with laser resurfacing. I'm not indicating that laser resurfacing is without complications, but it does offer better control.

Superficial Peels

Superficial peels are used to correct fine wrinkling or discoloration of the skin. They are not as invasive as deep peels and less caustic agents are used. Results are not as dramatic but there is lower risk of complication.

Physician-applied Alpha Hydroxy Acid Peels

Physician-applied alpha hydroxy acid peels are popular because this process has no down side and a lot of up side. This is more than the alpha hydroxy acid available at cosmetics counters in moisturizers of 8 or 10 percent solution. I'm referring to physician application of an alpha hydroxy acid in a varying concentration from about 20 to 70 percent. Over the course of a half-dozen applications, separated by two weeks, there is often a very significant reduction of superficial wrinkling, a marked decrease in blotchiness, and a general feeling of tightening and well-being of the skin with almost no risk.

Botox Injections

Botox, denatured botulinum toxin (the same toxin that causes botulism) is injected into an area of a muscle that is reacting too much and causing a wrinkle. It is commonly used to correct the horizontal lines of the forehead or the vertical lines between the eyebrows. When Botox is injected in these areas, it paralyzes the muscle and the forehead becomes completely smooth for the period of time that the Botox works. That's the good news. The bad news is that we can't exactly predict when the wrinkle is going to come back. It can come back on one side before the other, leaving a less-than-pleasant appearance. Some people find it worthwhile. I do not use it any longer.

Implants for Wrinkles

A number of implants have been used to lessen the depth of nasal-labial folds and for other deep wrinkles or folds. Sterile Gortex implants, the same material that lines your shoes or jacket, are threaded onto the skin in a wrinkle or to enlarge the lips. The product is inert and will stay permanently. The body weaves fiberblasts in, out, and around the Gortex so that it doesn't move. Results are reasonably good and sometimes excellent.

Another implant recently available for use in the nasal-labial fold is a soft plastic "tube" called Soft Form, into which tissues grow.

The down side of both of these is the implants can sometimes be felt or seen.

Liposuction

There is a place for liposuction at this time in life, which was not available ten years ago. The proviso for liposuction is this: The less you need it, the better the result.

Most people in their fifties have an accumulation of fat, on their bellies, below the umbilicus, and above the pubis. No matter how much they exercise, that fat stays. Excess fat can be removed by liposuction simply through a tiny incision through the belly button.

Many women have an accumulation of fat at the lower portion of the hips, on the outside, like a saddlebag deformity, and some fat on the buttocks themselves. Those areas can undergo liposuction through a little quarter-inch incision in the buttock crease. We can remove up to a quart of fat. The skin is thick and shrinks down immediately. Excess buttock fat or the riding-britches deformity can be completely corrected with this simple procedure done without general anesthesia. The accumulation of fat on the midportion of the abdomen can be similarly removed.

In addition, a little bit of jowl or double chin can be permanently removed by microsuction, which is liposuction using a small catheter and a slightly different technique.

Where Liposuction Does Not Work

Liposuction doesn't work on the loose fatty skin of the upper arm or on excess fat because the skin won't shrink adequately. It is not done on the inside of the thighs because that skin is too thin. When you remove significant fat, the skin doesn't shrink back and the procedure leaves an unsightly rippled look.

Eyelid Surgery (Blepharoplasty)

Eyelid surgery is probably the most commonly performed surgical procedure in the plastic surgeon's repertoire. More than 300,000 such procedures are performed annually. Blepharoplasty is popular because it works, it's relatively easy to do, and should be complication-free.

The operation usually is done under intravenous sedation and local anesthetic. It is most frequently performed on an outpatient or ambulatory setting.

If there are dark circles under the eye, a 25 percent solution of trichloracetic acid can be applied to the skin at the end of the procedure to bleach them out.

Blepharoplasty can be done with a surgical knife or with a laser. Most surgeons use the scalpel technique. The entire procedure—upper and lower eyelids—takes about an hour. After the surgery, the patient is in the recovery room for an hour with ice on her eyes, and she goes home. The sutures are removed three days later. She's back to normal in a week.

Clamping Eyelid Wrinkles

Clamping eyelid wrinkles is a less invasive procedure. It is used mostly for patients with excess lower-eyelid skin and wrinkles. A clamp is used to grasp and compress the excess skin, which is then excised with a fine scissors. The recovery is much faster than surgical blepharoplasty.

Face Lift

A face lift is a procedure in which we're trying to undo damage done by gravity. We attempt to put stretched, out-of-shape skin back where it was. Most women who are fiftyish can do well with less than a full face lift. These are the range of face lift options.

A *full face lift* involves an incision from the temporal hairline in the scalp down to the top of the ear and in behind the little cartilage in front of the ear, called the tragus. It's then tucked in behind the tragus, goes under the earlobe and halfway up the back of the ear, and down into the hair behind the ear. A tunnel is then made under the skin. The skin of the neck, cheek, and forehead is lifted up and replaced. That incision and the amount of surgery necessary depends on the extent of the damage we're trying to correct.

Most women in their fifties have a loosening of the cheeks, a deepening of the nasal-labial fold, and a little bit of puffiness and looseness around the jaw line. But they don't have a lot of loose skin under the jaw or on the neck. The first approach would probably be what I call an S-lift.

An *S-lift* utilizes half the full face-lift incision. The incision starts in the hairline, goes behind the trachus, and ends at the earlobe. There is no incision behind the ear. A woman can wear her hair up without worrying about a scar.

Through that incision, we tunnel under the skin, using liposuction to remove the fatty area of the incipient double chin and jowl, and then tighten what's called the SMAS (superficial muscular aponeurotic system), which is a fibrous layer under the skin that is continuous with the plasma muscle of the chin and neck. By tightening that, either removing part of it or just tightening it up with sutures, we can alleviate the nasal-labial folds and the looseness of the plasma muscle on the jaw line or under the jaw. The skin is redraped after the excess is removed. It is closed with a hidden suture woven under the skin and stitches or staples in the hairline.

Q. Where are face lifts performed?
A. Most surgeons perform face lifts in an ambulatory setting or in a private clinic with an anesthesiologist. The safest way of doing it is under intravenous sedation and local anesthetic. Medications used for intravenous sedation these days are metabolized quickly. No narcotics are used. Patients don't get sick or vomit afterward. The new medications, such as Diprivan, are so quick acting that you have to keep giving them to keep the patient asleep. There is virtually no risk of overdose. The safety factor is excellent. Everybody breathes easier, especially the patient. Because of the number of face lifts being done,

the use of ambulatory settings, anesthesiologists doing the sedation, and the new sedatives available, the face lift has improved.

Q. What is the recovery period for face lifts?
A. The recovery period is about ten days. The first five days one can expect to look dreadful. There is a great deal of puffiness, which is maximal at about the beginning of the third to the fourth day. By the fifth day, it will have receded significantly. By the tenth day, the puffiness usually is gone, but there may be some little lumps and bumps under the skin, which represent drops of blood or areas that were cauterized and may take a few more days to resolve. In general, after the S-lift, my patients are advised to go back to work in ten days; after a full facelift, they wait perhaps a few more days. Two weeks is a safe bet.

Q. Are face lifts painful?
A. There is no pain at all. The reason is that when the skin is lifted to be pulled, the little fine nerve fibers that run into the skin to give it sensation are broken by the surgery. It takes six to twelve weeks for them for to regrow. There's a sense of numbness in the skin during the early post-op period that prevents any pain. Sensation usually comes back completely.

Q. What problems can occur as a result of face lifts?
A. Problems of face lifts are legion. The most common one is a hematoma, a collection of blood under the skin that may occur at or after surgery. A large enough hematoma might require opening sutures to be drained. That happens about 1 percent of the time. Other problems are small amounts of bleeding or a stitch that breaks. Minor annoyances. The complication most feared is cutting one of the nerves that animates the face. That has been reported, but it happens exceedingly rarely. I've never seen it. A more common incident is a nerve injured by cauterization or from bits of blood causing temporary nerve weakness. Normal sensation returns in a few weeks.

Breast Surgery

Mastopexy (Breast Lift)

The most common breast surgery for women in their fifties is a breast lift, also known as mastopexy. Breast lifts are desired for the same reasons one considers a face lift—to fight the battle with gravity.

Elastin and collagen stretches and the breasts suddenly are facing the wrong direction. A breast lift is performed by tightening the skin brassiere. The breast is left in place. The breast tissue is never touched. An incision is made around the outside of the areola (the dark area around the nipple) and down to the fold under the breast. Enough skin is removed to be reconstructed in a fashion that lifts the breast higher, making a smaller skin brassiere. It's like taking a pie, removing a slice of the pie, and putting the pie back together. The results of this procedure are superb. The shape and height of the breasts are youthful and natural. The disadvantage is a scar around the areola and under the breasts. Those scars become skin-colored in about a year. This is a very well-tolerated procedure.

Breast Reduction

The same incisions are used for breast reduction as for the mastopexy. Many women with relatively heavy breasts who have gone through child rearing and a twenty-five-year battle with gravity find they have large, low breasts and want them lifted and reduced. The procedure is similar to the mastopexy, except that the wedge section of the breast is removed as well. The results are smaller, less full, and higher breasts. This procedure is usually received with a sigh of relief by the patient because we have removed a ten-pound weight.

Breast Augmentation (Breast Enlargement)

Breast augmentation is not frequently done in women over fifty for two reasons: They've come to grips with their breast size; and usually the breasts have descended low enough that breast augmentation would make them look worse.

Abdominoplasty or Tummy Tuck

Abdominoplasty consists of lifting all the skin off the abdominal wall from the pubis up to the rib cage, releasing the belly button (umbilicus) so it can stay where it is. The skin is pulled up, excess skin is removed, and the belly button is popped through the skin to a new location. All the skin from where the belly button used to be down to the pubis is removed. Everything is then sewn closed. In addition, the rectus abdominus muscles (the muscles of the belly) are sewn together at the midline, tightening them. In childbearing, there's usually a spreading of the connection between the left and right side of the rectus muscle. We sew them together to tighten the abdominal wall. This slightly reduces the waist. The result is a tight, firm, youthful abdomen.

The price you pay is that you virtually can't walk upright for four to five days. In about ten days the sutures are taken out. In three weeks you can resume activity. This procedure is done in the hospital under general anesthesia or in the ambulatory setting under an epidural.

Q. What can be done to improve the buttocks?
A. There are many procedures to improve the buttocks. Again, the less you need, the better liposuction will do it. For most people, you can improve the buttock area through liposuction, and nothing else is necessary. However, if the backside is really large, or if it's hanging and flabby, liposuction might make it worse. A buttock lift might be the answer. A buttock lift is excellent in the shape it yields, but it leaves a scar. That scar ultimately will become skin-colored. It will show when you're wearing a bathing suit.

Q. Tell me about an inner thigh lift.
A. You can tighten the inner thighs with a procedure that makes an incision up along the pubis. Over the course of years the incision seems to drop down onto the thighs and is difficult to disguise. In either the buttock or thigh lift, the more dramatic the change, the more risk of having a telltale sign of the surgery.

Q. What about flabby upper arms?
A. Nothing acceptable can be done. We can make the upper arm skin fit perfectly, but the scar is terrible.

Q. What about tightening hands?
A. There's no good procedures for hands. I suggest a twofold plan:

nightly or twice a day apply alpha hydroxy acid for a year and use a six-month course of prescription-strength bleaching agent to get rid of the brown spots and make the skin finer and tighter. Laser resurfacing of the back of the hand is a possibility. The disadvantage is the skin is raw for a week to ten days and there is significant risk of scarring. I haven't seen improvement dramatic enough to warrant laser surgery on hands.

Q. What is the future of cosmetic surgery?
A. There will be breast implants filled with materials that are more like silicone. Various organic gels are being tested that feel more like silicone, which was once the best we had.

Newer facial implants are being looked at that are softer, less permanent, and made of collagenlike substances.

Constant changes are taking place in the field of liposuction, such as ultrasonic liposuction.

Knowledge of what makes the skin age and how to deal with it is reaching a point where we can actually affect its aging. That's going to be the biggest step in the next few years.

Q. What should women be wary of?
A. Plastic surgeons and people who pretend to be plastic surgeons have done a great disservice in marketing and promoting technologies before we knew enough about them. One example is the use of endoscopes. The endoscope is great for looking into someone's belly and performing appropriate procedures, such as taking out a gallbladder. Endoscopes have some appropriate uses in cosmetic surgery. But physicians are using endoscopes for face lifts and forehead lifts. They're tacking up the skin and not removing it and giving a dot-and-dash scar instead of a long one, while achieving no significant result.

We're doing the same things with the laser. We have this tool and we're looking for a use. We have to be wary of jumping on the bandwagon of every gadget that some plastic surgeon talks about on television. There will be great advances, but they must be proven. There must be a good basis in common sense before we adopt them. We have a responsibility that we must not ignore.

Q. Has cosmetic surgery changed in the past decade?
A. Cosmetic surgery has changed dramatically.

Cosmetic surgeons are performing smaller procedures earlier, for maintenance, rather than making dramatic changes.

Liposuction, lasers, fat transplants, and alpha hydroxy acids are now a part of our everyday care.

The change from a hospital to an outpatient setting combined with the increased experience of the surgeons, and the increasing knowledge and interest of the patient, has made cosmetic surgery an everyday part of life.

Things that one does frequently become things that one does well. Because we cosmetic surgeons do it more, we do it better. Because we do it better, we do it more. Because we do it more, we improve the techniques and because of that we do it more.

Q. Do you have advice for women in their fifties who want to look better?
A. The idea is to keep looking like yourself. Don't wait until things are so bad that you'll need a dramatic change. It's silly and you're wasting the best years of your life.

37

What to Expect from Cosmetic Surgery

Robert Amonic, M.D.

Robert Amonic was a premed major in college and attended UCLA Medical School, graduating in 1963. He went to Yale for his internship and one year of residency and returned to UCLA to complete his general surgical training. In 1968 he joined the United States Air Force and served as chief of surgical services at an air base in Germany. After two years he returned to the University of California at Los Angeles to do a three-year plastic surgery residency. In 1973 he went into private practice while maintaining a UCLA faculty position, which he has held since that time. He is currently associate clinical professor of surgery and has a private cosmetic surgery practice in Santa Monica. Dr. Amonic is a board-certified plastic surgeon.

Q. Why do women seek cosmetic surgery?
A. Our society has established that a youthful look is desirable. Women's magazines focus on youth, thinness, activity, and health. A woman who reaches fifty may look in the mirror and say to herself, "It wasn't that long ago that I looked as young as the women in those magazines. Can I get there again?"

Q. Isn't it vain to want to turn back the clock?
A. Vanity isn't necessarily negative. Caring about your appearance and wanting to look your best is healthy.

Q. Where are the hot spots for cosmetic surgery?
A. Centers of excellence in plastic surgery usually are found in major cities. Public demand determines if a particular area is likely to have high-quality cosmetic surgical care available. New York City, Chicago, San Francisco, Washington, D.C., Miami, and of course Los Angeles are well-known "hot spots."

Q. Why do people accept the risks of cosmetic surgery?
A. Many people have a sense of invulnerability. They are highly motivated and believe that the benefits outweigh the risks. For the most part, cosmetic surgery is safe for a healthy person.

Q. Should a woman tell her family and friends that she's going to have a face lift?
A. If you tell people you're getting your face done, their immediate comment is likely to be "What for, you don't need it." Well meaning or not, this is a natural response. It's a knee-jerk reaction. They think they're being complimentary and supportive, when, in fact, they frequently are motivated by fear, misunderstanding, lack of information, or envy. The ego strength of the woman who wants the surgery must be strong enough to overcome the resistance of her husband, family, and friends.

Q. What about the husband who does not support his wife's desire for a face lift?
A. This is not uncommon. The man might feel threatened that his younger-looking wife could make him feel old. If a patient tells me, "I'll come in for cosmetic surgery when my husband is out of town," my response is "Don't do it in secret. If your husband is against it, bring him in to talk about it." Often his fears can be allayed, giving him the opportunity to become supportive.

337

Q. Who is the ideal cosmetic surgery patient?
A. There isn't a true ideal patient, but certainly someone who has the physical findings that will respond positively to surgery and the psychological makeup to deal with the realities of the outcome will make an excellent candidate. In other words, the potential patient with fixable flaws and realistic expectations can expect to do well.

Q. What are inappropriate reasons for having cosmetic surgery?
A. Psychological baggage. "I've been going to the bars and no one looks at me," or "My husband just left me, he's threatening to leave me, or he's having an affair," are examples of poor reasons to seek cosmetic surgery. These women often hope that the surgery will fix their problem. Of course it doesn't work that way, and the psychological backlash may be devastating. Disappointment and serious depression can set in.

Undergoing surgery to please someone else is an inappropriate motivation. "My boyfriend likes women with big breasts" is a terrible reason to have augmentation.

Q. How does a physician pick up on those wrong motivations?
A. The physician can get a feel for what the patient is thinking by asking a few simple questions. "What brings you here? Why do you want this?" If the surgeon is listening with a sensitive ear, the patient will usually reveal why she wants the surgery.

Q. How can a woman judge the surgeon's qualifications?
A. Ask your own doctor for a referral, or call the American Society of Plastic Surgeons referral service at 888-272-7711 to find a qualified surgeon in your area. The doctor's basic credentials (training, certification) can be found through the Directory of Medical Specialists.

Visit more than one surgeon; however, too many consults can be confusing, as each doctor is likely to have a different approach. Two or three should be sufficient. Question if that surgeon has been sued or has lawsuits pending, or if he or she has ever been denied privileges at a major hospital. This is public information and is available from the *National Physician Data Bank.*

All things being equal, the best thing to do is trust your instincts.

Let yourself respond to your inner feelings. If you like this person, if you feel safe in his or her office, if you talk the same language, then these are all good signs. If, on the other hand, you sense a lack of professionalism, if you get "bad vibes," then get out of there!

Q. What about the specialist in another field who is not certified in plastic surgery? For example, an ear, nose, and throat specialist (otolaryngologist) who does facial cosmetic surgery?
A. That can be all right if the physician is properly trained and certified and meets the criteria we discussed in the previous question.

Q. What if the woman wants to look better but doesn't know what she needs?
A. Most women know. They often don't want to seem vain, so they say "I don't know what I need, Doctor. What do you think?" My response is "It's not what *I* think you need that's important; rather, let's focus on what bothers you." This allows an open discussion on what might be the best surgical plan.

Q. What will a responsible surgeon do during this initial visit?
A. A responsible, reliable, conscientious doctor will not take advantage of the patient's vulnerability. He or she will be very careful not to suggest a fix for something the patient doesn't perceive as a problem. When the surgical plan is established, the doctor should demonstrate the procedure with photographs or graphics and discuss likely expectations, risks, and results.

Q. What is your routine before you schedule surgery?
A. During the first appointment the patient tells me what bothers her and together we decide on a surgical plan. I often show pictures of patients with similar problems and their postsurgical results. Then we go into an examining room, where she can look in a mirror, and, if possible, I demonstrate what she might expect from the procedure. I will then take photographs to be used on her return visit.

On the second visit, I review the surgical procedure completely, including the incisions that I will make, where they are, why I do what I do, the sutures I use, and when they will be removed. I talk about pain, bruising, when she can go out in public, and how long before her incisions will be fully healed. I try to cover all the risks ranging from death to disappointment, putting appropriate emphasis on the likely ones.

Finally, the patient will speak with my scheduling nurse and get information on the cost of the proposed procedures as well as details of pre- and postoperative management.

Q. Do most cosmetic surgeons tell patients about the trauma, pain, and the risks of the surgery?
A. If they don't, they're not acting responsibly. In fact, they could be medically liable. The patient is entitled to full disclosure in order to give an informed consent.

Q. Tell me about depression that may result from the trauma of a face lift or other procedure.
A. Regardless of how realistic a person is, there's usually an underlying fantasy. For example, the patient comes in expecting to look like a movie star and ends up looking like herself with tighter skin. Or patients look in the mirror a week or two after surgery and say, "I suffered all the discomfort, spent all that money; my husband told me not to do it; my children were against it; and everybody said I didn't need it, and I don't look a lot better." That's because two weeks after surgery you probably *don't* look a lot better. It takes longer than that. People frequently think they should be fully healed in a couple of weeks. They get impatient and sometimes depressed. It's a normal reaction.

Then there is the type A personality who is usually a control freak and likely to micromanage every detail of everything she is involved in. When she finally surrenders and puts herself in the hands of the doctor (or nurse, or anyone involved in the medical team), she becomes "dependent." This is exaggerated when the patient knows something about the process—if she is medically trained. It takes a while to return to normal, and during this time, she is likely to feel depressed. This too is a normal reaction. In a healthy person this type of depression is temporary and usually short-lived.

Q. Tell me about medical conditions or other problems that might preclude someone from having cosmetic surgery.
A. I recommend a complete medical evaluation by the patient's family physician before undertaking a major procedure. Several conditions, if significant, preclude surgery. Insulin-dependent diabetes usually is a contraindication, as is severe heart disease or uncontrolled high blood pressure. However, many times these conditions, when controlled, add minimal risk to the surgical procedure.

Q. What about risky behaviors?
A. Examples of risky behavior are smoking, heavy alcohol use, or drug abuse. Serious consequences can occur if these conditions are not recognized or imparted to the surgeon.

Q. Why is smoking hazardous to a face lift?
A. Smokers who undergo face lifts are at greater risk. The nicotine from smoking causes blood vessels to shrink, making them permanently stiff and inflexible. During a face lift, many of these smaller blood vessels are cut and the skin is lifted away from the fat layer (called undermining). The remaining blood supply for the skin comes from the central area of the face and must extend to the edge of the incision. If those vessels have been compromised from chronic use of nicotine, skin sloughs can occur (loss of skin due to insufficient blood supply).

In my practice, smokers or anyone who smoked in the past are asked to sign a separate release form that states that they understand that there is a higher risk of complications, including infection and scarring. The duration of the smoking habit, whether current or long ago, does not define the level of risk. Fortunately, the majority of patients with a smoking history do not have problems.

Q. What about medications?
A. Many medications affect the course of a surgical procedure, and we need to know whether a patient is taking them. Besides the obvious drugs that are taken to thin the blood, lower the blood pressure, control diabetes and other chronic diseases, some over-the-counter remedies can pose a problem. For example, aspirin and aspirinlike

medications (ibuprofen) can cause postoperative bleeding and hematoma. I give my patients a long list of medications that they must discontinue at least two weeks prior to surgery. In addition, I review their other medications to be sure there will be no adverse interaction of drugs or lapse of important therapy.

Q. Do some women become addicted to cosmetic surgery?
A. Addiction is probably not the right word, but certainly some patients become obsessed with the process. They take care of one area and then immediately see another problem. Or they see something that is good but want to make it better. It is the doctor's responsibility to be aware of the difference between normal and obsessive behavior and to help the patient cope with these feelings. Many physicians obtain a psychological profile before proceeding, while others have a sense of these problems and head them off before problems occur.

Q. How long will a face lift last?
A. The average face lift lasts six to seven years. This is, of course, just an average. Some can last much longer and some much less. Some determining factors include: age, skin type, skin quality (sun damage), hormone levels (especially estrogen), weight gain or loss, and the type of procedure performed.

Q. Why are so many physicians who are not plastic surgeons performing cosmetic procedures these days?
A. It is a fact of life that cosmetic surgery has become an economically driven issue. In this age of managed care, cosmetic surgery is one of the last medical areas where the patient pays for the services in advance and without the assistance of an insurance company or other payor. This has made cosmetic surgery attractive to many physicians who are receiving less and less compensation for their usual medical care. Certain procedures lend themselves well to other specialties that are closely related to plastic surgery. These include liposuction and laser skin resurfacing. These procedures are not exclusive to plastic surgery, and if the doctor is well trained and has a good reputation, there should be no problem. It is the responsibility of the patient to

verify the credentials and evaluate any doctor before proceeding with surgery.

Q. What is your advice for women in their fifties who are considering cosmetic surgery?
A. There is no "right" age, so if you are thinking about having cosmetic surgery, do your homework. Consult with several qualified doctors and either go ahead or postpone surgery and reevaluate in several months. Remember, if you procrastinate too long, time will pass during which you could have enjoyed the benefits of the procedure.

Cosmetic surgery is not for everyone, but with proper motivation and realistic expectations, it can be a very rewarding experience.

Index